No More Bananas

How to Keep Your Cool in the Collective Madness

No More Bananas

How to Keep Your Cool in the Collective Madness

Jeroen Kraaijenbrink

Effectual Strategy Press

Bananas
adjective [after verb]
/bəˈnæn.əz/ informal

very silly
very excited because of pleasure, anger, or another emotion

extremely angry or excited

(Cambridge Dictionary)

ISBN: 978-90-823443-5-6

Published by Effectual Strategy Press, Doetinchem, Netherlands - www.effectualstrategy.com

Cover image: clipart-library.com

Contents

PREFACE — xi
    Acknowledgments — xiii
    Other Books to Read — xiv

PART 1: PROBLEMS

CHAPTER 1: We Are Going Bananas — 1
    Some Effects of Going Bananas — 3
    What Is Going On? — 4
    But What about Real Problems? — 7
    Is There Hope? — 8
    How to Regain Your Senses — 10

CHAPTER 2: How Bananas Are We? — 13
    The Future of Bananas — 13
    Bananas Today — 15
    Bananas in the Past — 41

CHAPTER 3: The Science of Bananas — 47
    The Basic Banana Mechanism — 48
    Banana Biology — 51
    Banana Psychology — 52
    Banana Sociology — 55
    Banana Technology — 57
    Banana Economy — 60
    Conclusion: The Five Banana Forces — 63

PART 2: SOLUTIONS

CHAPTER 4: Leaving Bananaland   67
  How Great People Get Great   68
  Another Take on How to Do It   70
  The Nine Steps to Bananalessness   73
  Stages You May Go Through   75
  Your Personal Banana Demons   77
  How to Get the Most Out of this Book   77

CHAPTER 5: Step 1: Calm Down   79
  Switch Off Notifications   79
  Consume Less Information   83
  Stop Babbling   87
  Seek the Silence   89
  Channel Your Thoughts   93
  Conclusion   96

CHAPTER 6: Step 2: Let Go   97
  Stop Ruminating   97
  Cut Down on Planning   100
  Stop Controlling   103
  Forgive   106
  Release Stress   109
  Conclusion   113

CHAPTER 7: Step 3: Take Responsibility   115
  Quit Complaining   115
  Stop Blaming   120
  Speak Out   124
  Allow Feeling Bad   127
  Accept the Consequences   130
  Conclusion   133

CHAPTER 8: Step 4: Dethrone Yourself   135
Control Your Emotions   135
Stop Soul Searching   139
Enjoy Your Averageness   141
Embrace Your Unimportance   145
Celebrate Your Temporality   150
Conclusion   152

CHAPTER 9: Step 5: Build Character   155
Ignore Apps and Advice   155
Deviate from the Herd   158
Take a Risk   161
Guard Your Boundaries   164
Adopt a Work-Rest Rhythm   167
Conclusion   169

CHAPTER 10: Step 6: Detox Yourself   171
Challenge Your Beliefs   171
Rethink Your Aspirations   175
Question Your Habits   178
Filter Your Words   183
Change Your Yardsticks   185
Conclusion   189

CHAPTER 11: Step 7: Get Organized   191
Clean Up Your Stuff   191
Get Rid of Work   195
Stop Procrastinating   201
Multitask Sequentially   204
Plan for Uncertainty   206
Conclusion   209

CHAPTER 12: Step 8: Think Sensibly 211
   Assess Importance 211
   Check Facts 214
   Question the Source 219
   Explore Perspectives 221
   See the Bigger Picture 224
   Conclusion 226

CHAPTER 13: Step 9: Pay Attention 229
   Welcome the Unexpected 229
   Listen and Respond 232
   Monitor Yourself 234
   Read and Repeat 236
   Use Your Senses 238
   Conclusion 240

NO MORE BANANAS! 241

Preface

This is a self-help book. Literally. I have written it to help myself get rid of my bananas and withstand the collective madness around me. So, I am sorry, its first goal was not to help you or to save the world. My purpose was more mundane and self-serving than that: eliminate the bananas in my own head so that I could think, say, feel and act as a sensible individual rather than as some sort of hyper-alert copy of what others think, say, feel and do. I needed that and still need it. Every day.

But, despite this initial self-serving starting point, this book is also a self-help book in the usual sense of the word. Of course, I wrote it for you. And of course, it is meant to help you to get rid of your bananas as well. Why else would I spend all those hours conceiving this book, writing it, rewriting it and polishing it, and why else publish it in the first place? If it were just for me, I could have saved myself the effort. So, this book is as much for you as it is for me.

In this book, I share all the lessons that I have learned on my own journey out of Bananaland because I think they can help you as well. We are all human beings with a great talent for going bananas. Therefore, many of the lessons I learned are not just personal lessons. They are universal lessons that should be as useful for you as they were for me. So here you have it: a nine-step approach with no less than forty-five remedies for going bananas.

To manage your expectations, this book is not a success story. It doesn't tell you about all the heroes who have mastered the nine steps and got rid of all their bananas. And it most certainly doesn't tell you how great and successful I have been—because I haven't.

Success stories are interesting and inspiring. But they are not necessarily helpful. They are usually about hero-type people at a far distance from us ordinary people. I find it hard to relate to such stories, and it is far from evident that their unique experiences are helpful.

We learn more from ordinary people who have struggled and are still struggling. Of course, they should have their occasional successes, but it is their struggle from which we learn most. Because that struggle is telling us what they actually did to get rid of their bananas. Therefore, this book reflects the lessons I have learned, as well as lessons we can learn from others.

The book is intended as a guide for action. If all you do is read it, you won't be very successful in getting rid of your bananas. Because reading is not enough. To appreciate fully the power of the nine steps and forty-five remedies in this book, and get out of Bananaland, you will need to challenge yourself to do something. Bananas don't just disappear. They need active removal. This means there is work to do.

But you will be rewarded. If there is one thing I can say looking back at the past few years, it is that every part of my struggle was worth it. And even more worthwhile than I could have foreseen when I started my journey out of Bananaland. Now that I am rid of a large share of my bananas, I feel more relaxed and can think more freely and clearly than before. If you want that as well, I invite you to start your own banana detoxing journey. Not sooner, not later, but now.

If I can do it, you can do it. None of the nine steps and forty-five remedies in this book requires supernatural skills or special abilities, talent, knowledge, or experience. None of them. They are all things that anyone can do. They are practical things that don't require any higher order mindset, advanced meditation training or an enlightened mind. The only real difficulty is actually doing them and persisting. That is going to be your only real challenge. But if you can manage to do that, you can get rid of many of your bananas too. So join me!

Acknowledgments

Writing this book was easy. At least in one sense. Sometimes you hear an author say that their book "wrote itself," or that writing felt like "the story was already there," inside them, waiting to be told. For me, writing this book was a similar experience. Before I started, I knew more or less what I wanted to say, but while on my way I discovered that the book kind of wrote itself. Apparently, I had been sitting on my thoughts about bananas for a while already, and just needed to release them.

But writing this book was also difficult. Particularly, it was confrontational. As I said, this truly is a self-help book. While doing the research, making my observations and writing, I continuously confronted myself with my own bananas and tried actively to get rid of them. This wasn't always fun. And still, while going through the drafts and final version of the text, the book keeps working like a mirror, showing me where I can still improve.

Luckily enough, I wasn't on my own. Even though the actual writing was a solitary job, and even though all remaining errors, omissions and mistakes are mine, this book would not have been possible without the help of many others.

First, there are all the people who have knowingly and unknowingly provided me with their observations, facts, studies, blogs, newspaper articles, books and scientific articles about banana problems. They were a great source of inspiration for Part 1 of the book and have ensured I could make a substantial deep dive into the banana problem. Thank you for that.

Along the same lines, I would also like to thank the people who have—again, mostly unknowingly—pointed me at the numerous possible solutions that are out there or demonstrated them through their own behaviors. They include people I know personally, like my relatives, friends, neighbors, colleagues, and students. And they also include people I don't know personally: researchers, journalists, bloggers, entrepreneurs, monks, politicians, and even pop stars. You have been the source of ideas and inspiration for Part 2 of the book. Thank you.

In addition to this crowd of idea- and inspiration-givers, there is a small group of people who have volunteered to work actively on the book by reviewing drafts and sharing their feedback and comments. I'd like to thank them in person. Franke Jongsma, thank you for your detailed and critical remarks and suggestions and challenging me to keep the book personal and to the point. Ingrid Maas-Aalbers, thank you for bringing in more nuances and empathy through sharing your personal reflections on the book. Björn Kijl, thank you for your confirmatory remarks and additional sources and suggestions. And David Williams, thank you for the final editing of the book and for offering great value and support in answering my questions. Together, you have made this a better book.

Finally, I have to thank one person in particular: my wife, Caroline. She has read and reviewed the book in detail and pointed me at those sections where things were unclear or too much in your face. But more importantly, she has been the greatest source of inspiration for this book. Many of the remedies described can be traced back to her. And she needed them for a good reason. Not for getting rid of her bananas but helping me get rid of my own. Therefore, Caroline, thank you so much for joining and guiding me on my own journey out of Bananaland. I hope you will stay on my side until the very end.

Other Books to Read

As part of the research for this book, I also relied on what other authors have written about similar topics. As it turns out, there has been substantial and increasing attention to bananas and related subjects over recent years. While the total list of relevant books is too long to include here, I want to mention specifically ten 'brothers in arms' who also wrote books that help against bananas:

- Johan Nordberg (2016), Progress: Ten Reasons to Look Forward to the Future

- Steven Pinker (2018), Enlightenment Now: The Case for Reason, Science, Humanism and Progress

- Fred Luskin (2002), Forgive for Good: A Proven Prescription for Health and Happiness

- Timothy Ferriss (2007), The 4-Hour Workweek: Escape 9-5, Live Anywhere, and Join the New Rich

- David Allen (2015), Getting Things Done: The Art of Stress-Free Productivity

- Tony Crabbe (2015), Busy: How to Thrive in a World of Too Much

- Cal Newport (2016), Deep Work: Rules for Focused Success in a Distracted World

- Mark Manson (2016), The Subtle Art of Not Giving a F*ck

- Wil Derkse (2003), The Rule of Benedict for Beginners: Spirituality for Daily Life

- Svend Brinkmann (2017), Stand Firm: Resisting the Self-Improvement Craze

The first two form a reality check and plea for sensible and optimistic thinking. The next six contain a variety of contemporary approaches against bananas. And the last two invoke centuries-old approaches against bananas and translate them to the world of today.

Given that all the books address related topics, there is obviously overlap between these books and between them and this book. Some of the observations and points they make, for example, I also make in this book. But we all approach the banana problem from a different angle and in a different style, making them all worth reading separately. Therefore, if you are serious about ridding yourself of bananas, I can wholeheartedly recommend reading these books too. But now you are here, let's start with this one.

Part 1

Problems

1

We Are Going Bananas

We are living in a crazy world. Not because the world is so crazy, but because we are. With 'we', I mean us, adult human beings, together, as a group—myself included. Somewhere over the years, we have started to collectively lose our senses as a human species. This makes us do, think, say and feel strange things that don't make any sense.

Either in a documentary or for real, you must have seen schools of fish, flocks of birds or herds of wildebeest making extreme, unexpected and stressful movements when danger is signaled. Whenever an enemy approaches, the whole school, flock or herd moves from one direction to another in an attempt to escape the danger. This is pretty much how we, as grown-up people, often behave collectively.

The most accurate description that I can give for this behavior is that we have gone bananas. According to the Cambridge Dictionary, going 'bananas' means "very silly" or "to become extremely angry or excited" or "very excited because of pleasure, anger, or another emotion." And that is what our collective behavior often looks like: very angry, very excited and very silly.

Taken individually, we are quite reasonable people. Apart from the occasional exception—the lunatic, the sociopath, the frustrated—we are generally fairly sensible. We usually think about things and try to make the best of our lives. And we even care about others while doing so.

Collectively, however, we behave like a panicking herd of animals that have spotted a source of danger. As part of this herd, we stop thinking and acting by ourselves. Instead, we mimic each other and show exponentially strange behaviors that make little to no sense.

A clear example of this is Twitter—where the metaphor of a flock of birds is hardly a metaphor anymore. Through Twitter, messages spread globally in a matter of seconds, causing an explosive chain of reactions, the one often even more extreme than the other.

Take the #MeToo movement that went viral in October 2017. Of course, at the heart of it is a very serious and unacceptable problem— the widespread prevalence of sexual assault by men in power. However, the chain of events that this movement has set in motion and that has been fired up by the media is absurd. Suddenly, large groups of people felt indignant and upset. They sensed an untamable need to express this loudly, and publicly condemn the possibly guilty with outraged messages full of hate. And if someone had the guts to make a critical remark, they were immediately crucified too. Even the very fact that I call #MeToo an example of going bananas here, may upset some people who will go bananas about it while reading this very paragraph.

It is not only social media where collective madness takes over our ability to think reasonably. Admittedly, Twitter, and also Facebook, WhatsApp, Snapchat, Instagram or any social media app that is popular at the moment you read this book, play a big role in aggrandizing the collective lunacy.

There are countless other occasions though. A good example is the apparently irresistible force to follow consumer trends and buy stuff that others buy. Even though we may think we are living in a free society, where everyone can decide what to wear, eat, and do, we largely just follow the trends and do as everyone else does.

Take the superfood trend. With the exception of a few of us, a decade ago no one had ever heard of chia seeds, wheatgrass, quinoa, or goji berries—let alone considered for one second to eat them. And kale was still a boring vegetable that your grandpa and grandma ate. Today though, we MUST eat these foods or else we are DESTROYING OUR BODIES!!! (note the caps and exclamation marks).

In some cases, the superfood craze can even take extreme forms that are unhealthy or downright dangerous. An example is the (hyped) Silicon Valley craze to drink 'raw' unfiltered water because it still contains all the natural ingredients that have been removed from normal drinking water. These natural ingredients include minerals and ions. They also include bacteria and parasites. It is exactly by drinking such raw water that millions of people across the globe have died and are still dying.

"But these are just two examples!" you may argue. "And altogether it is not that bad!" or "At least *I* am not as sensitive to the collective lunacy as other people," you may think. But don't be too sure. I'll bet that, if you look honestly in the mirror and analyze your own behavior, you'll discover quite a few bananas there. At least I did when looking in my mirror, and found many. Too many. Far too many.

Some Effects of Going Bananas

Going bananas is like taking drugs. Sometimes it reflects instant heavenly experiences that make us feel better, more excited, or happier than ever before. This is the kind of "Oh My God!" (OMG) excitement when we go bananas in the sense of going crazy about a new gadget, experience, movie, meal, book or song. It is also the kind of bananas that we find on Facebook whenever we share, like, and comment on something to show how superbly great our lives are. Or the kind of bananas when we buy cryptocurrency stocks and see them double in value in a couple of days. OMG!

This kind of going bananas and its effects seem positive. They reflect a 'shot' of instant gratification. Like with drugs though, the gratification is usually rather short-lived. After a few days, minutes, or even seconds, the 'eternal' happiness feeling is usually gone. After clicking or swiping to the next message on your Facebook timeline, or after the next cryptocurrency crash, the temporary high is quickly replaced by a feeling of disappointment, envy, anger or panic.

Going bananas also has a darker side—with only negatives. Through our collective madness and constant comparison to others, we often feel pressured to show particular behaviors. Some examples: we 'have to' stay abreast of everything happening on social media, we 'have to' respond promptly to email and WhatsApp messages, we 'have to' do as our friends and family do, we 'have to' eat certain foods, treat our kids in a particular way, like particular movies, and so on and so forth. Or so we make ourselves believe.

This creates pressure. It stresses us out. It makes us feel uncertain. We lose confidence. It makes us anxious. It increases our blood pressure. It leads to insomnia. It gives us heartburn. Palpitations. Headaches. In short: going bananas is not good for us.

Many of us recognize these effects and seek ways to deal with our bananas. Over the years, for example, an increasing number of people have visited monasteries, and been for a short or longer retreat to enjoy the silence and to calm down. Furthermore, people engage in information fasting, digital detoxes, and tidying up courses to reduce the physical and virtual clutter that is bothering them. And mindfulness, yoga and meditation training have never been so popular. So, we are aware and work on it. That's great. But to avoid collectively losing our minds further, we need to step up our efforts.

What Is Going On?

I have used the metaphors of a school of fish, flock of birds and herd of wildebeest to describe our collective madness. If we were really a school, flock or herd of animals, and if there was real danger threatening us, our collective behavior would not be mad. On the contrary, it would make a lot of sense. Staying close together, copying each other's behaviors, and making unexpected collective movements are effective protection mechanisms facing an enemy we can't beat on our own.

However, we are not a school, flock or herd of animals. Sure, we are connected. As the famous 'six degrees of separation' idea goes, we are all no more than six steps away from each other. So, our friends connect us to other friends, who connect us to still other friends, and so on. In this way, any two people in the world are assumed to be connected in a maximum of six steps.

But being connected doesn't automatically mean that we are like a school, flock or herd of animals. With the exception of our closest relationships, we are not dependent on each other to survive and we are not physically stuck with each other 24/7. We are only loosely connected some parts of the day and are largely unconnected other parts of the day. Even if we are online 24/7 and chatting with our friends all the time, we are still not as connected as these animals.

And the dangers that make us panic aren't real either. Only rarely, we are in real danger. Usually, we are safe, and our lives are rather dull compared to that of the average animal or bird. Our lives aren't at stake, we don't have to worry about food, we have a home to live in, and so on. The kind of fears that make us go bananas are other, more psychological and sociological fears. They include:

- *Fear of missing out.* The fear of missing interesting opportunities, information or experiences while doing something else.

- *Fear of being alone.* The fear of being disconnected from others and feeling uncomfortable when on your own.

- *Fear of being left alone.* The fear of being lonely and being left behind in a world in which all others seem to move forward.

- *Fear of being ordinary.* The fear of not being seen or being ignored because you are not special enough for others.

- *Fear of being extra-ordinary.* The fear of being called strange and thereby being abandoned, criticized or ridiculed by others.

- *Fear of failure.* The fear of setbacks, mistakes, grief or pain because you think you can't deal with such feelings.

- *Fear of nothingness.* The fear of being called lazy and of your demons coming up when doing nothing.

Compared to being eaten, I would argue these fears are relatively insignificant. When going bananas, they control our minds and seem to be the most important things on earth. However, if you think about it as a sensible person, there is not much to fear. So long as you are reasonably confident in yourself and do not care too much about what others are thinking, saying or doing, you'll be doing fine.

So, what is going on? The main thesis of this book is that, in this postmodern society, we have abandoned all but one of our pillars of certainty. And, as a result, we have lost our individuality and so go bananas.

Postmodernism is a Western philosophy that came up around the 1950s. It is characterized by an attitude of skepticism, subjectivism and relativism, a denial of all structures, ideologies and certainties of the past and a general suspicion of reason. Today, this is no longer just a philosophy engaging a handful of philosophers. Rather, it has invaded our lives and become part of our mainstream, everyday way of thinking.

We can think of postmodernism as a way of thinking that liberates us from the preconceptions and boundaries of the past. It does away with the straitjackets of science, reason and logic and it makes sure we don't take things for granted. It gives a lot of freedom in what and how to think, feel and act. This sounds good.

But it also makes us feel lost. If nothing is certain anymore, what can we rely on? In the past, we had various pillars that provided us with a level of certainty that made our lives comforting. We had kings, emperors and pharaohs to obey. We feared them, but they offered us protection and predictability. We had gods, churches and priests to have faith in. They gave us the comfort of forgiveness and the promise of heaven. We had witches, magicians and alchemists to believe. They made us feel more certain about what would happen to us in the future. Or we had science, universities and professors we could depend on. They made us feel masters of the universe and showed us the truth about our world.

All of that, many of us—at least in Western society—have abandoned today. We don't accept any know-it-all leaders, we don't believe in an omnipresent god, we are suspicious of anything that is non-scientific and, with the many cases of fraud we are confronted with, we don't even trust science any longer either. Our postmodern thinking has flushed all these certainties down the toilet.

In our quest for certainty, grip and support, the only seemingly dependable pillar we have left is The Other—other people. This is our friends and families, but also celebrities or any other people we want to relate ourselves to. We look to them to get the desired feeling of certainty about what we should be doing. We copy their behavior, we take their opinions seriously, we try to please them, and we try to be as them. And since we are all doing this and aping each other, it is no wonder we go bananas. Together, we create and perpetuate our own vicious socio-psychological stress-cycle.

The interesting effect is that bit-by-bit we are losing our individuality. Often, you hear claims that we are living in an individualistic society. We don't care about others, we are ego-centric, and we engage only in self-serving behavior. That may very well be the case, since individual*ism*—the idea that freedom and autonomy are key qualities in a society—rules.

However, at the same time, we are more socially bound than ever before. Through the various fears described above, we hardly dare think for ourselves, be different, or be our true selves. Rather, we conform to what we expect is expected from us. This means that real individual*ity*—the things that make us unique as a person and different from others—is getting rarer and rarer. And so we go bananas.

But What About Real Problems?

Of course, we have real problems and real fears. We may be assured of food on our plate and have a decent home to live in. But we all have our own share of problems to deal with. Maybe you have an unruly child who drives you to despair or a demented parent you provide care to. Maybe you are in a dreadful fight with your ex or with your neighbors. Maybe you have suffered a trauma from something terrible that happened to you. Maybe you have a super stressful job that keeps you awake at night. Or maybe you have any other problem that is as real as it can be.

Problems like these make us easily lose our minds. They make us anxious, uncertain, sad, frustrated or angry. And they keep our mind continuously occupied. We keep on worrying and thinking about our problems night and day, and so they have a significant influence on everything we do. They make it so that we can't function as well and think as clearly as we would like.

Worrying, feeling lost and losing our minds because of these real problems, though, is perfectly sane. We aren't robots or cold, rational thinkers. So we can't avoid it. We even need it. To process the things happening to us, we need to worry and think about them, and we need them to disturb our lives. If we ignore them and pretend everything is fine, they will come back to us twice as forcefully later on.

And, of course, we look at others when we have real problems. We ask them for help and support, we look at how they deal with it, or we talk to them so we can share and tell our story. We want to know what they think, feel, say and do or we want them to listen. After all, together we are stronger than alone.

These behaviors are sane. Not silly. This means they are *not* what this book is about. Going bananas is not about our real problems and how we deal with them. Going bananas is about our imaginary or pseudo-problems. About the things which we make larger than they are. About our silliness in how we respond to things. About how we derive what we think, feel, say and do from others, and thereby create bandwagon effects and reinforcing cycles that make our minds derail. About being so occupied with our pseudo-problems that we can't effectively deal with our real problems. About not taking responsibility for the things we do. About not behaving as sensible adults.

Is There Hope?

Yes. There is hope. Because most of our problems and fears are not life-threatening and are largely imaginary, we can do something about them.

At root, the remedy is extremely simple: be yourself. You are you, so basically, being yourself is the most natural thing you can do. I don't mean the kind of 'be yourself' that would imply that you don't care about anyone or anything else. And I most certainly don't mean the kind of be yourself that is used as an excuse for 'intuitive' uncontrolled outbursts of so-called authenticity. You know, the sort of people who shout, sing, laugh out loud, or give you unsolicited advice about how to raise your kids because they authentically feel they should do that.

Be yourself refers to the quieter self that is inside you. The self you find through introspection and reflection—or by doing nothing. And no, I don't mean the self that results from over-analyzing yourself and digging deeper and deeper to find your 'true' self. Instead, it is the confident self that you experience when being happy or satisfied with something small. It is the self that cares about things and about others and knows what is right and what is wrong.

I'm sure you know what I mean. Maybe it has been a while since you experienced this self. Or maybe you made yourself believe it isn't there because you can't remember when you experienced it. This is understandable. In the social lunacy of today, your self gets easily suppressed and moved to the background. But it is there, and you know it.

While many of us, me included, find it extremely difficult to be this self and regain their individuality, there are people around us who are doing it all the time. Here is a list:

- Movie or book characters including Mr. Miyagi from *The Karate Kid*, Pippi Longstocking and Moana (*Vaiana*). They are all strong-willed individualistic characters daring to be different.

- Rockstar entrepreneurs such as Richard Branson, Steve Jobs and Elon Musk. They are famous for their unique ideas and approach and their headstrong disregard of conventional wisdom and public opinion.

- Political and religious leaders like Nelson Mandela, Martin Luther King and Mahatma Gandhi, who stood up for their belief in a better world and persisted despite all the threats and suffering.

But wait… "These are not real people," you may argue, or "they are real, but surreal exceptions and not like ordinary people." You are right. So, even though we can learn from them, they are so far out of reach that taking them as a role model might be too much of a stretch. But there are more ordinary people who manage to stay true to themselves as well:

- The mysterious monks who live a structured, dedicated and segregated life in a monastery. They successfully manage to keep the craziness outside and live a peaceful, silent life together.

- The mad scientists who ignore what others are telling them and continue their quest for the truth. They stoically manage to follow their own ideas and let others laugh at them.

- The hard-nosed politicians who follow their own convictions and convince others too. They manage to withstand the pressure of populism and fight for their own ideology.

"But…," I almost hear you object again, "…these hardly qualify as 'people like us'." You are right. They have chosen a rather particular career and made extraordinary sacrifices to follow their heart. Despite their perhaps inspirational way of life, they are exceptions too and hard to relate to. So, here's another list:

- Your outspoken aunt wearing her purple dress, carrying her own herbal tea and having a smiling face all the time. She manages to deviate from what 'everyone' finds 'normal.'

- Your imperturbable colleague sitting next to you in the flex room, who would continue working even if a bomb went off next to her. She can switch off her ears or so it seems.

- Your offline grandma who still writes letters on her old typewriter and whom you can only reach by wired phone, snail mail or by visiting her. She manages to escape the social media craze completely.

- Your nerdy neighbor who wears the 'wrong' jeans, laughs about the 'wrong' jokes and likes the 'wrong' music. He manages to stay totally ignorant about what is supposedly wrong.

- Your explosively energetic four-year-old who talks to her imaginary friend and sees cars where you see random scribbles. She manages to let her fantasy speak for itself.

Even though some of them look like outright anti-heroes, they are the real heroes in your banana detox. They are as ordinary as people can be. And yet, they do something that seems increasingly extra-ordinary: they withstand the collective craze, keep a cool head, and stay close to themselves. The good thing is that we can learn a great deal from them. Because what they do is nothing magical and doesn't require supernatural skills. This means that all of us can do it. So yes, there is hope.

How to Regain Your Senses

The road to regaining your senses is a bumpy and winding one. We are extremely attracted by The Other and go to great lengths to imitate and please other people and thereby lose our senses. However, as the beacons of light above show, there are people who can withstand the madness. They keep a cool head and stay grounded and true to themselves. And if they can do it, you can do it too.

But how? How to keep your cool in the lunacy? How to behave and be more like them? For these role models, it seems to come naturally. They seem to have an intuitive built-in feature that makes them less sensitive to others than us, ordinary people. While they will have the occasional slip and also join the lunacy, their default mode is being grounded.

This may be true for some of them. But certainly not for all of them. Getting and staying grounded doesn't come naturally to many people, including these role models. Take the monk, the scientist, the politician. Don't you think they are tempted to join the collective madness every day? And don't you think they spend a great deal of effort withstanding it? Of course they do. And take your nerdy neighbor and your outspoken aunt. Don't you think the same applies to them? Of course it does. They are human too, which means they also have their doubts and temptations. But, nevertheless, they choose to stay grounded.

The way to regain your senses is exactly that: regain your senses. I already referred to the school of fish, flock of birds and herd of wildebeest a couple of times. As these metaphors suggest, the behavior we show when joining the madness is animal behavior. It reflects a primary, animal-like response when in danger. We respond out of fear and let our ancient animal brains take control of us.

But we are not just animals. As human beings, we have a unique ability that makes us different from other species: we can reason. We have the ability to think about what we do, reflect on it, and decide to behave differently. We can affect our primary instincts and choose to ignore them. We might not be able to control them fully, but we can influence and neglect them. And this is exactly how we can keep a cool head and stay grounded in the collective madness. When we succeed in staying sensible and think about things before we let our fears and primary responses control us, we no longer have to join the collective treadmill. We can step out and become ourselves again.

2

How Bananas Are We?

Maybe you have read or heard the quote "No one ever went broke underestimating the intelligence of the public." This is pretty much what the collective madness I refer to means. It doesn't mean we are unintelligent individuals. It means that, as a group, we are not especially intelligent—and sometimes we are downright stupid.

But exactly how bananas are we? To find out, I have made an inventory of the numerous ways in which we are going bananas. As I soon discovered, bananas are everywhere. They invade about every aspect of our lives with disturbing effects. Therefore, be warned that reading this chapter can be seriously frustrating. Bear with me.

The Future of Bananas

To get a sense of where we are heading, it is always informative (and entertaining) to watch Sci-Fi movies. Even though such movies are of course largely fantasy, they usually contain just enough realism to make them interesting to watch—and make them a bit gloomy too. After all, who knows…? There could be some truth in aliens or robots taking over the world or in an undiscovered people with their own peculiar habits, clothes, and language saving the world.

In the light of bananas, and particular the future of bananas, an interesting movie is *Idiocracy*. This Sci-Fi comedy from 2006 by Mike Judge sketches a dystopian future in which the world (or at least the United States) has gone completely bananas as a result of 500 years of evolutionary reproduction. By the mere fact that people with higher IQs have fewer children than people with lower IQs, humanity has become increasingly stupid by out-breeding intelligence.

The story goes like this (spoiler alert). The protagonist Corporal Joe Bauers and a prostitute named Rita are selected for a secret military hibernation project. In 2005, they were sealed in hibernation chambers and supposed to be woken up a year later. However, the experiment is forgotten and, instead of being woken up one year later, Joe (and Rita) wake up 500 years later. In these 500 years, humanity has degenerated to a level at which Joe, who was 'the most average soldier' in 2005, is now the world's most brilliant intellectual.

The level of bananas in this future world is beyond imagination. People name their kids after corporate brands, and everything that is told in commercials is accepted as the truth. People's span of attention is about two seconds and they are immediately distracted by any ad-like communication or sale. They water their lawns and crops with a sugary drink called 'Brawndo: The Thirst Mutilator' because—even though it kills all plants—the mighty Brawndo Corporation has effectively convinced people that water is only good for toilets. As a result, there is a serious food shortage that no one knows how to solve.

The most popular TV program—Ow! My Balls!—is as stupid as its name suggests, and the blockbuster film called 'Ass' shows a two-hour close-up of someone's ass. The world is full of misspelled signs and people speak a dumbed-down version of English. Their math skills are at the level at which they can be made to believe that 30 billion minus 20 billion equals 80 billion. History is reinterpreted so that Charlie Chaplin was believed to be the leader of the Nazi party who set the world to war using dinosaurs. The 'Un' (United Nations) is celebrated as a great institution because it 'Un-Nazied' the world forever, and the president is a porn star and five-time TV wrestling champion…

Of course, this movie is fiction. But it is also *science*-fiction. And like other Sci-Fi movies, the scary thing is that there is truth in some of the assumptions on which it is based. As research shows, people with lower IQs have more children than people with higher IQs. Furthermore, even though IQ has gone up, the genetically determined level of IQ has dropped about one point over the past fifty years and is expected to continue dropping, by even more than a point over the next fifty years. If this trend continues, it would mean that, in the course of 500 years, the world's average genetically determined IQ would drop more than ten points. This doesn't immediately get us to the stupidity levels of *Idiocracy*. However, we only have to extrapolate the trend a little bit differently to end up there.

More important than the scientific truthfulness of this movie or our possibly degenerating genetic IQ, is the dystopian image of society that *Idiocracy* sketches. In the movie, people have completely lost their ability to think sensibly. Going bananas has become their default mode of 'thinking'. Even though we are not living in an idiocracy yet, and I hope we will never get that far, we can unfortunately recognize its seeds wherever we look around us.

And I am not the only one. Interestingly, the film's popularity is rising again. Furthermore, in 2014, *Rolling Stone* magazine called it "more pertinent than ever" in the year "11 AK" (After Kardashian). They conclude, referring to urbandictionary.com's definition of *Idiocracy*: "No, it is not a movie that was originally a comedy and then became a documentary quite yet. But just give it a generation or two."

Bananas Today

Even though *Idiocracy* is not a documentary yet, we are reaching respectful levels of bananas today. To illustrate this point, this is going to be a long section. It needs to be, because this helps with getting a sense of how deep and wide bananas have invaded our lives. You may feel that not everything applies 100% to you. If so, that's great. It means you haven't gone completely bananas yet. However, I also suspect that you will recognize quite a few bananas if you look honestly at yourself. At least I do. We can divide our bananas into eight categories.

1. We Don't Really Care About the Truth

A first and strong signal that we have gone bananas is our disrespect for the truth. Having been a university professor myself, I know the whole notion of 'truth' is a complicated one, and that we can never fully and objectively know whether something is true or not. However, according to any accepted scientific standards of truth that are used, there are facts that we cannot rationally deny.

A widely discussed truth that is denied even by presidents (at least one, or not, depending on which day you ask), is Al Gore's *Inconvenient Truth* that climate is changing and that this is to a large part caused by human activity. There is such broad and convincing evidence for this, that denying it really is bananas and shows a disrespect for anything that deserves to be called true.

But examples of not caring about the truth go to greater extremes than this. A good, extreme banana example is the fact that a significant number of people honestly believe that the world is flat. I don't mean Thomas Friedman flat, in the sense that our current world is one of global competition in which companies from all over the world have more or less equal opportunities due to technological advancement such as the Internet. I mean really flat. Physically flat—as a pancake.

Depending on which discovery we put most value on, we have already known for sure that the world is round since the 14th or 15th centuries, or even as long ago as hundreds of years Before Christ. Still, there is a group of people on this globe that actually believes the world is flat. It is not one-third of millennials who believe this—as is sometimes claimed. However, as a recent survey by YouGov of over 8,000 US citizens shows, it is still an astonishing *2 percent* of American adults who are *resolutely* convinced of this, and that the whole idea of a round world is a conspiracy theory. This adds up to *5 million* people, just in the United States. I find this outrageously bananas.

(Let me make an apology to US readers at this point. It is not my intention to suggest that you have gone more bananas than anyone else. However, somehow, studies like this, presidents such as the above, and movies such as *Idiocracy* tend to be from the US. Because of my personal bias, language and research approach, I may have found more studies and publications about your country than any other country. But throughout this book, I will assume that things are similar elsewhere).

Less extreme, but more widely spread, is the belief that the world is getting in worse and worse shape. We look back in nostalgia at the good old days when crime, poverty, pollution, etcetera were not as terrible as they are today. And we worry about how much worse it can go and in what kind of misery our children must live—if the world survives at all.

Such feelings are understandable. But they are also outright wrong. And increasingly wrong. As extensive research shows, with the exception of climate change the world is in better shape than ever before on virtually all indicators we can imagine (thanks Johan Norberg for putting all of this together in your book *Progress*). Whether it is life expectancy, equality, freedom, literacy, sanitation, food, poverty or violence, the conclusion is as convincing as it is strong and hard to believe; we are living in the best of times.

Of course, this doesn't apply to everyone. There are large groups of people who suffer from poverty, who are on the run as refugees, who have to fear for their safety every day, who die of curable diseases, and so on and so forth. And some people in some regions are worse off than ever before. However, taken as a whole, the world is in better shape than ever before.

Reading Norberg's book is good medicine for the truth-denial kind of bananas described above and a reason to become a rational optimist. Let me summarize a few of the impressive facts it presents:

- In the last 50 years, poverty has dropped more than over the preceding 500 years.

- Worldwide malnutrition has dropped from about 30% in 1970 to about 10% today—while the world population has doubled over this period.

- Worldwide average life expectancy has increased from 31 years in 1900 to 71 years today.

- The number of people killed per 100,000 people is lower than ever before in history.

If you need further convincing, read Norberg's book or Steven Pinker's more recent *Enlightenment Now*, which carries the same, fact-based optimistic message. And if you still need further convincing that we ignore, deny or are otherwise wrong in our beliefs, visit gapminder.org. This is the website of a Swedish 'fact tank' fighting the "devastating misconceptions about global development" by measuring global ignorance. Have a look at their interesting material and take their Gapminder Test to find out how far off you are. A confession: when taking the test while writing this book, I scored just above 50% and was universally too pessimistic. So, even while being aware that things are generally much better than we think they are, I didn't pass the test even close.

Not caring about the truth means that our beliefs are based on something else. After all, if it is not facts, there must be *some* reason why some believe that climate change is a Chinese invention, that the world is flat, or that we are living in the worst of times. We don't just make this up. We rely on sources other than facts in forming our beliefs.

One such source is Personal Experience—the experience that says "I have never noticed it, so it is probably not true" or "I have had this once, so everyone else must have had it too" or "I know a friend of my uncle's mother in law who had this remarkable experience, so it is must be true".

Yes, we may feel the world is coming to an end. Yes, we may experience the world as flat when we walk on it. And no, we don't literally experience global warming. But this says nothing about whether or not the world is actually coming to an end, whether or not it is flat, or whether or not climate change is real. Yet, we use Personal Experience all the time as a basis to judge whether something is true. This makes it an important source of bananas.

Another source is Baffling Stories. People are storytellers. We love good stories, especially ones that baffle our minds. We like hero stories, drama stories, success stories, misery stories, failure stories. And we especially like them if they are almost too good to be true; if they have this "No! Really?" effect. And that is where the problem comes in. Many of them *are* too good to be true. They are urban myths, misinterpreted reports, after-the-fact rationalizations, degenerated anecdotes, or just plain nonsense. But we like them anyway.

The story that one-third of millennials today believe the world is flat is such a story. It has a great "No! Really?" factor which makes us like it. But it is just not true. Other examples are the stories that we use only 10% of our brain, that sugar causes children to be hyperactive, or that ostriches bury their heads in the sand. These stories sound nice, have a great "No! Really?" factor, but they are nonsense.

If we would only like these stories as stories, there would be no problem. Then they would be just another piece of entertaining fiction next to novels or movies. However, the problem with these stories is that we must hold them as true to like them. A story is only baffling enough to get a "No! Really?" effect if we make ourselves believe it has actually happened. Because we *want* them to be true, we pretend they are true. We even want them so dearly to be true that, despite the data refuting these stories being nowadays at our fingertips, we don't check. But this doesn't make them true. Which makes Baffling Stories a great source of bananas.

A third source of beliefs that replaces facts and truth is the Majority Opinion. The larger the group of people that believe something is true, the more likely we assume it is true. After all, if so many people believe something, it must be true, right? The Majority Opinion is at work every time when we base our decisions on public ratings—the number of likes on Facebook, the number of retweets on Twitter, the number of stars on Amazon or Netflix, and so on. It is also at work in bestseller lists, blockbuster movies, and numbers of downloads: the more that people buy, watch, or download something, the better it must be.

As far as it concerns something subjective, such as whether you like a message, book or movie, this has not much to do with facts or truth. After all, there is no objective standard to decide whether they are 'truly' good or bad. As far as it concerns our beliefs of what is true, however, the Majority Opinion is a highly suspicious replacement for facts. The mere fact that many people believe something is true doesn't make it true. Take the belief that the world is increasingly uncertain, complex, and dynamic. We mainly believe this is true because we hear and see it repeated everywhere. We see it on social media, we hear it from friends, and we read it in magazines. But that doesn't make it true.

The same applies to the idea that the world since 9/11 is more violent than ever. We believe this because this is what we are telling each other. We hear and see 'evidence' every day. However, as referred to above, the exact opposite is true: we live in the least violent times ever in history, making the Majority Opinion a highly unreliable source to rely on.

A fourth source that serves as a replacement for truth in shaping our beliefs is Celebrity Opinions. For a long time, people mostly believed what prophets, priests, witches or druids were saying. These were assumed to be the bearers of truth because of their great visionary powers, or they represented God. Since the scientific revolution that started in the mid-1500s and that was propelled forward during the Enlightenment around 1700, this idea was gradually replaced by science as the source of truth. Instead of relying on the views of a select group of people, it was found that truth could be discovered through careful research. Of course, science isn't perfect, and many findings that we once held true have been replaced by others. However, the progress that we have made by relying on scientific principles rather than on individual 'bearers of truth' is astonishing.

Today, however, we seem to be regressing back to relying on the views of a select group of people. In a time of 'fake news' and 'alternative facts', we are increasingly suspicious about science and scientists and about facts and truth. In our search for sources to rely on, we have turned to celebrities. Whether it be pop stars, athletes, or actors, the mere fact that someone is well-known is now taken as an indicator that we should follow their views. We read their biographies, watch them in talk shows, follow them on Twitter, and listen to what they say. This is equally absurd, or maybe even more absurd than assuming prophets, priests, witches or druids know the truth. There is no link whatsoever between someone being good at performing, sports, acting, or playing the celebrity, and knowing more than the average person. This makes relying on their views to form our own, pretty bananas.

2. We Lose Our Sense of Nuance and Perspective

Losing a sense of reality by losing sight of facts is one form of going bananas. Overreacting to the things we see, hear and feel is another. And we are good at this. To start with, let's have a look at how we communicate, especially on social media. Take Twitter. I won't use actual examples because they are too offensive. But it is easy enough on Twitter to find extreme hate speech with all variety of death wishes against almost anything and anyone you can imagine.

Of course, hate speech is extreme. It is not representative at all of the average tweet. But the sheer number of hate messages that float around on social media like Twitter and Facebook is worrisome. And what is also worrisome is that this number and their level of extremism seems to be growing, too.

I recently read a study which said that my country, the Netherlands, is among the top countries when it concerns hate speech on Facebook. This makes me feel embarrassed. Once upon a time (and not so long ago), the Dutch were known for their open-mindedness and tolerance. The fact that a nation like this has one of the highest shares of hate speech on Facebook today shows that this open-mindedness and tolerance is disappearing—and that we urgently need a banana-detox.

In addition to my not-so-relevant personal experiences and concerns, there is also research on social media hate speech. Safehome.org carried out a study on hate on social media between 2008 and 2016. In particular, they studied the number of messages, likes, and followers of American hate groups (anti-muslim, anti-immigrant, anti-LGBT, anti-Semitic, white supremacy, black separatists). The sad picture this research shows is that, even though overall 'normal' Twitter usage has stabilized over these years, hate speech exploded in 2015 and 2016. The study found, for example, that the number of likes given to tweets by hate groups more than tripled between 2014 and 2015, and more than tripled *again* between 2015 and 2016. That is a staggering tenfold increase in just two years.

It is not only on social media and in hate speech where we go bananas. This also happens in our 'normal' communication and in the conventional media. Rather than saying something is remarkable, nice or good, we shout Amazing! Fantastic! Excellent! Wonderful! or Perfect! (with at least one but preferably more exclamation marks, or in full caps, and with lots of emojis). And rather than saying that one thing could be a bit better, worse or more than another, everything is 'the best', 'the worst', or 'the most' ever. And if something as ordinary happens as a friend showing up at our doorstep, looking in the mirror when fitting a pair of new jeans, or tasting a new flavor of ice cream, we put our hands in front of our face and scream Oh My God! (OMG!). And to stress that something is extraordinarily important to pay attention to, we put full stops after every word. Can. It. Be. More. Bananas?

In the newspapers, we can see extreme language as well. Of course, there have always been trash tabloids like *the Sun* (UK), the *National*

Enquirer (US), or *Bild* (Germany), with extreme page-filling all-caps headlines such as "WORLD WAR 3 IS COMING!", "HILLARY: 6 MONTHS TO LIVE!" and "DR. PHILL: RAGING MONSTER!" (all from *National Enquirer*). But also in more respected newspapers, this sensational style of writing is gaining traction. They adopt the same all-caps style (but still without the exclamation marks) in headlines such as "TERROR RETURNS" (*USA Today*), and "DEPORTATIONS TO BEGIN" (*Boston Globe*).

It's not only in the way we talk that we go bananas. It's also in the way we *think* that we are losing our sense of nuance and perspective. Even though *Fifty Shades of Grey* was a box office king and bestselling book, we seem to be increasingly engaging in dichotomous black and white thinking. Something is either good or bad, right or wrong, healthy or unhealthy, we either love it or hate it, want all or nothing, and you are either with us or against us—as US president George Bush framed it in 2001.

Of course, the world is not black and white. It doesn't even have just fifty shades of grey. With all its nuances, varieties and perspectives, it is offered to us in high-definition full color. But seeing that nuance is apparently something we have difficulty with. I don't know why. But I suppose this is our way of coping with the uncertainty and complexity that we experience. All the stuff we hear and see around us—about terrorism, new technologies, climate change, geopolitical changes, etc.—scares us. And in response, we seek for safe simplicity that we can handle: black vs. white.

Even though understandable, this is a banana response. As long as we don't have any mental disorders, we have the capability to embrace nuance and perspective in our thinking. We know the world is not black and white. We know food cannot be simply categorized as healthy or unhealthy. And we know that there is more than good and bad. But somehow, we seem to forget this all the time.

Such dichotomous thinking is characteristic of babies and small children. For them, the world is simple: as babies, they are hungry or not hungry, want to sleep or be awake, and smile or cry. And as toddlers and children, they are either best friends or hate each other. Their senses and brains have not yet fully matured and they are therefore not yet able to pick up the nuances that we can see as adults. As research shows, newborns even literally see only black and white in their first week after birth.

Dichotomous thinking is also characteristic of people with a mental disorder, such as borderline personality disorder. Because of their condition, they tend to see the world only in extremes. And this often has a crippling effect, causing feelings of great excitement and high hopes on the one hand, and feelings of depression, shame, anger and failure on the other. So, if we all had borderline personality disorder, our lack of nuanced thinking would be normal. However, so long as we are not all diagnosed, I take it as a sign that we are going bananas.

If we are losing our sense of nuance and perspective in how we think and talk, it automatically also affects the way we *act*. We do extreme things. While terrorism and other forms of extremism are of course the most obvious examples of this, they reflect the extreme behaviors of only a small group of people. But extreme behavior is more common than that.

A good example is the way we vote. In politics, we see polarization happening in many countries. This is perhaps most evident in the US, with its two-party system of democrats and republicans. While having two parties in itself already fosters dichotomous thinking, the divide between democrats and republicans on liberal versus conservative thinking has never been as great since we started measuring this in 1879, which indicates they have never disagreed more than today.

Also in other elections and referenda, our voting reflects black and white thinking. Protest seems increasingly more important than progress. Sure, I am biased towards the progressive side, but the kind of protest I mean has not so much to do with the traditional conservative versus progressive division. A substantial share of voters use their vote to vote against the existing regime. Populist parties and politicians profit from this. Even though some voters don't agree with them, and may even completely disagree, they still vote for them.

A conversation that I heard between a restaurant owner and a customer during a recent election was illustrative. The customer talked about how much she disliked the existing regime and that she also disagreed with this up and coming populist politician. But she would rather burn down the castle than vote for the existing regime. In her words (freely translated): "I know this populist politician doesn't offer any solution and will fuck it up, but I'd rather we all go to hell and blow up the whole country than that I vote for the existing regime." Considering that my country ranks amongst the happiest, wealthiest, most stable, and best-organized countries on the globe year after year, this clearly shows a lack of nuance and perspective—and a clear case of going bananas.

3. We Have Omni-Obesity

A third sign that we are losing our senses is the way we go bananas about gathering things—both virtual and physical. To paraphrase the infamous song by the rock band Queen: we want it all, we want it all, and we want it now. We want more information, more notifications, more friends, more followers, more likes, more bandwidth, more clothes, more sneakers, more money, bigger houses, larger cars, more holidays, more hobbies, more options to choose from, more features, bigger portions, longer bucket lists, more experiences, more types of peanut butter, and more blades on our razor—and we want it now. It seems we are addicted to everything that we can gather and get more of.

Does it make us happier? Of course not, or at least not for more than two seconds. And we know this perfectly well. We all have the experience of instant gratification when buying something that is immediately forgotten afterward. But the inclination to gather stuff and the fear of missing out on something are so strong that we just go on and on. It is like an addiction: even though we know it doesn't help us, the irresistible force of more is simply too strong for many of us.

We are repeatedly confusing quantity with quality here, and price with value. In shopping jargon 'good value' means cheap and a 'value deal' means we are getting more stuff that we don't actually need. But the mere fact that something is cheap (or 'free'), or that we get more of it (or 'all-inclusive'), doesn't make it more valuable. A product that you buy because it is 'good value' (cheap) is still more expensive than not spending the money. And the money spent on the stuff in a 'value deal' that you didn't want in the first place could also be saved to spend on something you really value.

We really go bananas if the 'good value' or 'value deal' is temporary. Picture the sprints people make and the fights people get into when there is a 'special', 'once in a year', or 'now or never' SALE—on Black

Friday, after Christmas, at the start of the season, at the end of the season, mid-season, etc. Do you get the picture? The perspective you are taking in your picture is revealing. Are you an outsider watching or an insider participating?

Even though it may be perfectly explainable that we behave like this, it is seriously bananas if you think about it. Fighting for the last Christmas tree? Pushing people aside to grab the last t-shirt that is the wrong size anyway? Trampling, shooting or stabbing people to death to buy a product? Come on. And no, I am not exaggerating. The last thing actually happens. Have a look at www.blackfridaydeathcount.com, which counts the number of deaths and serious injuries through Black Friday sales over the last decade. The numbers? 12 and 117 respectively when writing this. Could it be more bananas?

I am not preaching here. I am as guilty as everyone else. Not of the sales and Black Friday thing (which I avoid no matter what). But I am guilty of gathering stuff. So, rather than preach, let me confess. Even though I try to limit the amount of virtual and physical stuff that I gather (sometimes voluntarily, but largely stimulated and sometimes enforced by my lovely wife…), and even though I prefer to think that I am certainly gathering less than people do on average, I am probably as much a hamster as you are. Let me give some examples.

I'll start with the virtual stuff. I have 80 apps on my phone (no less than seven of which are for news and four for the weather) and slightly more on my laptop. I have 19 screens open while writing this. I have 13,700 PDF documents, 10,000 Word documents, 3,000 e-books, and more than 15,000 photos in my Dropbox account, seven active email addresses and over 30,000 read emails in my mailboxes. The most banana thing about this is that I find this normal.

Now let's have a look at the physical stuff (of which I am, perhaps just like you, honestly convinced that I am a less than average hunter-gatherer). I own 11 pairs of shoes, 24 pairs of socks, ten jackets and coats, 20 pants, and 23 t-shirts. And that *after* having sent the clothes I don't wear to a charity). Furthermore, I own three bikes, 837 books, and eight mouthpieces for my trumpet. And in our two-person household, we have 48 seats, 65 plates, 68 glasses, 78 spoons and 31 types of tea. Apparently, I think I need all this, but do I?

Now let's consider groceries and have a look at the varieties offered by the supermarket I usually go to—which is probably the most average supermarket in the country in terms of size and products offered. I went there and have counted the varieties they offer for a number of standard products. If you can ignore the strange looks you get from other customers and employees, I recommend you do the same to get a real sense of how much choice there is (or if you want to save the embarrassment, you can also visit their online stores, where the counting is done for you). So, here we go. In my probably most average supermarket in the country, I can buy:

- 200 types of breakfast cereal and 101 types of cracker
- 45 types of peanut butter and 115 types of jam
- 179 types of pasta and 94 types of rice
- 78 types of coke and 43 types of orange juice
- 405 types of beer and 526 types of red wine

And so on, and so on, and so on. These are all manufactured products, and you could argue they are all different and brand-specific. Could be, but the omni-obesity also continues with commodities. In my average supermarket, I can buy:

- 39 types of semi-skimmed milk
- 50 types of full cream butter
- 34 types of egg (all from chickens)
- 36 types of potato (excluding sweet, boiled or fried)
- 20 types of tomato
- 26 types of apple

Who on earth needs this? Nobody of course. But the stupid thing is that it does disturb me if my favorite type of cereal/pasta/beer/milk/etc. is out of stock. If I think about this, it doesn't make any sense. The only real reason I want to buy a particular product is mostly because I bought it before, so out of habit. And if I had only half the choice, or a quarter, or even 10 percent, I'd live on. Nothing would happen. But my banana omni-obesity makes me want these choices.

4. We Run Away from Real Experience

There is a lot of talk about 'experience' nowadays. We are living in an 'experience economy' where 'customer experience' is everything and where we consume 'experience travel', 'experience events', and 'experience gifts' in 'experience centers', 'experience rooms' and 'experience stores.' Despite all this noise about experience though, the paradoxical truth and the fourth sign of bananas is that we increasingly run away from real experience.

A clear example is how, using our smartphones, we observe and capture the world through a two-dimensional five-inch screen for sharing and later reuse rather than experiencing the real thing now. Whether it is concerts, museums or cities, look around you and see how many people are looking at their smartphone screens or tablets when observing something worth seeing. And some people I have seen even point at their screen instead of the real thing to tell someone else about a particular detail that they find especially worth mentioning. In this way, a concert, museum or city becomes quite a shallow experience.

Taking this narrowing down of our experience a bit further, we are living in a visual society today. Of all our senses, vision has by and large become the most dominant of our senses. We watch at how things and people look and basically judge them based on what we see rather than trying to grasp them with more depth—through listening, smelling, feeling or tasting. In this way, we are almost literally 'losing' our senses. Of course this is exaggerated, as we always use our five senses—consciously or not. But with our strong focus on the visual side of things, we push our other senses to the background and thereby create a reduced experience.

Interestingly, running away from real experience also works the other way around. Next to narrowing our experience by focusing on just one of our senses, we also narrow it down by scattering it over many things at the same time. Real experience is a focused activity in which we use all our senses and concentrate on one thing—or on nothing. However, we often divide our attention between multiple things at the same time: eating and reading and talking and listening to music and driving and so forth. As a result, our experience becomes so thinly spread that we do not taste what we eat, digest what we read, respond to whom we talk, hear which song we listen to, or see where we drive.

Even though we use different senses simultaneously in this way, we use them for different things at the same time. And the result is that we don't experience any of it.

A specific case of us running away from real experience is how we are always online and connected. We all have the experience of talking to someone while we (as well as the other side) at the same time use our phone to chat with someone via WhatsApp or check our Facebook account or email. The ubiquitous connection with others that we have with our smartphone means that whenever it is in sight, part of our brain is always somewhere else. Whether this is objectively seen as a good thing or a bad thing I don't know. But it does mean that we less-than-fully experience our conversation with the person(s) we are with. And I also know it annoys me big time when someone is doing it, especially when that someone is me.

The last case of running away from real experience is our fear of nothingness. Be honest, how often do you sit still and do nothing—not even listening to music? I bet hardly ever. We always have to be busy distracting our minds by doing something, watching something, listening to something or talking about something. It seems to me that we are afraid both of the demons in our mind that will come when we do nothing and of being called lazy.

The first of these fears is a psychological fear. Whenever we sit still and do nothing, our mind starts working and processing what our senses have experienced. This happens in an uncontrolled way, possibly leading our thoughts to places where we don't want to be. We don't want to think about something bad that someone said to us. We don't want to think about the difficult exam tomorrow. We don't want to think about the accident we had. We don't want to think about the mistakes we made. And so on. To avoid this, we distract our minds with reading, listening, talking or any other activity.

The second fear is a social fear. If we do nothing, we are afraid that someone will think the most terrible thing on earth of us: that we are LAZY. We are so obsessed with work, productivity and doing stuff in general today, that doing nothing is about the biggest sin there is. We can't just 'be' anymore. We always have to 'do'.

A good illustration of this is people's answer if you ask them how they are doing. Go back to the last few times you asked someone "How are you doing?" and recall their answers. If you get beyond the default "Thanks, how are you doing?" as a response, I bet at least half of the answers contain the word 'busy'—often complemented with adjectives like 'very' or 'extremely'. "How are you?": "Very busy", "Extremely busy", "Busy, busy, busy", "Busy as always", or "Don't ask, busy". In response, I usually answer that I have absolutely nothing to do and am bored to death. The half-smile that I get in return tells me that their 'busy' was not necessarily an accurate description of how they are doing.

A related example is people bragging about the number of emails they get per day or the number of unread emails they have sitting in their mailbox. In particular, the number of new, unread emails after people's vacations seems to be a strong indicator of success. The more you have, the more you are wanted? The same applies to the number of meetings we have. Apparently, having more meetings is good since it shows you are busy and wanted. Whether you are effective or efficient doesn't matter. So long as you are busy or can pretend you are busy.

Escaping from silence and nothingness is bananas. There is a reason why our minds start working as soon as we do nothing. This is the same reason that we sleep: we need to rest and process what we experience, otherwise, we can't function properly and both our physical as well as mental health will deteriorate. In other words, without it, we go bananas.

5. We Can't Handle Negatives

Yet another sign of our going bananas is that we seem to have unlearned how to deal with the negatives in our lives. Negatives are part of life. That is a simple fact. All of us experience problems, disappointments, losses and so on, all the time. But, we have an increasingly hard time accepting this and prefer to avoid negatives or make them disappear; this concerns both the actual negatives that we experience and the possibility that we might experience something negative in the future.

Let's start with the actual negatives. Somehow, we have ended up living in an eternal happiness society. If we believe what we hear and see around us, there is only one emotion allowed—happiness. We are supposed to smile all day, be energetic and enthusiastic about everything and everyone and have fun all the time. And as soon as something negative happens, we are blown away and get in a depression-like mood, or we choose to ignore it and pretend it didn't happen in the first place.

And that negative can range from impactful experiences like the end of a long marriage, to trivial things like having picked the wrong dessert in a restaurant.

The problem with this one-sided acceptance of the emotions that we want is that they only reflect how fairytales end: "And they lived happily ever after!" Real life (and the rest of the fairytale) is not like that at all. The truth is, that out of all the emotions we have, less than half of them are seen as positive. The others, such as anger, fear, sadness, pity, anxiety, boredom, disgust, and envy are negative. But they are just as real. They are as much a part of life as the positive ones.

If I sound like a Mister know-it-all, here is another confession: I can't deal with the negatives either, and try to avoid them whenever I can by avoiding confrontations, suppressing worries, ignoring pain, etc. Smart? Not at all. Bananas? Sure. Because there is no way around these emotions. Furthermore, as much an aphorism as it may sound—without pain, there is no happiness either.

The issue with emotions is that they are largely relative. What we experience as positive in one case, we may experience as negative in another. Take nothingness. If you have nothing to do week after week after week because you lost your job or are ill, this may lead to a feeling of unbearable boredom. But, if you just finished three 80-hour working weeks, having nothing to do may feel like an enjoyable relief and a moment of true happiness.

This points at another issue with emotions: we can get used to almost any situation. This flattens our emotions about these situations to close to zero. The consequence is that we can only feel the positive emotions if we have recently experienced the negatives as well. An example is that you only feel happy when succeeding in something if you also know the experience of failure. Furthermore, you only enjoy having enough money if you know the experience of not having it. And you only enjoy being pain-free if you had pain before. And so on.

This 'getting used to situations' has led my people—the Dutch—to become profound experts in what has become a national hobby: complaining. As referred to earlier, the Netherlands ranks among the best countries to live in on just about every scale that you can imagine. And we even *say* we are happy according to the *World Happiness Report* by the United Nations. But we complain. About everything. About our neighbors, about our schools, about our politicians, about the quality of food in airplanes, about the price of gas, about the traffic, about our public transport, about housing prices, about our national soccer team, about the heat, about the cold, about the drought, about the rain, about the wind, and about any other aspect of the weather.

So, we complain. Not because we are suffering. No, because of our *lack* of suffering. We are so successful in solving our actual problems and thereby avoiding the real negatives that we invent our own problems to complain about. It seems like there is a universal quantity of negatives that people need. And if nature doesn't provide them anymore, we create them ourselves.

Our (I am not referring anymore only to the Dutch) inability to handle negatives also projects towards the negatives that we might experience in the future. Over the years, we have developed a system of insurances, security measures, rules of engagement, protection mechanisms, quality systems and safety procedures that is so enhanced that we try to eliminate every imaginable risk in everything we do.

Take airport security. Of course, terrorism is a terrible threat. And of course, we want to fly safely and take measures to make that possible. So yes, we have carryon luggage restrictions, security checks, body scans and so forth. And yes, we want to collect some information about who is traveling to identify the possible terrorist. But asking for the name of your parents and contact details of your employer for a trip abroad? To me, these are signals that we can't accept that the absolute and guaranteed safety we are looking for is a fiction. Flying will never be 100% safe. It can't be.

Or take healthcare. We decreasingly accept that we get sick, old and die. Instead, we do everything to prolong our lives, improve the quality of life, and cure every health problem that we may have. And the people who do accept sickness, age and death and have peace of mind with it, we call fatalists, indifferent or cowards. Healthcare costs are going through the roof and any discussion about the costs and value of human life is not done. But the simple fact of life is—we get sick, old and die. Like with safety, there is no ruling out here.

Or take science. A large share of the funding for scientific research happens through highly competitive grants for which researchers must submit extensive research proposals. To get a chance of being awarded a grant, you often have to explain and more or less guarantee the outcome of the research as well as describe its practical usefulness and how it is going to be commercially exploited. So, you basically must have done the research before you can get it funded. This risk-avoiding process is good at protecting the downsides—the chances of complete failure—but it is also excellent at systematically erasing all chances for unexpected positive outcomes, which, I think, is the very point of scientific research in the first place.

Or take children. In our parenting, in our schools, in the playground, and in the products we buy for them, we try to protect them against any possible physical or mental risk. They can't go anywhere by themselves anymore, they have to wear safety gear, they have to be supervised, and they have to be protected against any harsh language, images or sounds. They also have to be protected against the most dangerous living creatures on earth: other children. An extreme case (at least I find it extreme…) is that at some schools, children are not allowed to hand out birthday invitations because this will harm the uninvited too much. If children are protected against such life-endangering events as not being invited to a birthday party, how can we expect them to build up the kind of resilience needed in the grown-up world?

I could go on, but I suppose you get the point. When asked individually, we know that life is full of negatives. But collectively, we have turned into absolute control freaks to protect ourselves against any possibly potentially slightly negative experience.

6. We Cry Out to Be Special

We are not only going bananas in the way we think and act. We also go bananas about ourselves. This is indicated by the sixth sign of us going bananas: we fear being 'average' or 'normal' and rather want to be 'special'.

There is a paradox here. As we will see below, the seventh sign of us going bananas is that we worship 'The Other' by taking them as reference points and source of universal truth. By doing so, we put The Other on a pedestal, making him or her more important than ourselves. At the same time though, we cry out to be special—or that our children, other family members or friends are special. So, we paradoxically make both ourselves and the other extremely important. Before you accuse me of pointing fingers: yes, I am guilty again and want to be special too. Why else write a book like this?

A first and general indicator of our cry for specialness is that, in whatever research is done, people on average tend to rate themselves above-average. As we might expect, this happens when it concerns positive characteristics such as generosity, patience and kindness. So long as we can attribute something positive to ourselves, we overestimate ourselves. Scientists even have a term for this: 'illusory superiority'. They also call it 'above-average effect', 'superiority bias' or the '*primus inter pares* effect'. These all refer to the same tendency to overestimate our own qualities and abilities compared to others.

Many studies have been done on this, and they all give this same result. David Dunning and Justin Kruger's research in this respect is so important that people refer to the 'Dunning-Kruger effect'. They conducted a series of studies in which people had to perform various cognitive tasks, such as solving logical questions or taking grammar exercises. When they asked participants to rank themselves, they found that, on average, *everyone* ranked themselves above-average—*including the lowest scoring 25%*. Along the same lines, others have found in a study amongst the faculty of the University of Nebraska-Lincoln that 68% rated themselves in the top 25%, and more than 90% rated themselves above-average in their teaching skills. And in a study amongst MBA students at the University of Stanford, it was found that no less than 87% thought they performed above average.

So, we all the time rank ourselves above average when it concerns our own positive qualities and abilities. Interestingly, something similar happens with problems and with negative qualities and abilities. Some people do this to an extreme extent. To seek attention, they invent stories about how they have been a victim of others' wrong-doing. Or they pretend to have a serious illness and simulate all the symptoms so that they are seen as a patient—and receive the attention that comes with it. There is even a name for this behavior: Münchausen Syndrome—named after the character Baron Münchausen in a book by Rudolf Erich Raspe, who fabricated exaggerated stories about his entire life.

Less extreme but more widespread is how we increasingly look for our own special pet-disease or pet-syndrome that gives us certain rights to be special. And if it is not us, it is our children who have them. Examples are:

- Self-diagnosed gluten allergy, dairy allergy, pet allergy and so on: all kinds of allergies causing physical overreactions to stuff that most other people have no problems with. Research shows a threefold increase of gluten-free diets in the US from 2009-2014, and Statista reports an estimated worldwide doubling of gluten-free products from 2013 to 2020. The interesting thing is that the number of people with an officially diagnosed gluten allergy (celiac disease) decreased by about 20% over that same period.

- ADHD (Attention Deficit Hyperactivity Disorder) and ADD (Attention Deficit Disorder): a family of disorders causing problems with paying attention. Research shows a threefold increase from 2002 to 2007 in the US and a sevenfold increase from 1990 to 2007 in Sweden. Part of that growth can be attributed to having better means of detecting such disorders. But the extent suggests that our willingness to accept such diagnoses has increased as well—especially for overactive children. At the same time, research in the Netherlands shows that actual medicine prescriptions for ADHD have dropped significantly over recent years.

- Autism, Asperger's, PDD-NOS (Pervasive Developmental Disorder-Not Otherwise Specified): a family of disorders causing a lack of socialization and communication skills. Research by the Centers for Disease Control and Prevention (CDC) in the US shows a large increase from 1 in every 2000 children diagnosed in the 1970s and 1980s to 1 in every 59 in 2014. This is a 3300% increase in half a century. The sheer magnitude of this increase is a clear indicator that there is more than biology at work here.

Of course, there are people who actually have these conditions and they suffer from them every day. However, they are often silent about their condition, embarrassed perhaps, wishing and trying to be 'normal'. There is also a group of people, though, who tell the world with a certain pride that they have a condition like this. They use it as an excuse for their behaviors, as in "I can't help being asocial because I have traits of autism," or as a trophy to show that they are special too. They would rather have one or more of such conditions than be normal or average—thereby avoiding responsibility for their own behavior and failing to do something about it.

We also exaggerate our problems in more harmless ways in our day-to-day lives. We are the unluckiest with the car we have bought, with the line we have chosen in the supermarket, with the taxes we pay, with the weather on our holiday, with the extent of adolescent behavior of our child, with our neighbors, and so on. Even though we accept that others have problems too, our own problems must be worse than theirs.

All these examples represent a fear of being average. If we can't be better than others in something, we find ways to be worse off, so long as we stay away as far as possible from the evil average. Because that would mean we are normal. And we want to be special, no matter what.

There is nothing wrong with a bit of overconfidence and a bit of complaining. However, the problem starts when we are taking our specialness too seriously. When we *really* think we are special, problems start to occur. We start behaving like victimized heroes. And the problem with that is that it makes us feel entitled—as if we have a special, exceptional position that gives us some special, exceptional rights. It makes us feel we deserve to be treated in a special way, to get special care and attention, or to be respected or pitied by others. In case you are wondering, yes, I am guilty too.

7. We Worship 'The Other'

So, we put ourselves on a big pedestal of specialness to feel better and to give ourselves explanations and excuses for our feelings and behaviors. At the same time, though, we do the same with The Other. We are living in an age where all certainties seem to have gone down the drain. We don't accept the word of gods, kings or priests anymore, and we don't believe science has the answers either. In the past, these gave us a sense of certainty we could trust and that gave us some peace of mind. Today, however, all pillars on which we can rely seem to have gone.

Therefore, we turn to the last resort: The Other. As we already observed above, there is a paradox here. We put ourselves on a pedestal to make ourselves more important than anyone else. But, at the same time, we put The Other on a pedestal too. My explanation for this is that both reflect a sense of feeling lost and insecure. We feel too insecure to be average or normal and therefore have to make ourselves special—in a good or a bad way. And in our insecurity, we look at the same time for something or someone to depend on. Since all traditional certainties seem to be gone, we cling to someone, anyone or everyone else, hoping they can show us the way.

A good example of this is our idol culture. We have always worshipped stars, be it rock, pop, films, soccer, baseball or basketball. Depending on the kind of music, movies or sports we like, we have our own idols. And some of us go completely bananas if we get the opportunity to see, hear, touch or smell them in person. We shout, cry, throw obscene objects, and even faint when this happens.

But this is not the kind of bananas I mean. What I mean, is that we take the mere fact that someone is well-known as proof that someone is omnipotent and omniscient. Once someone is a pop star or soccer star, we listen to their views and opinions. And not only about music or soccer, but also about anything else—politics, the economy, climate change, whatever. What they say must be true because they are famous. So, we ask them about their views in interviews, TV shows, magazines and so forth.

Scientists call this the 'halo effect'. It refers to our tendency to assume certain characteristics of people if we observe other characteristics. It leads to us often assuming that someone who looks attractive is also successful. This applies to our worship of celebrities too. From the mere fact that they are well-known, we deduce that they must be smart too and that their opinions are worth listening to.

It is not only celebrities we worship. We also worship our families, friends, colleagues and Facebook connections. We like to be as them and do as them, and we like them to like us. As a result, a lot of what we do is copying what they do. And since they do the same, we are copying each other, thereby creating a sort of exponential homogeneity in what we do, say, feel and think.

Examples abound. Take shopping. Even though we think we are autonomous individuals deciding for ourselves what we buy and wear, we end up buying the same shoes, shirts or jeans as everyone else. And also the same phones, cars, books, games, apps and houses. Of course, there is still variation: we pick the size and color. But for the rest, our choices are to a large extent dictated by what others do. What is left are trivial choices about marginal differences.

Another good example is how we celebrate Christmas. Through most of the year, we behave pretty sanely when it concerns decorating our homes. But with Christmas, we seem collectively to lose our minds. Suddenly, we put a tree inside our homes, develop a taste for red and green, and put enormous amounts of tiny lights on the inside and outside of our houses. Why? You would probably answer that it is so cozy, convivial, merry or otherwise pleasant. But the fact that we only do this around Christmas indicates it is a case of collective lunacy. Harmless perhaps, but still collective lunacy. Otherwise, this decoration behavior would be more evenly distributed over the year. It is the very fact that everyone else does it that makes us do it too. It makes us feel connected to The Other.

Our worshipping of The Other also appears in how far we go in keeping up appearances. We don't only want to do as others do. We also care tremendously about their opinions. This is most obvious on social media. If we were to believe the pictures we see there, everyone is always happy all the time doing the most exciting things you can imagine. We pick the right angle, enforce our camera smile, put up our thumbs, and inform our peers about the most amazing sushi, beer, trip, holiday or other experience we had. Or in our WhatsApp groups, we constantly share new, supposedly funny (typically violent or sexually oriented) pictures and videos and give each other a thumbs up for doing so.

Why? Because the next step is even more important: we want to be seen and we want some sort of appreciation. Or, in social media terms: we want 'likes'. While money is the mean currency to buy stuff and to show how successful we are on the commercial ladder, 'likes' are the main currency to show our position on the social ladder. And followers of course: the more followers and the more likes, the higher our status.

Your number of followers and likes are a good indicator of how much you worship the other. The more likes you have, the more important they are usually to you. And the more they affect your life. Just compare the level of self-inflicted social pressure of someone having to gather likes from all their followers every day with that of someone not using social media and minding their own business. The result of this has been nicely illustrated in what has become an almost instant classic episode of the *Black Mirror* series on Netflix: Episode 1 of Series 3 ('Nosedive'). In this episode, people rate each other not only online but also offline, on basically every part of their lives. While it is fiction, we just have to watch Uber drivers as an example, to see what this can do to you in reality.

Putting ourselves under the pressure of others also happens without social media and ratings. Let me give two more examples, one at work, the other at school. The best example at work is how we deal with being physically present. Research is clear. Being present does not have a correlation with how much work you do or how well you do it. Some studies even show that people perform better when working at home. Yet, the pressure put on people to be physically there is strong. The most scurvy form, perhaps, is asking supposedly funny questions such as "Did you oversleep?" when someone comes in at 7.30 am, or "Enjoy your free afternoon!" if someone leaves the office at 6 pm.

When it concerns our kids at school, we go completely bananas. The kind of judgments we have about other parents and the kind of craze we are enforcing upon ourselves is close to surreal. Take birthday treats. I don't want to sound too much like Statler and Waldorf from the Muppet Show, but come on… the circus and rat race that parents reinforce by producing increasingly esoteric creations is astonishing. If you don't know what I am talking about, query 'kids birthday treats' on Google Images to get a sense of what I mean. Why? For the same reason as before: because we worship The Other and want to be seen and liked by them.

8. We Don't Take Responsibility

We have arrived at the last category of bananas: we don't take responsibility for what we think and do. I am going to assume that you are an adult. This means you have quite a few responsibilities. Of course, you take many of them seriously. But we are also good at avoiding responsibility or shifting responsibility to others. At least, I am.

The first area where we shift responsibility to others is in our thinking. Wherever possible, we outsource our thinking to others and to technology so that we don't have to bother with it. One way in which this happens is through the earlier referred to ratings and rankings.

Instead of forming our own judgment, we pick the movie/book/food/company/etc. that has the highest rating. Others like it, so it must be good, we think.

But we don't only outsource our thinking to other people. Increasingly we outsource it to technology as well. We let apps and sensors do the work for us. Think about how much you rely on their built-in judgments in your day-to-day life—for example when driving your car, consulting your smartphone, or looking at the thermostat in your house. Technology is great. It makes our lives safer, nicer and more convenient. But it also leads to us not taking responsibility anymore for our judgments and decisions. Instead, we let our car, smartphone or thermostat instruct us what to do and what not to do.

The same happens with signs and signals. Rather than making a judgment ourselves, we look at what the sign tells us and follow that information. Take expiry dates. Rather than judging the quality of a product by smelling it and having a look, we assume it is still eatable before the expiry date and not eatable after that date. Or take traffic signs. Of course they are there to help us, but, at the same time, many of them take away the need to make any judgment for ourselves. Examples are signs showing a recommended speed, that you are approaching a sharp turn, or that the road is getting narrower. As a result, we crash our car if there happens to be no sign to rely on.

Or take product packages. They tell you that a product is healthy, for the elderly, or not suitable for kids under three, which most of the time you could judge perfectly well yourself. Or they tell you that your water is gluten-free and your apple contains no dairy. You may think this is exaggerated, but the gluten-free water claim can actually be found… With a tiny bit of thinking, most of us should be able to conclude that water has never contained any gluten (nor carbs, sugar, dairy, peanuts or fat).

We don't just outsource our responsibilities. We also walk away from them rather than face them. A remarkable example of this is 'ghosting'—someone you love or care about who suddenly vanishes without any explanation. As it turns out, it happens a lot in dating nowadays. But, as I have recently experienced myself, it also happens in business relationships. After having worked with my overseas business partner for over three years, he just disappeared from one day to the next. No email, call, WhatsApp message or whatever. Of course, breaking up a relationship is okay. But not even taking the responsibility to explain to the other side why, or at least letting them know, is bananas.

Another form of abstaining from taking responsibility is to blame someone else. We are good at that. Whatever happens to us is not our fault. Rather, it is their fault. If our kids misbehave or perform badly, it is the school's fault. If we have a disease, it is the doctor's fault. If we pick the wrong line in the grocery store, it is the cashier's fault. If a product breaks, it is the manufacturer's fault. If we use the product in the wrong way, it is also the manufacturer's fault. If we can buy the product cheaper somewhere else, it is the shop's fault. If our street is full of litter, it is the government's fault. If we are late for work because of a traffic jam, it is the government's fault. If we don't have a job, it is the government's fault. And if we have a job we don't like, it is our employer's fault.

We can always put the blame on someone or something else—a person, an institution, an app and so on. In some cases, we may be right. But in all the cases above, I'd argue the other side is not to blame. Shifting responsibility in this way is childlike behavior. As adult human beings we are supposed to take responsibility. After all, if we don't do it, who else is left? And if not us, who else is going to make sure that we are not going even more bananas than we are already going?

Summary

As you have had to digest a significant number of pages by now, let's summarize once more how we are going bananas today:

1. We Don't Really Care About the Truth
2. We Lose Our Sense of Nuance and Perspective
3. We Have Omni-Obesity
4. We Run Away from Real Experience
5. We Can't Handle Negatives
6. We Cry Out to Be Special
7. We Worship 'The Other'
8. We Don't Take Responsibility

Quite a list, no? Altogether, it creates a not-so-shiny picture of us. Of course, we act sensibly a lot of times, and of course, you may not recognize yourself in all eight, but I bet there are at least a few that apply to you—and probably more than a few. They most certainly apply to me. Not all to the same extent, but I am guilty of all eight.

So long as this is still within limits, there isn't any real problem. After all, who can or even likes to be sensible all the time? I don't. But as the previous pages show, the eight often are a problem. Frequently, we are going bananas at the expense of ourselves, meaning we are overdoing the eight. And this is not only harmful to us but also to others. Because we behave like a school of fish, flock of birds or herd of wildebeest, we influence each other and reinforce our banana behavior.

Bananas in the Past

History is always a good teacher, and certainly when it is about bananas. Knowing where we come from and how bananas have played a role throughout human history gives us perspective. And putting things in perspective is exactly the kind of remedy that can help against going bananas. Knowing a bit about our history also makes us understand that we may not be as special as we think we are and that current times may also not be as special as we think they are. Therefore, let us have a look at the past and learn from it.

In the very first paragraph of Chapter 1, I wrote that 'Somewhere over the years' we have gone bananas. That was not very precise. I guess you had in mind something like the last two to five years or so, or perhaps ten. This is not completely wrong. As far as I can tell, we have indeed gone more bananas in those years. But the history of bananas goes back further. Quite a bit actually. To show this, I first give some examples of how we have gone bananas in the past and then reflect on the whole feeling that the world is now more bananas than ever.

As it turns out, people have lost their ability to think sensibly many times in the course of history. Striking examples are the many cases of mass hysteria that we find over time. The most well-known and widespread example is probably the witch-hunts that took place in Early Modern Europe and North America in the 15th - 18th centuries. During this centuries-long period, an estimated 200,000 men and women were tortured, burned and hanged because they had supposedly made a pact with the devil. Imagine the kind of mass panic and loss of sensible thinking that caused this. A clear case of bananas.

Other, more local cases of mass hysteria are often related to some sort of disease that people think they have. There is the example of a 'dancing plague' in 1518 in Strasbourg. A woman named Mrs. Troffea began dancing in the streets and danced for multiple days. Apparently, she couldn't stop dancing because of some sort of infective disease. After a week, more than 30 others had joined her, and after a month there were no less than 400 people infected who danced continuously. Around that time, about 15 people died of the disease per day. Local physicians concluded that people had 'hot blood' and thought this could only be cured by dancing more to let it out. Therefore, authorities even paid musicians to make sure people would go on dancing.

It is not only hundreds of years ago that people went bananas because of some sort of fictitious disease. Over the last century, there have been plenty of examples. In 1962, thousands of children suddenly suffered from uncontrollable laughing in what is now Tanzania, resulting in dozens of schools having to close. And in 1967, hundreds of men in Singapore believed their penises were shrinking into their bodies and would eventually disappear. A few years later, in the 1970s, there was a wave of phantom pregnancies in London after a young woman checked into a psychiatric clinic claiming she was pregnant. Needless to say, none of this was actually true.

These are rather extreme and local cases of people going bananas. They show that there have always been (and always will be) groups of people going completely crazy about something. But, you may argue, in all those years the large majority of people were unaffected. They lived their 'normal' lives and things were generally okay. Compared to today, life in those centuries was relatively simple and predictable. But, today, we are living in a crazy world that is more uncertain, complex and changing than ever before. Such a world gives us more reason to go bananas than was ever the case in history.

Or does it? Is the world indeed more uncertain, complex, and changing than ever before and therefore more banana-prone than ever? It is at least a widely-shared belief. You just have to open whatever newspaper or magazine to find evidence for it. It seems to be particularly strong in the management and business press (although this might be my personal bias because of my background in this area). Browsing through various articles and online posts, you find titles such as:

"Winning in a Turbulent World" *(AT Kearney,* May 2012)

"How to Innovate in an Uncertain World" *(Forbes,* July 2013)

"The World in Transition" *(The Economist,* November 2014)

"Welcome to the New Age of Uncertainty" *(The Guardian,* July 2016)

"Thrive in a Fast-Changing World" *(MarketWatch,* February 2017)

"The World is About to Change even Faster" *(Bloomberg,* July 2017)

"Leading in a Disruptive World" *(The Guardian,* October 2017)

"Leadership Potential in Turbulent Times *(McKinsey,* April 2018)

"Strategy in an Uncertain World" *(Forbes,* January 2019, my post…)

And so on and so forth. The message is clear: the world is really different from what it was before. Due to technological advances, geopolitical shifts in power, climate change, etc., all our conventions are being tested and are about to be disrupted—we live in an era of transition with a lot of uncertainty at the verge of a whole new world.

Interestingly, this belief is not limited to the media or business press. Also in science we find it, as we can infer from the titles and themes of academic papers and journals. Staying within the field of management, let me give some examples from the past three years of themes for special issues of journals to which people were asked to submit their research articles. These requests are known as 'calls for papers'. They are meant to trigger researchers to do research and publish in a particular direction, leading to publication in about one or two years—so still to come while writing this. As such, they reflect the most up-to-date information about the themes that are found important today:

"Managing in the Age of Disruptions"
(*Journal of Management Studies*, Call for Papers 2016)

"Disruptive Technology and Innovation in Society"
(*Technological Forecasting & Social Change*, Call for Papers 2016)

"Management Innovation in an Uncertain World"
(*California Management Review*, Call for Papers 2017)

"Digital Disruption in Marketing"
(*Journal of Marketing Education*, Call for Papers 2017)

"International Business and Strategy in an Era of Global Flux"
(*Strategy Science*, Call for Papers 2018)

This list doesn't look so different from the list above, does it? We see the theme of an increasingly changing world clearly reproduced in both lists. But why bother? And why talk about this in a section that is called 'Bananas in the Past'? The reason is that I want to show you that the kinds of feelings of uncertainty and turbulence that we find today are not only a media thing. And I also want to show you that this way of thinking is not really different from how we thought in the past.

Now have a look at another list. This time it is a list of article titles that appeared in *Long Range Planning*, a key strategic management journal:

"Strategic Management: A New Managerial Concept
for an Era of Rapid Change"

"Defence Planning: The Uncertainty Factor"

"How Corporate Planning Responds to Uncertainty"

"Planning in a State of Turbulence"

Also, this list doesn't look so very different from the two lists before. It reflects the same idea that the world is changing and getting more uncertain and more turbulent than before. Now, make a guess when these articles were published. You have an idea? If not, make a guess.

The main hint that these articles did not appear today is that strategic management is introduced as a new concept in the first title.

Today, strategic management is an established field, so at least the first article can't be that recent. What would you say if I told you that all these articles appeared in the 1970s? Because that is when they were published: in 1971, 1971, 1976, and 1977 respectively. This means that the feeling of an increasingly unmanageable world was there already, about 40 to 50 years ago.

But it doesn't stop there. The feeling goes back a bit further. To get a sense of how far, I'd like to share a quote with you that I came across while doing the research for this book (thank you, Svend Brinkmann, for mentioning it in your must-read book *Stand Firm*). It reflects a concern about where the world is going. And, albeit formulated more eloquently than I did, it is similar to the concern that we are going bananas:

We have fallen upon evil times
and the world has waxed very old and wicked.
Politics are very corrupt.
Children are no longer respectful to their parents.

Now, make a guess again from which year this quote appears. I won't be disappointed with you if you are off by a couple of years. What do you think? Is it 50 years old? 100? More? Let's have a closer look then. The contents could definitely be said by someone you met today. Also today, children are not as respectful to their parents as their parents would like them to be, and politics and corruption are definitely words that often appear in the same sentence. Furthermore, the feelings that the world is waxed and wicked, and that today is a more evil time than ever before are widely shared. The language tells us though, that this quote must be a bit older. The wording is a bit outdated and probably not something that would be written in the 21st century. So, what is your final offer? 1900s? 1800s?

I am going to assume you were wrong. It may surprise you that this quote is ascribed to King Naram-Sin of Chaldea, 3800 years BC, and has been found as an inscription on an ancient tablet. Yes, 3800 years BC. That is almost 6000 years ago. That is a long time. It is slightly before Adam and Eve were born according to the Bible (which was in 3716 BC to be precise...) and hundreds of years before the first pharaoh of Egypt was installed. There was no social media yet, and even no pyramids—but nevertheless, there was a feeling the world was going bananas.

I can go on and on with giving examples like these for the period in between, but you get the point. Throughout the centuries, people have always shown banana behavior, and throughout the centuries, people have always had this gloomy feeling that things are getting worse and worse. This is important because it means that bananas are of all ages. Every generation before us showed banana behavior and thought the world was more bananas than ever before. Why? Let's explore that in the next chapter.

3

The Science of Bananas

The many examples in the previous chapter show how widely spread is our inclination to go bananas. When we look more deeply at why, it turns out that this is not so strange. On the contrary. Science gives us not just one reason why going bananas is a natural thing to do. It gives us dozens of reasons. The very fact that we go bananas is part of what makes us human beings. It has several functions that are elemental to our lives, and without bananas we would be missing an important part of what defines human behavior.

However, despite the fact that going bananas is something natural, it doesn't follow that we can't or shouldn't do something about it. Lying, stealing and killing are also human behaviors, and these also have a variety of functions that are elemental to human life. However, there is a widely-shared belief that such behaviors should be limited and controlled and only used in exceptional cases when absolutely necessary. This also applies to going bananas. It has its function but can be limited and controlled as well.

The purpose of this third chapter is to develop an understanding of why we go bananas. This is not meant to offer an excuse that we can't help it and therefore must continue going bananas. The reason I dedicate a chapter to the science of bananas is that I am an optimistic believer in the human power of sensible thinking. The only real remedy for bananas is to stay grounded, come to our senses, and use our human ability to think. This starts with understanding our own behavior, and this is where the science comes in. It offers us insightful explanations as to why we go bananas. And once we understand these, we can do something about our bananas.

The science of bananas is not just one science. It is a rich and varied science spread out over no less than five disciplines. In this chapter, I summarize these one-by-one. I will start by giving a simple explanation of the basic mechanisms causing us to go bananas. Thereafter, we will go into biological, psychological, sociological, technological and economic explanations of bananas.

The Basic Banana Mechanism

Going bananas is a mix of mad thinking and crazy acting and a mix of doing this individually and collectively. To understand how going bananas works, let's start with the simplest case: you go mentally bananas without any visible action and without any connection to others. When you go mentally bananas on your own, this means that you seriously lose your ability to think rationally for a while. Instead, you think up all kinds of crazy things, often in vicious cycles, making it worse and worse. In this way, you can end up in outright panic from something that starts as a small thought.

We all know how this works. Maybe you are a bit anxious about a presentation that you have to give or a new person that you are going to meet. That is all fine. But now you start to feel anxious about the fact that you feel anxious. You don't want to feel anxious because you don't like that feeling. You tell yourself there is no reason to be anxious and that you should stop being anxious. But the anxiety doesn't listen and stays, which makes you even more anxious. And this may go on exponentially until you go completely bananas from anxiety. You start sweating, your heartbeat gets as loud and fast as a drum jam session and your blood pressure is going through the roof. And then, once the moment is there, when you say the first three words of your presentation or meet the person you were supposed to meet, the anxiety evaporates as if it had never existed.

When you go bananas in this way, you are getting yourself into a vicious mental cycle. This happens all the time. Maybe not as extreme as above. If it goes that far, you are having an anxiety attack or a panic attack and you should maybe consult your doctor. But we often have quick chains of thought, propelled by our emotions and physical responses, that have a tendency to derail into thinking something that doesn't make sense anymore.

This doesn't just happen in isolation. There's usually a history before that of building up stress in a gradual way. If you go bananas about a presentation like in the example above, you probably already felt uncertain for a longer time and you may have had some bad experiences. Or, to take another example, if you go bananas about your neighbor putting his car in front of your house, there's probably already something been going on between you and your neighbor for a while. When you go bananas, the mental and physical stress that you have built up in the course of time is suddenly released.

This is how hate develops out of small angers, how frustration builds up out of something left unsaid, and how depression may result from feelings of uncertainty or loneliness. Of course, there are other mechanisms at work here as well—such as chemical ones in the case of depression and mental disorders—but it is through this vicious cycle that perfectly sane people manage to produce perfectly insane thoughts.

Going bananas goes beyond this purely mental process—and the accompanying physical symptoms such as an accelerated heart rate, sweating, and a dry mouth. It makes us often also *do* crazy things. Thus, in addition to going crazy in our heads, we also do stuff that doesn't make sense. We fill our houses with all kinds of stuff that we don't need, to compensate for a feeling of loss. We vote for leaders out of frustration rather than because we believe they can lead. We lose our temper and hit someone. And so on. As above, not all these behaviors can always be traced back to someone going bananas. There are always exceptions and cases where other things are going on. However, all these behaviors are also a result of perfectly sane people going bananas.

The kind of bananas resulting from our individual thoughts and actions is still manageable. Every now and then we lose our senses and do something stupid. That is okay if it doesn't harm others. However, it gets more interesting when we look at the collective level, at us as a group. We are social animals. This means we care a great deal about what others think and do. It also means that we tend to copy each other. And this is where we really go bananas.

In our thinking, we care a lot about what others think. We think we need to think as they think. And in our doing, we care a lot about what others do and we like to do as they do. It doesn't require a rocket scientist to see how this leads to an exponential growth in bananas that spreads like a virus. If someone thinks or does something crazy, and if a few others are thinking or doing the same, still others start thinking and doing the same making the bananas go viral.

A good example of this is the Ice Bucket Challenge that went viral in the summer of 2014. It started as a great initiative to create awareness of the motor neuron disease ALS and to gather donations. The idea was that you emptied a bucket of iced water above your head, captured it on film, shared it with others, and made a donation. This was a fantastic idea relying on the insatiable human desire to go bananas. It allowed us to go bananas for a good cause. However, it also went so bananas that people turned the cause into a means. Instead of making donations to ALS, they just filmed themselves while emptying a bucket of water above their heads to show others that they were part of this collective phenomenon. On their way, though, they forgot the donations…

When you go bananas, there is thus a three-step vicious cycle at work. First, you get into a mental cycle in which small thoughts get propelled through emotions into large headaches. Second, these thoughts result in stupidish actions that create undesirable effects, new thoughts and larger headaches. And third, through interaction and imitation, you absorb the thoughts and behaviors of others which further aggravates the headaches—and triggers others to go bananas too.

In combination, these mechanisms are strong. They show that we have some built-in features as human beings that make going bananas a very human thing to do. With such mechanisms at work, we may even wonder why everyone is not going bananas about everything all the time. After all, we think we are living in a crazy world that is more uncertain, complex and changing than ever before. Such a world gives more reason for going bananas than was ever the case in history. No?

Banana Biology

Our banana behavior has strong biological roots. As a species, we have evolved and developed a variety of features that make us who we are. Over thousands of years, our genes have evolved in a way that fitted the environment we were in. In the whole world of other species, this has led us to be homo sapiens—which, interestingly enough, means something like "discerning, wise, sensible human being." Perhaps a good one to remember when you find yourself going bananas…

This evolution has led to the physical characteristics that we have: our large heads, the fact that we stand on two feet, our teeth, the place and shape of our ears and eyes, our hands, our lack of hair, and so on and so forth. The same evolution has also equipped us with some particular mental baggage. Of course, with our super-large brains, we are supposed to be smarter than any other species. To a large extent, that brain is our way to survive. But, it has also equipped us with some peculiarities that help us go bananas.

As species, we are group animals. For thousands of years, we have lived together in relatively small communities or in small settlements where we were completely dependent on each other. The group was everything and survival was virtually impossible without it. This meant that deviating from the group was a dangerous thing to do. You didn't want to run the risk of being expelled from the group because that most likely meant you would die.

This group mentality is just as much present today. We are wired to be group animals. And this is one of the reasons for our banana behavior. We are wired to look at others and conform to how they behave because that is what made us survive over all those centuries. The issue today though, is that we are connected to so many people that trying to conform is an impossible task.

If you are living together in a group of 20 to 50 people, or even in a small village of up to a few hundred people and that is all you care about, conforming to the group norms is a relatively easy and smart thing to do. However, if you are connected to over a thousand people spread across the globe with whom you can communicate 24/7, conforming to group norms is impossible. The sheer size and variety of the group make it impossible to do this.

Evolution has brought us some even more advanced features that help us go bananas today. Some scientists argue that human intelligence did not evolve mainly to survive in the physical environment, but primarily as a means of surviving in large and complex social groups. The British anthropologist Robin Dunbar called this the 'social brain hypothesis'. It says that we have developed a set of social skills such as empathy, altruism and friendship, but also deception, coalition forming and manipulation to be able to survive in a complex social group.

As you can imagine, these skills are put to an extreme test in our heavily complex social world today. Even though we have developed these skills, it seems unlikely that our genes have caught up with the pace at which the complexity of our social networks has grown. So, we are stuck with skills that have been elemental for survival, but that also cause us trouble today.

One such particular skill is based on what is called the 'theory of mind'. It is our ability to understand the thoughts, beliefs, desires, intentions and emotions of other people and put ourselves in their shoes. Unlike any other species, we realize not only that we have these abilities but also that others do too. And to quite some extent, we can understand the perspectives of others. This enables us to explain and anticipate what they are thinking, believing, desiring, intending and feeling, and thus what they are likely to do. This skill is an essential part of being human and of surviving today.

The flipside is that this same set of biologically endorsed social skills makes life in the age of Facebook tiring and complicated. There are so many other people whose thoughts, beliefs, desires, intentions, and emotions we have to explain and anticipate, that it can fully stress us out. Next to the well-known information overload, this leads to a *social overload,* an overload of social connections through which we attempt to form a theory of mind and respond. And that is the kind of thing that is causing us to go bananas.

Banana Psychology

We can also explain a great deal of our banana behavior if we look at it through a psychological lens. Cognitive psychology is especially helpful here, as it explains the way we process information and make decisions.

As human beings, we are not computers. This means we are not processing all available information and taking calculated, algorithmic decisions. We are also not *homines economici*, the rational profit-maximizing abstraction of people that economists have long used in their scientific models. No, we are human and think in a human way.

While entire libraries have been written about this, I'd like to zoom in on one particular explanation of how we think: dual process theory. This widely accepted theory says that our brain processes information and makes decisions in two different ways, which are referred to as 'System 1' and 'System 2'. System 2 reflects the conscious, rational thinking that we apply when making deliberated and calculated decisions. It is rather slow with limited capacity and makes judgments and decisions in an analytical, step-by-step manner based on logic and systematic reasoning. System 1 reflects the unconscious, more intuitive and automatic reasoning that we apply in virtually all other situations. It is more associative, effortless and creative than System 2. When System 1 is at work, we are hardly aware that we are thinking. It is about a million times faster than System 2 and we apply it all the time.

In our current society, we are mostly focusing on System 2. That is what our education focuses on and how we are supposed to make decisions. We are stimulated to think before we act, define clear criteria, systematically compare all options and come to a rational conclusion. If we had to rely only on System 2, we would have gone completely bananas a long time ago. Imagine having to think consciously about every tiny decision you make…

So, luckily, we have System 1 and we apply it in about 99% of what we do. That makes life a lot easier. But also System 1 has some built-in features that help us go bananas. The tremendous speed, efficiency and automatism of System 1 is possible because it takes shortcuts. They are called 'biases', or 'heuristics' and enable us to make very fast decisions based on a few cues. You can imagine that in the socially complex world we are living in today, relying on such shortcuts is the only way to be able not to go completely bananas.

But, like in the theory of mind explanation above, these shortcuts have a flipside too since they lead us to respond to particular cues which are not necessarily the right ones and they also help us go bananas. To see how, let's have a look at a few of these shortcuts:

- *Availability heuristic.* We overestimate the likelihood of events that we can reproduce easily, such as a plane crash or someone winning a lottery. This makes us easier to convince by a single vivid story than by cold statistics.

- *Exposure effect.* We like people, products and other things more, the more we are exposed to them. This means that the more often we see a product or advertisement, the more likely we are to like the product and buy it.

- *Scarcity heuristic.* We value scarce things more than things that are abundant and want more of the stuff we can get less of. This is widely used in sales ('end of season sale!', 'two left!', 'two others are viewing this option now!') to make us buy more stuff.

- *Confirmation bias.* We look for and recall information that supports our pre-existing ideas more than information that goes against these ideas. This makes us selective in what we see and what we don't see.

- *Authority bias.* We attribute greater value and accuracy to the opinion of an authority figure, irrespective of whether that person is right or not. We also are more influenced by their opinion, meaning we are more likely to think and do as they say.

- *Conformity bias.* We have the tendency to look at others and accept their thoughts and behaviors as correct. As a result, we do as they do rather than exercise our own independent judgment. This is also called the bandwagon effect.

- *Framing effect.* We are sensitive to how things are framed. We respond differently when, for example, something is framed as a loss or gain. A variation is the *anchoring bias*, according to which we rely too much on the first information we get about something. Smart bargainers use this through their first bid.

- *Consistency bias.* We want to be consistent in our behaviors. If we say A, we believe we should also say B. This can also lead to an *escalation of commitment bias* when we persist in something even when this is not the best thing to do anymore.

The good thing about these biases and heuristics is that they allow us to respond quickly. Rather than systematically evaluating all options and acting too late, we quickly pick the one that, for example, others chose (conformity bias), some expert recommends (authority bias), or the one we have always chosen (consistency bias). Even though this approach may not always produce the best outcome, it mostly ensures that we don't pick the worst option and that we at least do something. Thus, it helps protect us from the downside.

The same biases and heuristics, however, also lead to some of the issues described in Chapter 2. The availability heuristic, exposure effect and framing effect mean, for example, that we have an inaccurate picture of the truth. And smart commercial use of the scarcity effect means that we want more of everything. And conformity bias and authority bias mean that we watch closely what others do so that we can do as them. This means that, next to our biologically built-in banananess, we are also psychologically well-equipped to go bananas.

Banana Sociology

Sociology also offers useful explanations of our banana behavior. It is not only our genes and neurons that assist us in going bananas, but also the way we are raised and educated has a big impact. So, it is both 'nature' and 'nurture' which together equip us with everything we need to go bananas.

Various sociologists, philosophers and developmental psychologists have studied the way we develop ourselves as human beings. Some study how we mature from infant to adult; others study how language and our ability to communicate affect our identities and abilities; and still others study how we exchange and interact with each other.

What these studies have shown, is that the way we think, feel, talk and act is to a large extent a result of our interactions with others. We are socialized creatures that develop our identities and abilities through interacting with other people. Knowingly, but mostly unknowingly, we take our parents, partner, siblings, and close friends as role models and model our own thoughts and behaviors according to theirs. The result is that, in addition to some genetic effects, we often look a lot like them in how we think and feel and what we say and do. It turns out that we are pretty good imitators.

Furthermore, the mere fact that we learn a language and communicate with others also has a profound effect on how we see ourselves. Even stronger, some argue, only through language and interaction can we truly learn about ourselves and develop our identity. It is language, they say, that allows us to think about things, other people and ourselves in the first place. By the words we learn through language, we can formulate thoughts about our world.

Okay, maybe I have lost you by now. All of this sounds rather philosophical—and it is. But it should give you a sense of how socialized we are. Both other people and the very fact that we have learned to talk to them have had a deep effect on who we are, on how we think, and on what we do.

The result is that the whole idea of us being autonomous, authentic, subjective, strong-willed individuals is a bit of a myth. We may think we are, but for the most part, we are not. We are far more a product of our social environment than we want to admit. A large share of what we do is directly the result of us being socialized by others. In other words, we do things largely because we have been socialized to do them.

The good thing, of course, is that this whole socialization process has made us who we are and taught us the skills needed today. Through socialization, we have grown mature and learned a great deal about how to survive in today's complex society. Without socialization, we would have gone bananas instantly and completely. Imagine you were born 10,000 years ago somewhere in the middle of Africa and now wake up in Manhattan with a smartphone tied to your hand with a couple of hundred unread messages in WhatsApp, Facebook and Snapchat, and you are watching a YouTube video of someone playing a videogame. You see the enormous amount of socialization that a fifteen-year-old today has already gone through?

But like our biological and psychological baggage, this social baggage also has a flipside. Exactly because we rely so much on socialization, our current identity, thoughts and behaviors are also very much shaped by our interactions with others. The number and variety of socialization triggers today is so overwhelming that we can't cope with them.

No wonder we go bananas. Just look again at the eight categories of bananas of the previous chapter. In the search for our own identity in this social overload, it is no wonder we cry out to be special. And it is no wonder we run away from negatives, responsibilities and real experiences. We just can't deal with all of them. They are too much.

Banana Technology

The previous three sections focused on the personal, human side of explaining bananas. Zooming in on our biological, psychological and social background, we got a reasonable understanding of why we go bananas. But obviously, there is also a technology side which propels a couple of things. So let's have a look at banana technology.

We are using all kinds of technology that helps us go bananas. Think, for example, about cars. Cars have helped us by enlarging our world. Through our increased mobility we can travel further, see more and different things and meet more and different people. This has exposed us to much more information than we had before. The same applies to trains and planes, which have further enlarged our world. And this larger world leads to more triggers to go bananas.

Or think about automation. Through automating large parts of our work and household activities we have more time now for other things. Rather than requiring all our time and energy for physical work, we have time left to read, talk, meet people, find information and so on. This means we have more time and opportunity to go bananas too.

Technology also helps us go bananas in a more subtle and profound way. Technology is great. It makes our lives safer, nicer and more convenient. But, as research shows, the use of technology also reduces our critical thinking ability. This is our ability to assess something ourselves, make a judgment, take a position, etc. Because technology takes a lot of thinking off our plate, it reduces the need for us to think for ourselves. Here are some everyday examples:

- Driving from A to B based on the route your navigation system suggests.

- Deciding whether you will go outside based on what your weather app is telling you.

- Having your phone or smartwatch tell you whether you have already had enough exercise today.

- Looking at the clock to see whether you fancy some coffee or whether you are hungry.

- Having your coffee machine tell you when it needs cleaning.

- Looking at the thermostat in the room to see whether you feel cold or warm.

In all these cases, the use of technology is convenient. But we could have used our own brain instead. And by not using it, we gradually lose our ability to think. This goes slowly, but it happens. Because the mind is like a muscle. If we don't use it, we lose it. And losing that ability is a problem because it means that we don't think about things ourselves anymore and we take things for granted. In this way, despite its convenience, technology helps us go bananas as well.

There is one type of technology with clearly the largest effect on our bananas: information and communication technology (ICT) in all its variations. Even though the term ICT seems outdated and has been replaced by 'digital' nowadays, I nevertheless stick to it because it captures what this technology is about: information and communication. Being information and communication animals ourselves, it is exactly our increased access to information and communication that makes ICT have such a substantial effect on our thoughts and behaviors. And it is ICT that, of all technologies, contributes most to us going bananas.

I want to zoom in on four ways in which ICT helps us go bananas. The first, and most obvious one is the sheer amount and variety of information we get exposed to today through ICT. Through the Internet, email, WhatsApp, Facebook, Twitter, Snapchat, Instagram, news apps, weather apps, and other apps, we get so much information bombarded at us by so many people that we almost have to go bananas about it. This creates information overload and social overload that only a few of us can withstand.

A variation of this is that ICT helps us to capture everything we do. On our smartphones, laptops and in the cloud, we have thousands of photos, videos, messages, songs and documents that we can keep forever. There is no shelf space or desk or room size that forms a physical limit to the quantity of things we can store. Nor is there a bag size that limits the amount of information we can carry with us. This means we are not only overloaded by new information but also by information from the past. Everything we have ever produced is still immediately accessible, wherever, whenever. Combined with all the new information coming to us every day, and our omni-obesity, this forms an almost lethal banana cocktail.

Second, ICT also helps us run away from real experience. There is so much second-hand and third-hand experience available that our own first-hand experience easily gets oppressed. In the recent past, thought-up third-hand experience in the form of movies, books, music and comics was the main alternative to our first-hand experience. However, increasingly, the more authentic second-hand experience of people posting their own photos, stories, videos, vlogs, blogs, and podcasts is quickly taking over. As these experiences are one step closer to us than the third-hand experience, they are an even stronger distraction from real experience than third-hand experience.

An interesting phenomenon along these lines is people watching other people play games. Rather than playing the games themselves (which I would still count as first-hand experience, even though the game is, of course, artificial), they sit and watch how others do it. After my initial skepticism, having watched a few of them, I can see the attraction. You are seeing someone you can relate to doing similar things to you but in a better or more interesting way. Given our socialized nature referred to above, it makes sense that we enjoy stuff like this.

ICT also helps us avoid real experience through 'screenization'. It turns our 3D experience into a screen-size 2D experience of the world. In Chapter 2, I already referred to this with the example of people watching a concert or sports game or visiting a museum indirectly through their camera rather than directly through their eyes.

Third, ICT also leads to the information and people you are exposed to being highly selective. Of course, this has always been the case. If you were a Catholic in the past, you talked to Catholic people, went to Catholic school, read Catholic magazines, etc. But our search engines, personal ads, and social media exacerbate this selectivity enormously.

The 'filter bubble' that we are exposed to in this way results in our seeing a colored picture of the world.

Combined with our built-in confirmation bias and conformity bias, this has a direct effect on the issue of losing our nuance and perspective. If we are only exposed to information and people like us, how can we develop a nuanced perspective? And if people lack a nuanced perspective, we shouldn't be surprised if this leads to the kind of extreme outburst we see in online hate speech. The selective exposure leads to the development of groups within which people feel increasingly similar and connected, but between which they feel increasingly different and divided. The polarization that results from this is a fertile ground for growing bananas.

Finally, ICT helps in creating fake information. In the recent past, we knew something was real because it was captured on photo, audio, or video. This counted as hard evidence that someone had said or done something or that something was true or not. Not anymore. We have been accustomed for years to seeing manipulated photos through the advanced photo editing software that many of us use (and through the cover models on our glossy magazines). But, more recently, the editing technology has become so advanced that we can also produce audio and video that is hardly or not at all distinguishable from the real thing.

This makes deciding whether something is real or not a challenge. Through the advance of deep fake technology, there is hardly anything anymore that we can trust at face value. And this also works the other way around: we also can't distrust something at face value either. This situation creates fertile ground for people claiming that something is fake news. No wonder we have become suspicious about the truth.

Banana Economy

A final force at play that helps us go bananas is our economy. Our current capitalist system offers the perfect conditions for going bananas. Don't take me wrong. I am a capitalist too and I am still convinced it is the least problematic system that we know to date (if implemented in the spirit of its founding father, Adam Smith). But in combination with the four previous forces, it can grow a lot of big bananas too.

First, there is the idea of economic growth as the main indicator of progress and as a necessity for the system to succeed. Simply put: more is better. It means that, to keep the system alive, every year companies need to produce and sell a bit more than last year. This makes a fruitful combination with our omni-obesity. After all, we need people to buy all that stuff.

This perfect match makes the system easily get out of hand so that selling and buying become the main driver. Not as a means of progress, but as an end in itself. It leads to people buying stuff not because they need the stuff or even want the stuff, but because they want the experience of buying the stuff. Of course, who am I to judge, leading my luxury life. But bananas it is.

A second, and obviously related way in which our economy fosters banana behavior, is through marketing, sales and advertising. Companies have become real stars in understanding and exploiting our human weaknesses. Like no other, they are experts in biases and heuristics and know how to convince us to buy their stuff.

Once upon a time, sales efforts were still primarily directed at the System 2 part of our brains. Sales people and ads told you exactly why you would need a particular product, what you could use it for, and how it was better than competing products. They explained the main features, how it should be used and why that would help you. Based on this information, you could then make a reasonably rational decision to buy a product or not.

But companies discovered a long time ago that this is not how we decide whether we buy things or not. Only in exceptional cases, for products we care about and which we understand, are we using our System 2. For the rest, though, we let System 1 decide. Of course, if I asked you, you would tell me you wouldn't let yourself be fooled by advertisements. But you are wrong. A main feature of System 1 is that you make your decisions largely unconsciously. So, you are not even aware you have decided something, let alone that you know what led you there. This means that the entire marketing apparatus of all companies combined is exactly focused on us going bananas about their products and services.

Politicians use this too. Some of them are stars at playing the public through triggering System 1 responses. Spreading fear and uncertainty is a good example of that. Politicians have a certain authority. This means our authority bias makes us sensitive to what they are saying. And in their speeches, they bring in inspiring examples (availability bias), tell us there is only a short time left (scarcity heuristic) and focus on those most susceptible so that once they are on board, others will follow (conformity bias). And so on. In an environment where such skilled people are deliberately triggering our banana mechanisms, it is no wonder we go bananas.

Finally, we have the media—TV, newspapers, magazines and the like. Our capitalist economy doesn't only run on supply and demand of products or services. There are also the media that are in the business of selling information, or 'news'. And this same media also plays a big role in what we get exposed to and what not.

Generally, the media have most interest in publishing everything that is not average, normal or expected. This means that, in their coverage, the media have a strong built-in banana bias. Everything that reflects the majority or things we would expect is non-interesting. The media focus on the exceptions, the outliers, the strange, the extreme, the unexpected. Because these have 'news value'. This means that whatever we hear, see or read in the news is by definition not representative of the state of the world. But with our availability bias, framing bias and the exposure effect referred to earlier, we are wired to believe it is. This means that, like advertisements, the media are giving us exactly the kind of information that we are sensitive to and are thereby directly helping us to go bananas.

Along these lines, I recently read the disturbing news that the reach of 'pulp news' through social media sites such as Facebook and Twitter is now larger than the reach of 'real news' through the professional media. Pulp news is news that is only written for the sake of drawing attention, without regard to whether it is true or not, thereby generating traffic and advertisement income. The fact that pulp news now reaches more people than real news shows the enormous effect media have on our bananas.

Conclusion: The Five Banana Forces

As you see, there are no less than five strong forces that all help us go bananas. As human beings, we have our biological, psychological and social baggage that makes us well-equipped to go bananas. And we are living in a society where our technology and the economy create the ideal conditions for letting our bananas flourish. Together, these five forces create an almost irresistible tendency to go bananas. In this light, it is perfectly understandable that we engage in all the types of banana behavior summarized in Chapter 2.

But don't let this put you off trying to beat your bananas. Even though the forces are strong, they can be beaten. And the best thing is that beating them doesn't require any supernatural skills. As it turns out, we are also perfectly equipped to counter these forces. Many people show this every day. They manage to keep a cool head, stay grounded and withstand the collective madness. In the rest of this book, you will learn how they do it and how you can do it too.

Part 2

Solutions

4

Leaving Bananaland

As Part 1 showed, we are going pretty bananas and there are strong forces that push us to do so. But this doesn't mean at all that we have to sit down and accept it or that we can't do anything about it. On the contrary, as I found out while doing the research for this book, there are no less than 45 remedies for bananas. The following chapters lay out these 45 remedies in nine steps.

The solution to bananas that unfolds in these steps is that you get grounded again. This helps you to get back on your feet and keep your individuality. Rather than letting yourself be driven by collective lunacy, following the nine steps will help you get more control of your thoughts and behavior. And regaining your senses in this way will help you get more control of your life. It did for me, and so it can for you.

But before you rush to the steps, it is important to realize that making any meaningful changes to your life is hard work. The steps are not steps that you can simply execute once. They require your continuous attention and a lot of practice. Your banana habits have become part of your everyday way of thinking and doing. This means that replacing them with other habits may take a while.

This is not meant to discourage you. Most certainly not. It is meant to give you a realistic picture of what you can expect. This should help to motivate you to continue when things take longer and aren't going as well as you hoped. This is perfectly normal. Too many self-help books and self-help gurus suggest that making changes is easy. You just have to follow their X-step plan to an epiphany or join their expensive two-day seminar and you'll live happily ever after. But life doesn't work like that. To help you make some real change, this chapter therefore discusses the overall attitude and approach that you need in order to follow the nine steps successfully.

How Great People Get Great

Why do some musicians get famous? Why do some athletes win the Olympics? Why do some entrepreneurs create hugely successful companies? Why do some scientists win Nobel prizes? Why do some authors write bestsellers?

Because they are talented, right? Sure, without their talent they wouldn't have gotten there. After all, you need to have a bit of luck with your genes. But the real answer is that they work damn hard. Whether you ask them or look at any of the many studies done on successful people, the conclusion is always the same: being successful in anything requires a lot of sweat, pain, effort, patience, and failure. It requires hard work and perseverance. Just look at the following quotes by some successful people in different disciplines.

Success is no accident. It is hard work, perseverance, learning, studying, sacrifice and most of all, love of what you are doing or learning to do.—Pele

All life demands struggle. Those who have everything given to them become lazy, selfish, and insensitive to the real values of life. The very striving and hard work that we so constantly try to avoid is the major building block in the person we are today.—Pope Paul VI

Talent is cheaper than table salt. What separates the talented individual from the successful one is a lot of hard work.—Stephen King

*The three great essentials to achieve anything worthwhile are: Hard work,
Stick-to-itiveness, and Common sense.*—Thomas A. Edison

Writing music is not so much inspiration as hard work.—George Gershwin

To be able to put a lot of hard work into something, you need to really want it. That is also what research on 'grit' shows: only people with passion and perseverance reach the top. Of course, in trying to overcome your bananas, your goal is not to reach the top. There is no top. There is only you who wants to feel better, be more effective or be a nicer person. But that requires the same passion and perseverance to make it happen.

I can't see how you could be 'passionate' about not being bananas. Imagine someone saying "Oh, I am so passionate about not going bananas. I love it!" The very fact that you are passionate about it is a clear sign you are not ready yet to let your bananas go. But what passion stands for here is that the only way to succeed is if you really want it. And this applies certainly to not going bananas anymore. Given that our banana habits are so deep in our veins, you need to really want to get rid of them to actually start getting rid of them. So, in that sense, both passion and perseverance are needed.

Only hard work is not enough. You can work very hard but not achieve any results. You can practice and practice and practice without getting any better at something. This happens when you practice in the wrong way. If you repeat the same thing over again, you are unlikely to make any progress. This means it is not only the number of hours or sweat you put in, but also the way you do this. You need to practice smart, not just hard.

Scientists have a name for it. They call it 'deliberate practice'. If you apply deliberate practice, you try to improve one thing at a time in a systematic and focused manner. When you are trying to achieve something, you observe what is your main weakness and try to improve on that. Once you have succeeded in that, you focus on your next main weakness and work hard to improve that one too. And so on and so forth. So, you deliberately pick something you are not doing in the right way yet and practice until you have improved it, before you move on to the next thing.

Deliberate practice implies that you constantly reflect on your progress. When practicing, you keep a close eye on whether you improve in what you are trying to achieve. And if you are not making progress, you adjust how you practice. This means that you try to learn from what you do. Thus, in a nutshell, deliberate practice works like this:

1. You identify the thing or aspect that you want to improve.

2. You practice, practice and practice to improve it.

3. You monitor whether you are improving.

4. If you are not, you adjust your way of practicing until you have found a way that works for you.

5. Once you are satisfied with the improvement made, you start again at 1 for the next thing or aspect that you want to improve.

This works for musicians, athletes, entrepreneurs, scientists, authors and anyone else who wants to improve their skills significantly. And it also works for getting rid of your bananas. Therefore, I recommend using these principles of deliberate practice when going through the remaining chapters. Of course, you can read them first at a glance. But if you want to make improvements, the best thing is to focus on one step or even one remedy at a time and work on that. And once you are happy with your achievements, you move on to the next.

Furthermore, in the same way as becoming great in music, sports, etcetera, you will have to maintain the other steps and remedies as well. Once developed, every skill needs to be maintained so as not to lose it. Maintenance is easier than development, but it needs to be done. There is thus no finish line or end point to aim for. Keep this in mind.

Another Take on How to Do It

We often look at the great achievers to learn how to become better at something. They are the stars, the heroes, the people that inspire us to achieve something great as well. That makes sense. After all, they show that great achievements are possible and how to do it. However, there is also a different, and perhaps unexpected, place to look for inspiration: the monastery.

"The monastery?" you may ask. "How on earth can we learn how to get rid of our bananas from monks and nuns who have completely disconnected from the world?" But that is exactly why we can learn from them. They manage to live in this world and at the same time not let themselves go bananas. And as you'll see, the way they live and their basic attitude—with the important exception of their religious core—is at its heart not that different from our heroes.

When looking at the monastery, I took my inspiration from monastic life in the spirit of Saint Benedict, or Benedict of Nursia, a Christian Saint who lived around the year 500 AD. His 'Rule of Saint Benedict' is one of the most influential religious rules in the Western Christian world. This rule contains a lot of surprisingly practical advice on how to live a monastic life. Unlike some other religious documents, it is extremely down-to-earth and free of mystique and symbolism.

Of course, you don't have to become a monk or nun to rid your bananas. Also, you don't need religion for that. But there is a surprising number of things we can learn from Benedict's Rule and from the way monks and nuns live. That is also one of the key points of Benedict's philosophy: you are supposed to apply it and integrate it in everyday life, also if you are not a monk. If you are interested, Wil Derkse's *The Rule of Benedict for Beginners: Spirituality for Daily Life* helps you do this.

Throughout the steps outlined in the next chapters, you will find ideas that can be traced back to, or are also found in, monastic life. At this point, though, I would like to zoom in on the general attitude and approach that can be found in Benedict's Rule. This rule is meant to explain how to achieve something really hard, in this case becoming a fully dedicated monk. And from this, we can learn a great deal about how to achieve something else that can be really hard too: liberating ourselves from our bananas.

It starts with your basic attitude. Benedict tells us always to stay a novice. You have to feel like a novice and behave like a novice, even if you are already advanced at something. This is interesting and humbling advice. It makes you realize that there is always something to learn and that you are never there yet. It also makes you realize that there is always someone to learn from, even if you are the highest boss or greatest person on earth. This attitude helps you focus on the things you are not good at yet and to improve them—an element that we also find back in the deliberate practice idea.

Another main principle outlined in the rule is perseverance—or *stabilitas* as it is called there. It means not walking away from something you have committed yourself too. So, despite the hard times that you will face, you need to go on and not stop and escape into something else. This we also find in our heroes' advice. But what I particularly like about the idea of *stabilitas* is that it takes away any grandeur. It is a grounded way of saying that once you commit to something, you stick to it. You are going to need this attitude to get the stickiest bananas out of your head.

A third important principle is Benedict's version of continuous improvement: *conversatio morum*. It is a bit hard to translate, but it means something like 'conversion of life'. It refers to making changes. According to Benedict, we are not only supposed to stick to something, but also engage in continuous, step-by-step change to improve. For Benedict, life is a continuous journey in which you keep on improving yourself all the time. The word *conversatio* implies a commitment to live faithfully and keep one's mind open. Broadly translated, it means we should stay optimistic and open to any ideas or help that we find along the way. So, you are not just sticking to your own improvement plan but, on your journey, you welcome and appreciate any help or opportunity that you may encounter. Having such an open attitude is going to help you a great deal in getting rid of your bananas.

This brings me to the fourth and probably initially most deterring aspect of Benedict's rule: obedience (*obedientia*). Benedict tells us to be obedient to our superiors and each other. That sounds old-fashioned and against today's strong focus on freedom, equality and self-determination. It would be if it meant that we follow someone else's orders blindly. But that is not at all what *obedientia* means.

The term *obedientia* comes from the Latin word *audire*, which means listening. What it stands for, is that you listen attentively and look carefully around you and embrace any advice or suggestions that you can get—and that you act accordingly. It means you are always trying to learn from what others do or tell you and that you implement their advice. So, you 'obey' signals you are getting and not just think by yourself that you are right.

Interestingly, *obedientia* means almost the opposite of blind obedience. It implies taking responsibility for your own life. You are supposed to make the best of it, and seriously consider any input you get and act if this is the right thing to do. So, you don't hide behind others, or behind being busy, or behind having some sort of special inability, or behind being entitled to deserve exceptional treatment.

I suppose you are getting a sense now of what Benedict is trying to tell us in his Rule. The four principles discussed above belong together and add up to an image of us persevering to continuously improve our lives with a humble attitude while carefully paying attention to any help and opportunities that come our way.

The Nine Steps to Bananalessness

To master anything, there is always a variety of steps or levels that you should go through. Although there are many routes to making progress, you need to go through certain stages which cannot be skipped and which you should approach in a particular order. We see this, for example, in education, where you start at elementary school and go through high school before you can go to college. The idea of this is that you first need to learn a set of basic skills before you can move on to more specific or advanced skills. Another example is the belt system in martial arts, where you first have to earn a variety of colored belts before you can earn your first level of black belt. So, there is a particular order in how to make progress.

The same applies to your road to bananalessness. There are things you first need to have in place before you can move on. This means that there is logic in the order in which the steps are presented in the next chapters. Of course, you can deviate from this order and also go back and forth. But my recommendation is to start with the first step and only proceed to the next step once you have mastered it to a reasonable degree. This will increase your chances of getting rid of your bananas and it will keep you motivated since you keep on making progress—one step at a time. So here are the nine steps.

Step 1: Calm Down

The first step on your journey to bananalessness is to calm down your mind. If you are going bananas, you are too full of thoughts and feelings to act sensibly. Therefore, before you can make any progress, you need to calm down. As you will see in Chapter 5, the way to do this is to shut off the noise and drastically reduce your information intake.

Step 2: Let Go

Your next step is to stop trying to control the many things that are beyond your control. Going bananas is also a result of keeping too many balls in the air. Once you drop a significant number of them, you will calm down further and free enough brain space to continue your journey out of Bananaland. Chapter 6 will help you achieve this.

Step 3: Take Responsibility

Once you have calmed down a bit and let go of some bananas, the next step is that you take responsibility for the fact that you are going bananas—and for your life in general. You can only make further progress if you accept that there is nothing and no one else to blame and that you are the only one responsible. This step is discussed in Chapter 7.

Step 4: Dethrone Yourself

The next step is a bit of a nasty one—at least for me. Getting rid of your bananas implies that you have to dethrone yourself. This means realizing that you are not as important as you think you are and that anything you worry about isn't so important either. Chapter 8 describes how to do this in a way that makes you feel better rather than worse.

Step 5: Build Character

Now that you have put yourself with both feet back on the ground and taken responsibility for your banana journey, you can start reclaiming your own individuality. That is what this fifth step—and Chapter 9—is about. It helps you to ignore your inner call to conform to what others think and do and live your life in your own way—even if that goes against accepted norms.

Step 6: Detox Yourself

Going through steps 3 to 5 helps you develop the right attitude to beat your bananas. These three steps are emotionally the hardest ones since they imply reconstructing yourself. Once you are that far, it is now time to start detoxing yourself. This means that you start cleaning your mind from all the clutter about what you are supposed to believe, aspire, say and do. Chapter 10 should help you with this.

Step 7: Get Organized

In the previous steps, you have mainly worked on your mind, on improving the way you think. That is clearly the most important part of getting rid of your bananas. However, you also need to work on the way you work, on how you plan and organize things. This helps you reduce the chances of falling back to your old banana behaviors. Chapter 11 focuses on this.

Step 8: Think Sensibly

In the first seven steps, you have made yourself banana-ready. After the noise-canceling of Steps 1 and 2, you have worked on your character in Steps 3-5 and cleaned up your internal and external clutter in Steps 6 and 7. This should enable you to stand firm against the never-ending flow of bananas thrown at you. Now, in the last two steps, you are ready to take in information again. Chapter 12 describes how you can do this without going bananas, by developing and using sensible thinking.

Step 9: Pay Attention

In the last step, you make yourself fully ready for this banana-rich world. Step 8 taught you how to think and act more sensibly so that you can separate the bananas from the other fruit. In this final step, you learn how to actively seek to take in new information and connect to others while staying calm at the same time. As you will see, Chapter 13 describes how to pay careful attention to the things that matter.

Stages You May Go Through

The process of getting rid of your bananas resembles kicking the habit of drug addiction. Of course, there are differences, but this resemblance makes sense. Going bananas is a bit of a drug addiction. Chapter 2 showed how invasive the addiction is, and Chapter 3 gave various biological, psychological and sociological reasons why we have such a strong inclination to go bananas. This makes ridding your bananas close to getting rid of a serious drug addiction—although usually without most of the physical effects.

The fact that getting rid of your bananas has striking resemblances to recovering from an addiction means that, in each step, you are also likely to go through a series of mental stages. Research shows that we go through a couple of stages in almost any relevant change in our lives. Well-known in this respect are the 'coping' stages of dealing with a loss, trauma, or externally imposed change such as being fired or discovering you have a chronic disease. Along these lines, you may find yourself going through the following mental stages while facing your bananas:

- **The 'Uh-Huh' Stage.** In this stage, you read about a particular banana or step and think: Okay, that makes sense, people are that crazy and they could indeed benefit from a step like this.

- **The 'Not Me' Stage.** While the banana or step you read about may be applicable to others, it doesn't apply to you. After all, you are doing fine and are certainly not as bananas as others.

- **The 'Oh Shit' Stage.** After your initial denial, you realize that what you read *does* apply to you. You may be shocked because you are more bananas than you were ready to admit.

- **The 'I'm a Failure' Stage.** While still trying to find evidence that you are not bananas, you know you are. And you loathe yourself for it. You may get angry and call yourself a failure.

- **The 'Poor Me' Stage.** After you have put yourself down, your anger turns into self-pity. You don't see how you can change, and you feel like a helpless child. Others should solve your problems.

- **The 'Farewell Banana' Stage.** With pain in your heart, you get ready to say goodbye to your banana habit. Having been your dependable companion, you feel sad about letting it go.

- ***The 'Nothingness' Stage.*** After having said goodbye to your banana, you wait and see. You don't give any special attention to it anymore and just do whatever you do.

- ***The 'Done, Next' Stage.*** At a certain point in time, you realize that your banana habit is gone and replaced by a non-banana version. You are ready to move on to the next step.

Your Personal Banana Demons

Even though all nine steps are important in ridding yourself of bananas, it is likely that there are one, two or maybe three that are especially important to you. Everyone has their own specific pitfalls and weaknesses. Mine are Step 4 (Dethroning Yourself), Step 5 (Building Character), and probably Step 2 as well (Let Go). I tend to make myself and the things I do far too important and find it hard to stand strong against the social norms around me. And I am also not good at letting things go, even though I know that would be better for me.

You will have your own personal banana demons, the steps that are most difficult for you. This means they require extra attention. You probably won't be able ever to master them fully, but that is okay. You don't need to be a banana champ. In line with the attitude and way of working described above though, these steps will always require your attention. You need to be aware of them and keep working on them in order not to regress back into Bananaland.

How to Get the Most Out of this Book

As should be clear by now, the best way of using the rest of this book is not just to read it and put it back on your bookshelf or in your folder of read e-books. Of course, you could do this, but the chances of any lasting effect are then close to zero. As this chapter has argued, making change is hard work, which can be as confrontational and difficult as recovering from drug addiction. If you just read the book and put it away, you are probably not getting beyond the 'Uh-huh' and 'Not Me' stages. You think it is interesting, but now let's go back to work.

To get the most out of this book, the best thing is to go through it step by step, or even remedy by remedy, within a chapter. So, you read a chapter or section, let it sink in and think about how you could adjust and implement the suggested remedies in your life. *And then you do so.* You are prepared to go through the stages above, and, while doing this, you persevere with an open mind and take any help and opportunity coming your way.

While reading the book, you have to continuously make the translation of what you read to yourself and to your own life. The steps and remedies are general, but this book is colored by my personal experiences and perspective. These may not be the same as yours. You have your own experiences and perspective. This means that, rather than taking things literally, you should see the steps, remedies and examples as seeds of inspiration that help you guide your own journey out of Bananaland. So, let's get started.

5

Step 1: Calm Down

The first step on your banana liberation journey is that you calm down and probably cool down too. The fact that you are going bananas means you are in an overheated stress mode. You can't think or do anything sensible in such a mode. This means that, before being able to do anything else, you need to create sufficient silence and room in your head. In this chapter, you will learn five ways to do this. The first two are noise-cancellation remedies that help you block the external noise. The other three are more targeted at reducing the internal noise that is going on.

Switch Off Notifications

One of the most banana-inducing mechanisms is notifications. You know, the signals you get when a new email, message update, or phone call comes in. They are well-meant, seemingly convenient, and we all use them. After all, as omni-obesitists and social animals with a strong fear of missing out, we want to know when someone has tried to reach us or when new information appears.

But notifications are intrusive and disturbing. The main issue with them is that they are pro-active. They appear when someone or something new pops up—not when we ask for them. As Chapter 3 explained, there are biological, psychological and sociological forces at play that make us sensitive to external signals. Our human genes, brains and habits are programmed to respond to them.

On the one hand, notifications are a trigger of excitement. They mean something new has come and we haven't seen it yet. Our curiosity leads us to want to know what the new thing is. But notifications could also be a sign of danger. A sudden light-flash could mean fire or lightning and a sudden sound could mean someone warning you or an approaching enemy. While new emails, messages, updates or phone calls aren't particularly dangerous, there is this primary fear response at play that makes each notification cause a little bit of stress.

Getting a few notifications per day is okay. Then they are handy and they cause the mild levels of stress that make our lives enjoyable rather than boring. As experiments with locking people up in completely dark and sound-isolated rooms show, we need signals from outside. Without them, we go rapidly insane—far beyond bananas.

But coming in large numbers, notifications cause stress. And the amount we get nowadays, it doesn't matter anymore whether it is excitement stress or anxiety stress. Our body basically responds to both in the same way, thereby disturbing whatever we were doing.

I suppose some of you are now in the 'Uh-Huh' or 'Not Me' stage. You nod and agree that many people have problems with notifications, but not you. Either you are not getting so many notifications or you don't feel any stress because of them. Maybe you are right and that is good for you. But to make sure, let's concentrate for a moment on the extent to which you are possibly exposed to notifications. Let's focus on your notification hub: your smartphone. First, consider the types of notifications you can get; for example, to be informed about a new email or WhatsApp message:

- Sound – one time or repeated until you have responded
- Spoken word – apps talking to you

- Vibration – also one time or repeated
- Banner – a pop-up message that you can tap or swipe away
- Badge – the tiny red circle with the number of unread messages.
- Lock screen – message on the screen of your locked phone
- Notification center – the place where all notifications are shown

That makes no less than seven types of notifications for a single message in a single app. Now multiply that by the number of apps you are getting notifications from. For example:

- Traditional phone calls and text messaging
- WhatsApp, Facebook, Instagram, Snapchat, Twitter, LinkedIn, Pinterest, or any other social media app you are using
- System updates, upgrades, app store, etc.
- Maps, navigation, and parking apps
- News and weather apps
- Games and any other apps you are using

And now multiply that by the average number of notifications you get per app per day. Of course, the total you then get is a bit of an insane number, and I suppose you are not using all types of notifications for all your apps. But still, it is a lot. Research shows that the average smartphone user receives about 50 to 80 push notifications per day (and that is all ages—imagine the average 15-year-old). Assuming you have about eight hours sleep time in which you don't look at them, this is about once every 15 minutes while being awake—every day.

And that is only your smartphone. Obviously, it is the most notable source of notifications. But it is certainly not the only one. Next to your phone, you may also have a tablet and computer giving you similar kinds of notifications (and potentially exactly the same, since you are getting much of the same stuff as on your phone). And there are many more notifications you get than only through those devices. Think about regular snail mail, advertisements, commercials, flyers, and cold-calling calls you receive. These are also pro-active and cause the same kind of excitement stress or anxiety stress as the notifications on your phone. No wonder we go bananas.

The good news: you can switch them off. All of them. Even though it may be a bit hard to find, you can switch off all notifications on your phone, tablet and computer, including the badges in your app icons. Furthermore, you can refuse all advertisement flyers, door-to-door papers, and commercial calls you receive, and you can watch TV without any advertisements, or stop watching TV at all. Therefore, the first remedy on your journey out of Bananaland is easy. Switch off your notifications and you are done.

If your fear of missing out is getting in the way, you can try one of the following two approaches. First, you can reduce the number of notifications step-by-step. Switching off sounds and vibrations for anything but phone calls and text messages is a good start. None of the other things is urgent, so you can easily ignore them for a while. But the fact that someone can always reach you, and that you will hear or feel it when they are trying, might give you the peace of mind you need for starting your new notification detox. And once you are used to that, you can start switching off pop-up messages, badges and any remaining notifications app after app, until you have arrived at your personal maximum bearable notification abandonment.

The second approach is to go cold turkey. Your goal is not necessarily to switch off all notifications forever but to experience how liberating this could be—and thereafter drastically reduce your day-to-day notification intake. You can decide, for example, to go for a vacation in which you completely disconnect for a week or so. To give you peace of mind this time, you could still have your phone switched on for calling (but no Wi-Fi or data) and set up autoresponders in, for example, your email so that people know you won't respond. Now experience the tranquil rest this gives you, get used to it, and after your disconnected week switch off as many notifications as you can bear.

Both ways work. And you probably will need to repeat them regularly. Without being aware of it, you might have increased your notification receipt again in the course of a couple of weeks or months. Once you realize this, start switching off again. Personally, I need the second approach repeatedly. I have succeeded reasonably well in reducing my notifications along the lines explained above. But about once or twice per year, I need to disconnect and experience again that virtually none of the notifications matter. This helps me switch off a few more, and thereby reduce my chances of going bananas. Therefore:

Banana Remedy 1.1: Switch Off Notifications
On your phone, tablet, computer, snail mail, or any other channel, switch off as many notifications as you can. And then switch off a few more to find out that you can do with even less.

Consume Less Information

Closely related to the first remedy, the second remedy to calm down is to reduce your information consumption. We are not only being disturbed by notifications. Also in other ways, we get so much information bombarded at us, that we just must go bananas. Think about all the information you get daily via news apps, the Internet, TV, radio, talking to people, reading magazines, and so on and so forth. When we compare that to the amount of information people got, 1000, 100 or even 10 years ago, it is astonishing.

Research by Zenith showed that, in 2009, the global average time spent on any type of media consumption per day was 411 minutes - including interacting with others through social media. That is slightly less than 7 hours per day. That is an insane number, I'd say. But if you think that is a lot, this had grown to an estimated 463 minutes per day in 2018. And if you think that is a lot, the numbers for the US are 578 and 633 respectively, which is more than 10 hours per day of media consumption in 2018. How can you not go bananas from that?

The interesting thing is that we actively seek most of the information for ourselves. Or at least, we expose ourselves to it. Of course, we are bombarded by others, but it is we who choose to pay attention. I explicitly say *choose* to pay attention here, because it is indeed a choice, even though it might not feel like that. We may feel overloaded or overwhelmed and that we can't do something about it. But since we are doing it ourselves, we can do something.

And that is good news, since it means we can stop doing it and reduce our information consumption. The only thing we need to do is consume less by ignoring mainly the information that is thrown at us. Of course, as omni-obesitists, we know that this is only easy in theory.

Getting more information is addictive. It is again our fear of missing out that is at play. "But what if I miss something important?" you may ask. But that is the point. You rarely do miss something important.

There is a strong social norm that we should be informed. We are supposed to follow the news and know everything about our families and friends—even if they are Facebook 'friends'. We are supposed to catch up with people, remember their birthday, have seen the latest viral video on YouTube, know about the plane that crashed on the other side of the world, or about the cat that was rescued from a balcony 5,000 kilometers away.

We have to know all of this because…because of what? Because something terrible happens if we don't? Because we will be expelled by our friends and families? We might think so. But the reality is that surprisingly little happens. You live on if you don't know all of these things, and I bet no one will even notice if you do not. But you feel more relaxed and relieved if you don't have the stress of catching up with everything knowable that you might need to know.

Of course, there are some things that you shouldn't miss. If your house is on fire, if your uncle is remarrying, or if your best friend has passed an important exam, you probably want to know. But you are more likely to pay attention to such important events if you are not fully overloaded with non-information. Less is clearly more.

There are a lot of things that you can do. Instead of presenting you with an endless list, let me share what I did to reduce my own information intake. This was most certainly necessary since I have a strong inclination always to look for more information. If there is such a thing as information addiction, I'd be sensitive to it. This means that I always have to keep a watch on my information gathering behavior. So, here are the five things that I have done—and which I can recommend to you too:

- Stop watching TV, especially commercial TV. I don't mean the screen, but the channels. It is a couple of years now since we haven't had a receiver anymore at home. This was a really good decision. Sitting passively in front of that screen and switching channel after channel after channel made me braindead. It is information consumption for the sake of information consumption. Occasionally, when I am in a hotel, I switch on the TV there and go through all the channels. The fact that, after about 100 channels, I still haven't seen anything interesting, tells me that I don't miss anything. Not even mildly.

- Abstain from news. This is a bit controversial. After all, we are supposed to follow the news and know what is going on in the world. But I became obsessed with this, and felt I *had* to read the newspaper and scan all headlines in my news apps all day. Canceling my newspaper subscription for a year and reducing my headline scanning felt like a liberation. Recently I renewed my subscription, and, interestingly, my temporary newspaper detox has worked. I can now read it when I want, not because I must. And, more importantly, I now read it to *understand* things not to just *know* about them. That is a crucial difference. It means skipping the attention-grabbing headlines and reading the deeper, more critical journalistic pieces. In this way, my news detox has been a double-edged sword cutting my bananas: less news overload and more putting things in perspective.

- Stop using Facebook and never start with Instagram, Snapchat and the like. Years ago, I created a Facebook account, went on the look for 'friends', followed them, liked their stuff, etc. And it was sort of interesting to see all these expressions of happiness and success, and all the funny, remarkable or otherwise interesting contributions. But it was stressful too. It brought me the social stress to keep up with everyone else, and the cognitive stress to keep up with the endless stream of updates. I still have an account, but not looking at it for the last two years has brought me more free time and a more relaxed life. And I have found that I don't miss out on anything important and don't now feel any tendency to look.

- Avoid, silence, and ignore WhatsApp groups. WhatsApp groups can be a useful and efficient means of communication. But they are also a source of social and cognitive stress. You get less information there than on Facebook, but the information you get is pushed to you and the pressure to conform is greater.

We all know the feeling of "I should react too, and in a funny, clever and original way." My way of dealing with this is threefold: 1) avoid WhatsApp groups that are not strictly necessary, 2) silence too-active groups, meaning that all notifications are switched off for that group while still receiving the messages, and 3) ignore much of the content that is sent around there, especially the photos and videos. This helps.

- Limit my amount of Googling. This is a tough one for me. I am curious and a perfectionist in seeking the best answer to a question. And once I stumble upon something interesting, I get easily distracted and want to know more about that as well. That is not a healthy combination with Google. It leads to endless searches and to consuming large amounts of information in a short time. Therefore, what I try to do is avoid searching in the first place. Whenever something knowable pops up, I try to ask myself whether it is really necessary that I know it. If not, I don't search. I am not really successful in this, but based on the occasions it works, I can recommend it, since it helps me to calm down and keep my senses.

While you could try to do the same as me, the best thing is to ask yourself what works for you. You probably have different information addictions to me. But reducing your information intake in whatever way is going to help you calm down and withstand the collective craze.

The point is, not to completely disconnect and become completely ignorant of what is going on around you. Not at all. The point is that you focus on the essence, on the most important things and reduce all the noise around it. This leaves you more time and brainpower to pay attention to the things that matter. Therefore:

Banana Remedy 1.2: Consume Less Information

Ignore the inner voice saying that you should keep abreast. Drastically reduce your information intake. Limit your exposure to media-pushing information (TV, Facebook, WhatsApp, etc.) and search less.

Stop Babbling

We are not only going bananas through all the information noise that gets to us. We also go bananas through the noise that we produce ourselves. What I mean is the endless stream of words that we produce without real meaning. Call it babbling, blah-blah, bullshit, mumbo jumbo, gibberish or word vomit; it is the nonsense talk for the sake of talking.

I suppose you know what I mean: you have started a response without knowing where it will go, but you keep on talking because you have started talking. Or you express your strong opinions about something without having a genuine opinion, or actually you don't care. Or, to avoid silence, you just talk about the weather, someone else's misfortune, or something in the news. Or you make jokes or try to be funny all the time for the sake of contributing to a conversation. Or you interrupt people with the first thing that comes to your mind. Or you simply repeat what others said before.

Of course, small talk has its purpose. We are social animals and it feels awkward to stay completely silent or immediately engage in a deep conversation with a total stranger. So, some small talk is needed as a social glue to get to know and bond with others and to get a conversation started. But if we engage in small talk or other forms of babbling all the time, this creates noise.

This works two ways. First, your babbling creates noise for others. They have to listen to stories that go nowhere, opinions that are not real opinions, non-informative stories about the weather, supposedly funny but actually annoying contributions to a conversation, or they are interrupted all the time by your untamable urge to speak. So, through your babbling, you are baking bananas for them.

But it also works the other way around. Your own babbling creates noise for yourself too. You hear yourself say words that you don't mean, or you talk about things that you are not even interested in or have an opinion about. You are creating a word cloud that clouds your thinking and conflicts with what you actually feel or want to say.

This creates stress. Saying one thing, while not having anything to say or wanting to say something else creates an internal tension. While talking to someone about the weather, or giving your funny or witty response, you hide the fact that you have absolutely nothing to say or would like to talk about something that matters to you. Going against what you would like to do creates internal stress.

It also makes your brain work unnecessarily hard. When, in a conversation, you start a babble story that isn't what you want to say, you have to overheat your brain to keep the story going because you have to continuously think up the next part of the story. Because you are talking from the head rather than from the heart, your brain has to work hard. I know from extensive experience, this can be tiring.

There are a couple of things you can do. The first is obvious: talk less. I know this isn't at all as simple as it sounds, especially if you are a talkative person. But it doesn't require any supernatural skills either. Anyone can do it. So, the next time you are with someone or in a group of people, try to talk less. Let moments of silence occur if they occur. Don't try to fill them with words but keep your mouth shut instead. Initially, this may feel like you have to suppress something that needs to get out. And you may also feel uncomfortable since we are hardly used anymore to sitting together in silence. But I am sure you will start liking it after you get used to it.

It is easier if there is more than one person present. It means you can talk less without there necessarily being a seemingly awkward silence. In that case, practice letting others do the talking. Rather than engaging in a word battle for the longest, funniest or cleverest contributions, you sit back and observe. This helps in three ways: it adds less clutter to the conversation, it cools down your brain, and it gives you time to reflect on what you see and learn from it. The last is especially useful, since it may help you see that there is indeed a lot of babbling going on rather than real communication—which may reduce your talking appetite.

Another variation that you can use to reduce the amount of babbling is to suppress your initial impulse to respond. Your goal is not necessarily to talk less but to talk differently about the things that you want to say. It is often our impulse to respond immediately that creates the mumbo jumbo. Therefore, whenever you feel the urge to respond, wait a couple of seconds before you do so. You don't even have to count to ten. Five seconds should be enough to channel your initial response and calm down.

It also helps if you combine this with physically holding back. Our body and mind are intertwined. This means that physical actions can have a direct effect on our minds. Babbling is often a result of us being too eager to respond. We lean forward, anxiously looking for the slightest opening in the conversation which we can fill with our words. If we lean back instead, with our backs against the back of our seat, or with our head straight up rather than leaning forward, this creates a sense of calmness too. Try it and you will see.

Finally, in case you can't tame your urge to speak, ask a question instead of saying something. Rather than overloading the other person with your babbling to fill the silence, ask them something. And ask them something you are genuinely interested in. So, if you ask them how they are doing, ask them in a way that shows you really want to know.

Asking questions has three advantages. First, questions are usually short and thereby asking them stops you from babbling. You can hardly use more than two sentences to ask a genuine question. Second, asking questions shows you are interested in the other person. Most people like this, and if the main point of your conversation is to establish or confirm your relationship with them, questions work well. Third, asking questions gives you control over the conversation. This means you can help others babble less as well, and talk about more interesting stuff. This brings us to your third banana remedy:

Banana Remedy 1.3: Stop Babbling
Reduce the number of words you utter and focus on the things that are worth saying. Suppress your impulse to respond. Lean back and ask questions instead of saying things you don't want to say.

Seek the Silence

The first three remedies are targeted at decreasing the external and inner noise that you are facing and that is triggering your bananas. The fourth remedy for that same noise is to actively seek moments and places of silence. So, rather than canceling the ongoing noise, you can also deliberately seek moments and places in which nothingness dominates.

Most people are not good at experiencing nothingness. It has become about the biggest sin one can commit. It is the one thing we avoid, no matter what. We have to be 'busy' and active to the extent that we don't have any idle time anymore. All our 'free' time is scheduled. We have to go to our dinner reservation at 7pm, we have to show up in the gym at 8pm for our group session, we must visit our grandparents and friends in the weekend, and we must have an exhausting all-you-can-see-do-and-eat holiday three times per year.

And when we are alone for a while, or face a slight moment of potential boredom, we immediately fill it. We listen to music, we switch on the TV, we read a magazine, or, most likely, we pick up our phone to fill our time with smartphoning—aimlessly checking any updates on the news or social media apps on our phone with the single purpose of having something to do.

In our quest for filling our time with action, we forget the importance of reflection, contemplation, of letting our mind flow to places without trying to control it. But the importance of silence cannot be overestimated. This is nicely illustrated with a quote that the philosopher Hannah Arendt uses. It is a quote from Cato, a Roman statesman who lived more than 2,000 years ago: "Never is a man more active than when he does nothing, never is he less alone than when he is by himself." Makes sense, doesn't it?

We need silence and nothingness to function properly. As the first half of this quote indicates, we need it to process all the information we get, to let things sink in, to let our subconscious do the work it is supposed to do, to calm down, to avoid getting bananas. It is for this reason that it is these moments of silence after hard work when we often get the best insights and ideas.

As the second half of the quote hints, we also need silence and nothingness to come to ourselves, to form our identity. We need it to think about others and about our relationships with them. In our silence, those relationships gain in meaning. Silence allows us to appreciate them more and to feel better about our relationships with friends and families while being alone, rather than spending our time with them babbling.

Seeking silence means two things. It first means that you literally seek silence. You go somewhere or lock yourself up in a place where there is hardly any information input: as little visual and auditory distraction as possible. This could be a particular room in your house, or a place outside, or a church, or any other place where there is silence. This is the easy part.

Seeking the silence also means that you seek silence in your head. So, when you are at your silent place, you should make sure that you don't fill your head with all kind of banana thoughts. Thus, no to-do lists, I-should-have regrets, puzzles to solve, whistling, humming, or replaying music in your head. Those are distractions, and sneaky attempts of your brain still to fill the silence with bananas. Don't.

This doesn't mean that you are not allowed to think about anything. On the contrary. That is the whole point. You should let your thoughts flow without any attempt to control them. While some would argue that you need to ban and suppress any thought that pops up, I don't believe that works. At least it doesn't work for me, because it makes me frustrated about my inability to control my mind.

How to seek your silence? Like the other remedies, there is nothing inherently difficult about this fourth remedy. You don't need any superb skills or supernatural powers, and anyone can do it. But given that we have virtually lost our experience of it, let me give examples of what you can do to actively seek the silence—both physically and mentally.

The first thing you may think of is meditation, yoga, or any of the many mindfulness training methods available today. That could work. But it also might have the opposite effect: that you are so obsessed about it that you go bananas about the fact that you do meditation, yoga or mindfulness and let everyone know on your social media. Also, if it is something you go to once a week or so, it may become too special and not enough part of your daily life. Don't take me wrong. There is a lot of value in this kind of training, but remember that it is merely a means not an end. The reason I mention this, is that these things seem to be hyped quite a bit and if you join the club like many others you are staying inside the same banana mill instead of leaving it.

You could also visit a monastery every now and then for a couple of days, or visit a church when there is no service and sit there. Even if you are not religious, the whole atmosphere is one of silence and calmness, which could help you find your silence as well. This is what I occasionally do. Close to where I live, there is a Benedictine monastery where you can stay as a guest for a couple of days. You more or less live with the monks and follow their daily rhythm. Unlike in a silence retreat, you aren't forbidden to talk, but the habit is that you don't. And there aren't many other distractions either. The calmness of mind this creates was a revelation for me the first time.

These are all 'special' things you can do. They help, but the real way to seek silence, is to seek it in your everyday life—at home, at work, etc. The easiest, and at the same time toughest way to do this, is to just sit on your couch or chair and do nothing. Don't watch TV, don't listen to music, don't read, don't talk, don't look at your phone. Sit there and do nothing. When doing so, you might feel all kinds of impulses that you need to suppress. But once you are through that, you will experience a calm. This way is easiest because your couch or chair are waiting there, and you don't have to go anywhere. It is toughest because you are doing nothing while being somewhere where you are used to doing something. Your old habits make it hard to change and may give you a feeling of guilt that you are doing nothing.

To make it easier, it can help if you can at least watch something. Watching fire or water works especially well. You can go outside to a river, or lake, and watch the water move. Or you can light a fire and watch the flames. This will give you the feeling that you are at least doing something, even though that something is merely watching. But that can be easier than sitting on your own couch and doing nothing. Also, walking in the forest works—so long as you follow a path that you already know and can look around without having to think about your route. Accordingly:

Banana Remedy 1.4: Seek the Silence

Find moments and places where you can be alone in silence. Don't do anything except letting your mind go and process all the things that you have seen, heard, felt or done.

Channel Your Thoughts

The fifth remedy for keeping your calm is to control your thoughts. This remedy is most targeted at not going bananas since it directly concerns the banana mechanism in your mind: our ability and tendency to quickly have one thought after the other thereby causing a chain of thoughts that derail at accelerating speed.

In Chapter 3, we already saw that the basic banana mechanism is a mix of mad thinking and crazy acting, and a mix of doing this individually and collectively. As we also saw there, this easily leads to vicious cycles in which you think and do increasingly remarkable things. To get a good sense of what we can do about it, let's first look at four commonly-found variations of this cycle.

1. **The Self-Destructive cycle.** The first variation goes like this: *I made a mistake—I am stupid—I am a complete failure!* It starts when you make a, usually small, mistake. Then you think yourself stupid that you made a mistake. And then you think yourself even more stupid because you think yourself stupid. This ends up with thinking that you are an outright loser or failure.

2. **The Apocalyptic cycle.** This variation represents doom and gloom thinking and goes like this: *If this—then that— and…OMG!* It happens when your imagination is taking over in thinking about what could go wrong, what the result will be, and how that will lead to new possible problems.

3. **The Rewind and Replay cycle.** A third variation of banana thinking is the never-ending loop where you keep on repeating something with no progress. It goes like this: *I shouldn't have done that—I shouldn't have done that—I shouldn't have done that!* It happens when you keep on blaming yourself for something that can't be undone.

4. **The Alternative Past cycle.** Looking back at something you wish you had not done can also lead to a fourth cycle that goes like this: *If I had not… —but instead would have …—then this would not have happened!* Such backward-looking, if-then thinking is futile because you cannot change the past.

All four cycles are useless. The first two lead exponentially to extreme thoughts about yourself and the world, and the last two lead you into an endless self-punishing loop. It is easy to see how they make us go bananas. They don't provide any actionable outcomes and thereby lead to nothing but making us feel terrible.

But what to do about them? How to channel your thoughts? The answer is, again, simple in theory but harder in practice. In theory, you 'just' stop thinking in this way. Once a thought comes up, you 'just' stop yourself and break through the vicious cycle. You tell yourself "enough!" and come to your senses again.

In practice this is hard. The problem is that, once (and if) you notice your thinking is getting into one of these cycles, you are usually too late. By the time you notice it, you are already far on your way to bananas. You have already half-lost your senses, which makes it hard to think rationally and bring yourself to a halt.

This means that one of your strategies needs to be to know your pitfalls so that you can avoid them in the first place. If you think about it, you will see that there are always particular cases when your mind starts living its own life. Maybe it is when you are nervous about something, or when you read about certain things, or when you meet particular people, and so forth. Of course, the idea is not to avoid those events. That will only make you more scared and more bananas. But you want to avoid triggering the chain of thoughts. Knowing your pitfall situations increases the chances that you can bring your thoughts to an early halt.

Another way to channel your thoughts is to develop a standard stopping mechanism. Something as simple as taking a deep breath and counting to ten could do the job. It will make you focus your attention for a short while on something else—your breathing—rather than on the chain of thoughts. This might be enough to stop the chain ending up in bananas.

If this is not enough, you can also set yourself a time limit during which you are allowed to let your thoughts run in cycles. Once you notice you are in one of the cycles above, you set a timer of ten minutes, and allow yourself to go crazy. But after the ten minutes, you stop. In this way, you keep the banana thinking contained. And rather than setting yourself the impossible target of never doing it again, you allow yourself to do it for a short while. For me, this has worked many times.

As a variation, you can also set a time for banana thinking every now and then, or even at fixed time intervals. For example, you may plan ten minutes twice every day during which you allow getting yourself in the Self-Destructive, Apocalyptic, Rewind and Replay, or Alternative Past cycle. Like before, after these ten minutes you force yourself to stop and go on with what you were doing or planning to do. In this way, you don't control your thoughts, but you do control when you have them. And this will diminish your urge to go bananas at other moments.

If you don't succeed in doing it on your own, and you are lucky enough to have a partner or friend who is willing to help you, you can also let them do the stopping for you. You can ask them to tell you to stop whenever you go bananas. And to enforce it, you can agree on some repercussion if you don't. You can decide, for example, that you do ten push-ups, that they throw a glass of water in your face, that they call your boss and put you on the line, or anything else that gets you out of your vicious banana loop. This works. I know from experience.

A final way to channel your thoughts is to do exactly the opposite: you deliberately make yourself think the gloomiest worst-case scenario. And the point is that you exaggerate bigtime. So, for the Self-Destructive cycle this means you start telling yourself in extreme terms why you are the worst loser on this planet, and for the Apocalyptic cycle you come up with the worst results that you can possibly imagine. With the Rewind and Replay cycle, you tell yourself why what you have done is indeed the worst thing on earth. And with the Alternative Past cycle, you explain to yourself why you indeed should have known better and could have known everything in advance. By exaggerating in this way, you'll soon see that what you are telling yourself is so ridiculous that this breaks the cycle. Hence, the fifth remedy to calm down is:

Banana Remedy 1.5: Channel Your Thoughts
Control the vicious thinking cycles that make you go bananas. Stop them by knowing your pitfalls, planning how long and when they can take place, or make them extreme to get yourself back to reality.

Conclusion

The first step in your battle against your bananas is to calm down. In this chapter, you have seen five remedies for achieving that:

1.1 Switch Off Notifications
1.2 Consume Less Information
1.3 Stop Babbling
1.4 Seek the Silence
1.5 Channel Your Thoughts

Once you have gone through this first step and mastered it to a reasonable extent, this paves the way for the other eight steps. It is important to take this step first. Before you can do anything else in an effective way, you first need enough calmness. When you are no longer overloaded with all kinds of external or inner noise, this frees your mind enough to go on with the next step.

Of course, this doesn't mean you need to be completely Zen after this step or perfectly master all five remedies. That will never happen. Remember the previous chapter, where I argued that getting rid of your bananas is a never-ending process, in which you will always have to persevere, learn, and see yourself as a novice. That applies to this first step as well. You are never done.

But there is a point when you feel you can go on. Only you can tell this. But you will know it. It is when there is enough room in your head to think clearly every now and then. Through working on the various remedies for a while, you will experience the 'Done, Next' stage when you are ready. This is the point when you know you can go on to Step 2.

6

Step 2: Let Go

The first thing you have done is to limit your information intake. This was a crude measure to make sure you reduce the chances of new bananas entering your mind. Step 2 serves a similar purpose, but now the focus is on your mind itself. A significant proportion of our bananas result from us trying to control things that we cannot control. Trying to control things and people that are out of our control is a great source of bananas. We can put in large amounts of effort without any result—except getting progressively more frustrated. Letting things go is therefore an important second step on your road out of Bananaland. In this chapter, we will explore five remedies that can help you with this.

Stop Ruminating

Remedy 1.5 suggested that you can break through the vicious cycles by bringing your banana thinking to a halt. The basic idea was that you force yourself to stop the vicious cycle by setting clear limits to when and how long you allow yourself to go bananas. There are also subtler ways to achieve this. One of them is to stop ruminating about unproductive thoughts and replace them with more productive ones.

A way in which we keep our brain busy with unproductive thoughts is by always trying to explain things. Being children of the Enlightenment, we are raised with the idea that everything has a reason and that everything needs to be explained. From our earliest childhood, we learned the idea of cause and effect: if we cried as babies, then we got attention (and food or a diaper change). And the rest of our lives we have continued this way of thinking: if we prepare for an exam, then we get a higher grade, if we speed on the highway, we get a ticket, and so on. This has taught us that for every effect there must be a cause. So, if we got attention, then it must have been because we cried. If we received a higher grade, then it is because of our hard work. And if we got a ticket, then it is because we were speeding. Whatever the effect, there always is an explainable cause. Or so we think.

Often, looking for explanations is useful. If we make a mistake and think about what caused this mistake, we might discover how to avoid making the same mistake in the future. When we look for explanations in this way, we learn from what we did and improve for the future. That is useful and is the basic principle of learning and scientific progress. Even the very fact that we *can* explain is one of the essential differences between us and all the other species inhabiting this world. So, it is definitely something to cherish.

However, our same inclination to explain things also creates bananas. This is the case when there is no evident reason why something happened or when we can't do anything about it. A lot of things happen for no particular reason. They just happen. Call them coincidence, lack of attention, nature, misfortune, fate, or divine intervention; they are beyond explanation. Why don't we have a higher IQ? Why did someone not smile back? Why didn't someone answer our email? Why did we forget to buy milk? Why did lightning strike the apple tree in our garden? There are no satisfying answers to such questions.

The generic problem with trying to explain the unexplainable and with any other unproductive thoughts (such as the four vicious cycles referred to in the previous chapter) is that they are *limiting* thoughts. Rather than helping you, they limit you. They take your energy, capture your brain power, and keep you away from engaging in more productive, fun or interesting things. A remedy for dealing with such thoughts is to bend them towards thoughts that help you rather than limit you. To do that, you can ask yourself five questions whenever a not-so-useful thought pops up:

1.   Is my thought correct?
2.   How do I feel with this thought?
3.   How do I feel without this thought?
4.   Which of the two feelings do I prefer?
5.   What other thought could be helping me?

An example. Suppose your thought is: "I am a failure because I have failed the test." With the first question, you analyze whether this thought is correct. This tells you that you have indeed failed the test, but that this of course doesn't mean that you are a failure. Then you ask how you feel having this thought. It makes you feel, for example, insecure, small, miserable, or unworthy. Then you ask how you would feel without this thought. You probably would feel more confident, relaxed, happy, or at least okay if you didn't think you were a failure. Then you move to Question 4. The answer to that question is rhetorical: it is always the second option that feels better. But it is nevertheless useful to confirm that to yourself.

Finally, you answer the most important, fifth question and look for thoughts that can help make you feel better. This could be thinking the opposite of your initial thought ("The fact that I failed this test does not mean I am a failure" or "The fact that I failed this test doesn't say anything about whether or not I am a failure") but it could also be thinking something else that helps, such as "23% of the candidates failed the test and I don't see them as failures", "Hey, I made the test and that is already a sign I am not at all a failure", or "If I am honest, I didn't prepare too well for the test in the first place".

Answering these questions isn't the same as pepping yourself up. It is not "You can do it!", "You are great!" or any other positive pep talk you can give yourself. It also isn't the same as telling yourself to stop thinking like this ("Come on, you know you are no failure", "Here we go again…", or "Stop thinking like this!"). The point is, to use your rationality to reprogram the way you think in a way that it makes you feel better. Instead of ruminating about the limiting thoughts, you let them go and bend them towards thoughts that are helping you. Accordingly:

Banana Remedy 2.1: Stop Ruminating
Stop looking for explanations for the unexplainable and accept that many things just happen. Bend your mind from ruminating about limiting thoughts to producing thoughts that help you.

Cut Down on Planning

With looking for explanations, we try to control the past. And because the past can't be controlled, this makes us go bananas. Something similar applies to the future. Sure, we have some influence on it, but we can't fully control or predict it, and most certainly not in the long-term. Trying to is futile and again eats up a significant share of our energy and brain power, thereby increasing our chances of going bananas. And if our predictions and plans are wrong—which they usually are—it can make us go even more bananas. So, there is plenty of reason to cut down on your planning efforts.

Like looking for explanations, we are conditioned to plan. We are told to think before we act, prepare ahead, and plan our careers. We carry a calendar on our phone, have meetings planned far in advance and even fill our evenings, weekends and holidays with plans. And at work, we engage in project planning, make strategic plans and have various planning systems. So we plan. We learn it at home, at school and at work: planning is good because it prepares us for the future. And the future is the most important thing there is, so we must plan for it.

But the problem is, we can't predict the future nor plan for it. Of course, some things are relatively predictable. It is reasonable to assume the sun will still get up tomorrow and also in five years. Or that there will still be Internet, electricity and cars. Or that people will still eat rice, chicken and carrots, and keep on buying new stuff. But those are high-level and general predictions. They say hardly anything about *your* life. When it comes to more concrete questions like whether you are still in the same relationship, what job you will have, and what your health looks like in three years, there is no way to predict this.

We usually apply two rules of thumb in trying to predict the future anyway: we extrapolate the past, and we make it better. Extrapolating the past means that you basically assume that things will stay the same. You assume you still have the same partner, job and health as today. But we are also optimistic, so we usually think things will be better: you will be even happier with your current partner, have a better job and will be healthier than today. When looking ahead, we don't envision ourselves being divorced, unemployed, or in a hospital, right? This means we are optimistic simpletons when it comes to predicting the future. As a result, any plan is biased. We plan for the extrapolated optimistic future that we expect. But, most likely, that is not the future that will unfold. And thus, our plans will be wrong.

But what then? How to live our lives if not by planning them? "Carpe diem!" some would say, or "Seize the day!" if they don't speak Latin. Maybe that is indeed the right motto, as it stimulates you to experience today rather than to worry about the future. Personally, I am not so much a *carpe diem* guy. I tend to think about things and am too much a matter-of-fact person to embrace wholeheartedly such a motto.

But you don't have to. You can also let go of your tendency to plan and predict things without the need for a *carpe diem* mentality. The main point is to acknowledge that many things in the future are out of your control and that trying to control them makes you go bananas. Like before, the simple answer here is—don't. Don't plan far ahead and especially not in detail. There is no point in doing so because the future will unfold differently to how you expect now.

"But my life will be a complete mess if I don't plan ahead!" you may say, or "I need those plans. They give me structure and direction so that I know what I am working towards!" Not really. Life is messy, and the only thing that these plans give you is a fictitious feeling of comfort. When you make detailed long-term plans, you create a false certainty for yourself that gives you some comfort. Such plans are no more than comforting stories through which you tell yourself that things will be stable and better. It is alright to have them so long as you don't take them too seriously. If they help you keep your calm, great. In that case, they might even help you against going bananas. But if you really believe in them, you run into trouble. Because the future will unfold differently. Believing your plans will make you go bananas because there is going to be a mismatch between what you thought would happen and what really happens.

If you need further convincing, also think about the opportunity costs of planning. There are two kinds. First, think about how you could otherwise use the time that you spend on planning. Instead of carefully planning every minute of your next holiday, you could have used that time to spend with friends, read a book, or anything else you like doing. And instead of meticulously planning the new interior of your living room, you could have started or even finished it.

Second, think about all the unexpected opportunities that you miss by focusing on realizing your plans. If you plan, anything unexpected is a disturbance. You try to ignore it and stick to your plan. Thereby, you close yourself off to better or more interesting alternatives. This could mean that, on your carefully planned holiday, you completely miss the beautiful part of the city that you are crossing because you have your eyes focused on the map and your mind set on getting to the next tourist attraction. These are your opportunity costs. Take those into account whenever you find yourself making detailed plans.

Cutting down on planning doesn't mean that you completely ignore the future. Of course, it makes sense to think ahead a bit; for example, about how you will pay your bills after you have stopped working. After all, you don't know how old you will get and in what condition you will be in. But you do know that, if you get beyond a certain age, you can't work anymore. Not preparing for that is denying some simple facts of life and not taking responsibility. But apart from such generic preparations, try to refrain from making any long-term plans. Instead, focus your attention on the present and on the next few steps that you will take. Those can be planned with some accuracy. But when it concerns the longer-term, only focus on the big picture, not on the details. Therefore, if you want fewer bananas:

Banana Remedy 2.2: Cut Down on Planning

Plan less, especially when it concerns details and the long-term. You can't control the future and your predictions will be wrong anyway.

Think about the opportunity costs of planning, and let go.

Stop Controlling

Next to trying to control our past and future, another source of bananas is trying to control the things and people around us. You can't control the world around you. Of course, you can try. And you will probably have some occasional successes in trying to control others and the things happening to you. But you will fail most of the time. I have tried, but with very limited success. Whenever I tried to force and enforce things that I wanted to happen and that required the involvement of others, I failed. In fact, trying to control things out of my control was mostly a means towards more bananas. The harder I tried, the more frustrated I became, the harder I tried… and the more likely I got into one of the vicious banana cycles described before.

Letting things go can be hard. Definitely if you are uncertain, a perfectionist, a control freak, or all of them at the same time. But my experience is that when you allow it, there is a great payoff. All you need to do is to get out of the way and give the rest of the world the chance to bring helpful and interesting stuff to your path. Woolly as this may sound, even a hardnosed realist and trained academic as me had to admit this over the years. I have had too many experiences where letting things go brought me something valuable after futile attempts to make them happen myself. It brought me clients, business partners, friends, new career directions and, looking back, probably my marriage as well.

I suppose you have similar experiences that trying to control things out of your control doesn't work, especially if it is other people that you are trying to control. Or the other way around. You probably have experienced moments where someone was trying to control what you should be doing and where that didn't work, because it made you resist.

An example. I assume you have visited a fashion store where an overly eager salesperson rushed towards you within two seconds of you entering the shop with a friendly but obtrusive "How can I help you?" Or the ones who keep on giving you compliments about how great everything looks that you try on. How did that make you feel? It always gives me a choking feeling that makes me want to escape the store rather than buy something. The reason is that the salesperson is too eager in trying to control my shopping behavior. If she waited and let me mind my own business, I probably would have bought something instead of running out of the store as soon as I could.

If we object to others trying to control us, we can assume that others also object when we try to control them. After all, we are all people and we don't like to be controlled by others. We might like some guidance, and we differ substantially in the extent to which we appreciate direction. But no one likes to be controlled. We value our independence and freedom too much for that.

But we do like to control and be in control. Partly, that is useful. It means we take responsibility and care about whether something is going as it should. But when it concerns controlling things out of our control, it gets us bananas. This is especially the case when we try to control things with our mind, when we think hard about something in the hope that doing so will make something happen. We did this as children when we wished for a particular birthday present with all the power we had. We also do it when we fall in love and hope with our entire heart that the other side will fall in love with us too. Or when we do a job interview or take a test and, after the fact, we want to make sure the result is positive. In all such cases, we somehow assume that we can influence a situation through pure brain power—through thinking, hoping and wanting something strongly.

Of course, we can't control things like this. We are not magicians and we can't steer the world with our brains. And, of course, we know this. But, nevertheless, we often keep on trying whenever we wish or hope for something. But wishing and hoping aren't very effective mechanisms for getting things done. If we can't control things, the better option is to let them go.

Letting things go doesn't mean you quit everything you do and go and sit waiting and hoping for something to happen. That would be just another form of trying to control things. After all, that implies that you have decided that *now* is the time that something unexpected should happen. It suggests that you, through some form of magical telekinesis, can mobilize the things and people around you to let something happen now. It doesn't work that way.

What it does mean, is that you really let things go. It means stepping back, relaxing, and stopping worrying about things that are beyond your control. You focus on the things that are within your control, and for the rest, you see what happens. You can't control them anyway, so why try? It makes more sense to spend your time otherwise and give things a chance to happen.

To make it a bit more woolly and hippie-ish, it helps if you try to 'actively release' things. This means that, rather than merely not trying to control things, you deliberately let them go. Instead of keeping them locked up in your brain, you try releasing them from your brain.

One effective mechanism for this is visualization. Through visualizing things in our mind, we can start to see things differently in real life as well. For letting things go, one way of visualization is to pretend that you send your thoughts into the air. So, wherever you are, close your eyes, calm down for a couple of seconds, and picture for example that you shoot envelopes with messages out of your head into the air. Or pretend you can open up the top of your head and let your thoughts escape like a bunch of balloons reaching up to the sky. Do you feel how this clears your mind?

For a long time, I have thought this kind of visualization exercise to be utter nonsense. How can imagining a picture like this help? I don't *do* anything, so how can there be any effect? Until I experienced that it works. There is no magic involved. The mere fact that you rid your brain of all the futile controlling thoughts opens your mind. And by doing so, you allow other things to evolve in a more natural way. And even if it doesn't work, letting things go in this way feels good anyway. So, give it a try.

Meditation is another possibility. When meditating, you focus your mind on something else other than your thought-controlling thoughts, or on nothing at all. Rather than worrying about stuff and trying to control it, meditation helps you to free your mind—not only while meditating, but also thereafter. There's a thousand different ways of meditating. Some require advanced skills and take a long time to perfect. Others are simple and can be easily fitted into your busy scheme. A basic exercise you can do is this: sit straight up on a chair, close your eyes, breathe in and out slowly through your stomach, and pay attention to how you breathe. I do this at the start of every day for five minutes, and that small change of my morning ritual has made a significant difference in how relaxed I start the day.

You can also write things down in a diary or notebook. Like visualization, writing the stuff down that keeps your mind busy is a good way of letting go. Rather than keeping them in your head, you trust your thoughts to your paper or screen. This means you don't have to control them anymore, and the result is that they don't control you anymore. When you write things down, the point is not to write excellent prose. The point is to let your thoughts flow while you write. Don't worry about typos, grammar mistakes or even readability. It is not the result, but the process that matters. And you, nor anyone else is probably going to read the stuff you wrote anymore anyway. Accordingly:

Banana Remedy 2.3: Stop Controlling

Don't try to control the things and people that are out of your control. Like you, they don't like to be controlled. Let go and give them the chance to evolve and unfold when and how time is ready.

Forgive

Another great source of bananas are the things of the past that we keep on being angry about. We are angry with our ex for cheating on us, we are angry with our parents for not giving us the attention we needed, we are angry with our neighbor for having put his fence one centimeter in our garden rather than his own garden, and so on. And we keep on being angry, even though such events go back years or even decades. Carefully preserved anger like this is a great source of pain and frustration, and it can eat up a lot of our energy and brain power.

The answer is forgiveness. Forgiveness is not something soft or vague, or something grand that you need to do with great gestures, tears and dramatic orchestral music (as in Hollywood movies). Forgiveness also doesn't mean that you forget or ignore what happened or how you feel. Furthermore, forgiveness is not something you do for the other person. They might long have forgotten they did something to you, or haven't noticed it at all, or they don't care. Forgiving them is not meant to help them. It is meant to help you.

Forgiving someone is an effective way of letting your anger go. It helps you get rid of your pain and frustration and it helps you free your brain so that you can think, feel and act in a more sensible, non-banana way. Forgiving is not easy, especially when your feelings of anger have been carefully preserved and nurtured for years. And it is even harder when you think you have forgotten those feelings while they are still there, lying dormant somewhere in a back corner of your mind.

The starting point for forgiving is realizing that whatever other people did to you, they rarely did it to hurt you personally. Even more, they probably didn't even think of you while hurting you. For you, you are the center of the universe. But for them, you aren't. This means that most of what they did and do doesn't concern you personally. You just happened to be the object of their behaviors or were affected by them in a non-intentional way.

Partners don't usually cheat to inflict pain on each other. They just fall in love or let their hormones take over. Parents mostly don't deliberately mistreat their children. They just struggle with raising them and aren't perfect. And neighbors usually don't put their fences deliberately one centimeter on the wrong side of the boundary. They just don't measure very accurately. So, whatever happened to you that you are angry about, it is important to realize that the other side virtually never did it with the deliberate intention of hurting you and only you.

The second thing to keep in mind is that, even though the other person might have been responsible for our initial pain, it is us who have maintained and nurtured it over the years. We are responsible for how we feel. Not them. Deliberately or not, we have chosen to keep on mourning and complaining and to keep those feelings of anger intact. So, we are responsible for the fact that we haven't let things go and allowed our pain to eat up a significant share of our brain power and energy. Not them.

Realizing these two key things opens the door to forgiveness. But forgiving remains hard. Therefore, to make things a bit more practical, I borrow a technique from Fred Luskin's book *Forgive for Good.* When we are angry at others for what they did to us, we keep this anger alive through what Luskin calls our 'grievance story'. This is the story you keep on telling yourself and others about how someone has mistreated you and how you were a victim of their behaviors. In the examples above, they are the stories you tell yourself and other people about how you were a victim of something your parents, your neighbor or your ex did to you.

Relating your grievance story a few times is good. It helps you clarify your thoughts and get support from people. But repeating it over and over again is detrimental—to your mental and physical health, as well as your relationships. No one likes to hear the same stories time and again. And, worse, repeating these stories makes you go progressively more bananas about your feelings and the unfairness of life.

The detrimental effect of grievance stories shows how powerful stories are and how much they affect our lives. But they are stories. They reflect your version of what happened and the version you keep intact as a foundation for your carefully maintained feelings of anger. This means that you can also change the story and thereby change how you feel about what happened.

The key is to turn your grievance story into a hero story. Rather than being the victim, you create a story in which you are the hero. There are various ways to do this. You can focus your story, for example, on how great it is that you survived the mistreatment in a good way. Or you can focus on how the mistreatment has shaped your character and made you who you are. Or you can focus on how it brought you good things that otherwise would not have happened—like meeting particular people or getting an unexpected opportunity.

The strongest mechanism to turn your grievance story into a hero story is focusing on what Luskin calls your 'positive intention'. This is the bigger aim that you were trying to achieve when you got into the situation in the first place—good health, meaningful work, learning, mastering a skill, discovering new things, and so on. When you focus your story on that, you draw your attention away from the hurt and towards the bigger picture. This helps you think about the things that matter to you most and thereby help you let go of your grievance story.

An example. Suppose you are angry with your ex for cheating on you. Your grievance story about this may go something like this "I hate my ex because he deceived me. I loved him so much, but he broke my trust by dating with this {not so nice description of his new partner}. I can never trust anyone again and will remain alone for the rest of my life!"

If you think about your positive intention behind this, it may be that you strive for a loving and stable relationship. You had this intention before you met your ex and you still have it. At that time, it was your ex who helped you achieve this. Now, after cheating on you, it isn't your ex anymore. But the positive intention remains. You still want to have a loving and stable relationship with someone. When you focus your story on the more general positive intention that is driving you, you are less likely to go bananas about it. I know from experience how hard it can be to change your story like this, but it is definitely worth the effort.

As a final note, I want to emphasize that what applies to forgiving others also applies to forgiving yourself. You might stay angry at yourself about something you did in the past and that you regret. But that was the past, and you can change how you feel about it now in the same way as described above. You didn't do something wrong on purpose and it is you who is keeping the grievance story alive. Change it into a hero story by refocusing it on your positive intention and thereby forgive yourself. So:

Banana Remedy 2.4: Forgive

Stop preserving your angers from the past. Take responsibility for how you feel by forgiving others and yourself. Turn your victim story into a hero story by focusing on the positive intention behind it.

Release Stress

All four remedies above focus on letting go of particular thoughts. They require knowing what you are trying to control and then letting that go. In addition to that, you can also let go in a more general, undirected way. This can help to release some more bananas, especially if you are not entirely sure where they came from.

There are both mental and physical exercises that you can do to release some of your banana-causing stress. Let's start with a mental exercise. I already mentioned the power of visualization. Also for stress release, visualization can be effective. The following exercises have helped me in cases when there were too many stress-causing bananas floating in my head.

Take a dining chair or any other object on which you can sit up straight. Sit up straight and close your eyes. Breathe in and out calmly from your stomach for a minute or so. Now picture yourself covered with all kinds of sticky stuff. This can be anything: toffees, sticky notes, duct tape, glue, peanut butter, or anything else that is sticky. These sticky things represent all the bananas that are bothering you: a difficult task at work, a remark someone made, a relationship that doesn't go smoothly, a too long to-do list, and so on and so forth. So, you are all covered with nasty sticky stuff that is bothering you.

Now imagine your skin is made out of Teflon—the non-stick coating on your grill and frying pan. Keep your eyes closed and visualize how all the sticky stuff is falling on the floor. Your skin is made out of non-stick coating, so nothing sticks to it. Imagine that the various bananas that are bothering you don't stick anymore and fall to the floor like leaves falling from a tree. It doesn't matter whether you follow them one by one or all at the same time. If you visualize this convincingly enough, you'll start noticing you feel freer and stronger. Liberated from the sticky stuff, you have more room to move freely around. You have fewer bananas in your head and this should make you feel better— physically and mentally.

You can also try another visualization. Again, sit straight up on a dining chair with your eyes closed, and breathe in and out through your stomach for a while to get into a calm mood. Now imagine yourself with a protective cocoon around you about the size of how far your arms can reach. If you watch sci-fi movies, you can picture it as the kind of force-field protection shield as in Star Wars or Star Trek.

This force-field cocoon represents your personal space. Now imagine you fill it completely. This means you break out of the straitjacket of your skin and fill the space. So, you grow, a bit like the Incredible Hulk (as you see, movies have their purpose...). Like with the Teflon image, this visualization should make you feel freer and stronger too. As such, it should help you keep the bananas out of your personal space so that they don't bother you anymore.

While it works when applied in general, the force-field cocoon visualization also works when applied to specific situations. Suppose you are very nervous about a presentation you have tomorrow. Now close your eyes and imagine it is tomorrow and you arrive at the place where your presentation is. But before you open the door, you bring up the image of your protective cocoon. Once you have filled it and feel stronger, you go inside and imagine you give your presentation. I'll bet this makes you feel less anxious, both now and tomorrow. In this same way, you can apply this visualization to anything you are anxious about—whether it is in the future, the present or the past.

Next to these mental exercises, you can also do physical exercises to release stress and let things go. Our efforts to control things that are outside our control and to nurture unproductive thoughts can lead to a lot of physical tension being built up in our bodies. You feel it in your shoulders and neck, in your stomach, and maybe in other parts of your body as well. No matter how relaxed you are, you are affected by the things happening around you, and your body and mind respond. Letting go of that stress physically helps you get out and stay out of Bananaland.

There are hundreds of ways to do this. I don't mean drugs, smoking or alcohol. They only cover or soften the stress for a while so that you forget about it, but they don't help you release the stress. I mean the more physical exercises such as any type of massage, hot stone treatment, yoga, jogging, sex, walking, reiki, or breathing exercise. Some may work for you while others don't. I want to single out two specific exercises because they help me get rid of my own tensions and stress.

The first exercise, you can do both sitting or lying, whatever you prefer (you probably want to do it out of sight though…). Again, close your eyes. Now open your mouth and throat as wide as you can and breathe freely through your mouth (now you know why you want to do it out of sight). Place your forefinger and middle finger on the side of your face, in front of your ears, at the height of your earlobes. This is about the place where your jaw is connected to the rest of your skull.

Now start moving your fingers slowly with a little bit of pressure in small circles in a backward direction (up on the side of your face, down on the side of your ears) while still keeping your mouth and throat wide open, breathing freely. Do this for about ten seconds and then put the same fingers right behind your ears and move them in circles in the same way. Do this also for about ten seconds and then go back to the front.

After a while—half a minute, a minute—you will probably get the inclination to yawn. Give in and yawn, as much and deeply as you have to. Because that is the whole point of doing this exercise: getting you to yawn. Through yawning you release stress. Feels good, right?

If it doesn't work, you can try adding another step: stretching your face. Drop your jaw as far as you can, lift your forehead as far as you can and open your eyes as far as you can, and hold for 5-10 seconds. This looks really ridiculous (another reason why you want to do this out of sight). But it can help to release stress and, when you relax your face again, you might now feel an inclination to yawn.

There is one more exercise I'd like to suggest. I learned it from my karate sensei (don't overestimate me, I am still a beginner). It takes a bit longer—10-15 minutes or so. This time you should be lying—in bed, on the floor, or wherever you can lie with a little bit of space around you. Lie on your back with your legs a little bit apart and your arms next to you with the palms of your hands facing upwards. Make sure you are lying on an even surface, so don't use a pillow or anything. Try to completely relax every part of your body and breathe slowly from your stomach.

Now close your eyes, spread your fingers, and stretch your hands backward as if you are sending a beam of energy from the palm of your hands (again, superhero movies come in handy). This means you should feel some tension in your hands because of the stretching. But make sure the rest of your body is still as relaxed as it can be.

Keep on lying in this way for 10, 15, 20 minutes, and just see what happens. Maybe nothing happens the first time. No problem. Do it again tomorrow or next week. At some point, though, you could feel that your hands start trembling or shaking. This is good. It means the stress is leaving your body. Don't worry about it, even if your whole arms are starting to move in an uncontrolled way. That is exactly what should happen. After all, you are doing this to let the stress go.

Sometimes the trembling and shaking can go much further. Your entire body could start shaking. This can feel eerie the first time you experience it. It can feel a bit like the girl Regan in the film The Exorcist, in the scene where the demon is leaving her body. It is not as scary as that, but it is nevertheless a strange feeling because of the uncontrolled movements of your body. But don't worry, let it go. Whether it is your hands or your entire body, the shaking will stop after a while. And now you can relax.

As these exercises show, you can't beat your bananas with only your head. Sure, using your ability to think rationally covers a large share of the things you can do. But your body has a role too. As a 'head person', this took a while for me to accept. And if anyone had told me about the exercises above ten years ago or so, I wouldn't have taken them seriously and would have just laughed. But they work. Therefore:

Banana Remedy 2.5: Release Stress

Let the stress flow out of your body by doing targeted visualization or physical exercises. This helps you let go, especially in cases when you don't know where your bananas exactly come from.

Conclusion

After shutting down the main banana-causing noise in Step 1, Step 2 focused on letting a substantial share of your bananas go along the lines of the following five remedies:

2.1 Stop Ruminating
2.2 Cut Down on Planning
2.3 Stop Controlling
2.4 Forgive
2.5 Release Stress

Together, these remedies should help you relax more and let things go rather than trying to control them. This is an essential step because so long as you don't release some of your bananas, they stand in the way and keep you from going through the next steps. And so long as you try to control things that cannot be controlled, you will just grow more bananas in your head. This is why letting go comes as the second step on your journey out of Bananaland.

To be clear, letting things go doesn't mean letting yourself go. Not at all. You should let things go that you can't control because trying to control them is futile. But you should definitely not let yourself go. On the contrary, getting rid of your bananas means working on yourself so that you control your built-in banana modus. So, rather than trying to control other things and people, an important share of what follows is about controlling yourself. This starts with taking responsibility for the things you say, do, feel and think.

7

Step 3: Take Responsibility

After you have calmed down and let go the things that are out of your control, you are ready for Step 3: taking responsibility for what you think and do and for what you *can* control. This is an important next step since it also means taking responsibility for your own banana detox journey. It is you and only you who can do this. Of course, you can ask for help and support but, at the end of the day, it is you who needs to take the steps. Like the previous chapters, this chapter contains five remedies to help you do this. Altogether, they should protect you against victim behavior and help you accept life as it is. On average, life is no picnic or box of chocolates with only variations of happiness to choose from. But it is also far from terrible or something that just happens to you.

Quit Complaining

As already referred to in Chapter 2, complaining seems to be a national sport in my country, the Netherlands. We excel at it. We complain about our job or lack thereof, about our neighbors and family, about heat and cold, about rain and drought, about the government and institutions, about traffic jams and the railways, endlessly. And yes, I'm as guilty as anyone. I too complain and nag far more than I should. We all do. And often about things that aren't even worth complaining about.

We like it so much that we even invent imaginary problems to complain about. Of course, some people sometimes have good reasons to complain. They are in really shitty situations and have every right to complain. But, complaining about the color of the paint in your hotel room, the view from your second-floor apartment window, the ten minutes of rain in your weekend, or the length of the line in your supermarket? These don't seem to be particularly valid reasons for complaining.

It seems to me that there is a direct relationship between how wealthy we are and how much we complain. The wealthier we are, the more we complain—and about increasingly trivial things. The main reason for this relationship that I can see, is that being wealthy makes us feel entitled. It makes us feel we have special rights. Because we are wealthy, we deserve a perfect world where everyone and everything serves us. And as soon as this perfection is broken through some minor issue, we are entitled to complain because we deserve better.

Any idea how much we complain? There is research about this. A recent study in the UK shows that we (or at least Brits) spend an average of 22 minutes per day complaining. And interestingly, on Mondays, that average is 34 minutes. This adds up to about three full working weeks per year. Research also shows that Brits complain about eight to ten minutes per day *just about the weather*—and it is especially people aged between 24 and 35 who do the complaining.

Complaining serves multiple purposes. If we are dissatisfied with something, a product or service for example, complaining can help us get problems resolved or get us our money back. Used in this way, complaining can be instrumental. Complaining also has emotional and social purposes. One of them is venting. If we feel dissatisfied, complaining is a way of blowing off steam, which makes us feel better. Complaining is also a way of distracting ourselves. Rather than paying attention to our real problems or concerns, we complain about trivial things that are harmless because they are not about us. Yet another purpose of complaining is social bonding. Complaining together is a way of interacting that gives us a topic to talk about and a feeling of togetherness.

So, complaining has its purpose. But it is a fine line. When used properly, complaining helps us. When we address our complaints to the right person or organization, it can help solve the problems we experience. And when we complain with a bit of humor and self-mockery and don't take our complaints too seriously, complaining can be an amusing way of communicating and social bonding. However, all too easily, even supposedly funny complaints can create a negative atmosphere that serves no purpose. Not for us and not for those we complain to. Complaining then becomes a fertile ground for bananas.

Mostly we complain to our peers, who can't do anything but nod and complain with us. That doesn't help us. Furthermore, research shows that venting doesn't make us feel better. On the contrary. As it turns out, complaining and listening to complaints increases our stress levels, making us feel *more* stressed rather than less. And, as far as social bonding is concerned, complaining is just another form of babbling for which better forms are available—such as showing genuine interest in each other, asking questions, and talking about things that do matter. So, besides the occasional and targeted instrumental complaint, complaining doesn't help us and it harms us most of the time.

Like the other remedies in this book, quitting complaining is easy in theory. It doesn't require any special skills and it doesn't ask for any big sacrifices. And it is rewarding. Quitting complaining makes you feel better, and you can spend the half hour of extra time per day on other things. But because complaining is so much part of our everyday life and has become so much of a habit, quitting complaining can be hard in practice.

But there are various things you can do to make it happen. One of them is to give yourself a fine for every time you complain or nag. This may sound a bit silly, but it does work. Giving yourself a fine makes you aware of the fact that you are complaining. It takes you out of the automatic mode and makes you reflect on what you are doing. As such, the fine is a way of signaling. But the fine also makes your complaint less rewarding. If you have to pay something for every time you complain, complaining has a clear and visible price.

There are two things important in fining yourself effectively. First, the fine should be significant. For some, 50 cents is enough, for others, it is 5 or even 50 euros, dollars or equivalents. The point is that you should feel the fine and be annoyed by the fact that you need to pay it. Second, you need someone to help you signal the complaint and agree what fine you should pay. If you have a better half, he or she is usually the best person because you spend a great deal of your time with them. And probably, they suffer most from your complaining in the first place, so paying them the fine is not a bad idea…

You can also reduce your complaining the Monty Python way: always look on the bright side of life (I'll leave it up to you whether or not you include the sticky whistle tune). What this means is that you focus your attention deliberately on the things that you like, that make you feel happy, satisfied or good in any other way. In his book *Forgive for Good*, Fred Luskin uses the metaphor of a TV for this. As he argues, we all have a remote control which we can use to switch channels in our head. Instead of watching the Complaint channel, we can switch to the Happiness channel, the Grateful channel, the Beauty channel, or the Love channel.

This starts with realizing that you have a choice and that the Complaint channel is just one of many channels that are available. Even though your TV might be on the Complaint channel by default, it is just a channel. Once you realize this, you can start trying other channels and watching shows other than the usual ones. So, rather than watching *My Unfair Life*, *Poor Me*, or *Miserable Country* on your internal Complaint Channel, have a look at *Lucky Me, My Lovely Husband* or *Amazing Achievements* on your own Gratefulness channel, Love channel or Beauty channel. Like on a real TV, there are numerous channels and shows to choose from that focus on the bright side of life. And the best thing: you can watch them on demand, wherever, whenever, for free!

A third way of reducing your complaints is to aggravate them *ad ridiculum*. Using this strategy, you enlarge your complaints and their consequences as far as you can to the level that they become absurd. For example, whenever you complain about your daily traffic jam, you spell out how terrible it is, what else you could have done with the time, how much you suffer from sitting behind your steering wheel, etc. Or when you complain about the weather, you tell yourself how much of a victim you are that this, of all days, is the day when rain decided to fall to punish you, and how you are the unluckiest person on earth that this should happen to you. Using this strategy should equip you with a healthy dose of realism that makes you appreciate that you are complaining about nothing.

Another way of creating some realism is to relativize the complaint by thinking of others who are worse off. There are always people who are worse off—especially when you are complaining about things not worth complaining about. So, when you are in a traffic jam, think of people in longer traffic jams, or those who can't afford a car, or those who don't have a job to drive to. Or when you complain about the government, think of countries where government is virtually absent or is messing things up big time. By focusing on people with bigger problems, you downplay the gravity of your own complaint.

The last thing you can do is look behind your complaints and find out why you complain in the first place. Only rarely is the cause of a complaint what you are actually complaining about. That is a distraction. I don't think we complain about the weather, our neighbors, or our hotel because these things are what we are seriously disturbed about. We complain because we are frustrated about ourselves. About the things we didn't do or say, or about our own behavior, or about choices we made but secretly regret. That's at least how it works with me.

To find out what is behind your complaints, you need to reflect on your complaining behavior. Don't ask "Why?" That only leads you to thinking in circles around the complaint itself. For example, when you ask yourself why you complain about the rain, your answer could be that you don't like getting wet. And if you ask why that is, your answer could be that you don't like your pants sticking to your legs, etc. That doesn't get you anywhere.

Instead, whenever you complain, ask yourself: "What am I frustrated about?" or "What *other* thing am I frustrated about?" The trick is not to look at the subject of the complaint itself, but at what else may have caused it. You probably won't get your answer the first time, or even the tenth time. But thinking about this every now and then when you find yourself seriously complaining can eventually give you some useful insights. And when you get to an answer, take responsibility and do something about it. Accordingly:

> **Banana Remedy 3.1: Quit Complaining**
> Stop complaining about trivial things, especially if it serves no purpose other than venting or bonding. Fine yourself, focus on the bright side, relativize your complaints or find out what you are frustrated about.

Stop Blaming

The previous remedy referred mostly to our emotional response to disappointment and frustration. Rather than taking responsibility, complaining means telling ourselves we are victims. This also applies to blaming. When we blame someone, we also put ourselves in the position of victim of their behavior. The difference is that, with blaming, we seek someone else who can be held accountable for our misfortune.

We blame a lot. We blame our boss for underpaying us. We blame our friends for not inviting us enough. We blame teachers for our low grades. We blame the fast-food industry for our obesity. And we blame the government and 'the economy' for everything else.

Blaming and complaining are both backward looking. They focus on undesirable situations and on ruminating about those rather than on finding solutions. Of course, like complaining, some blaming is useful. Some of the things that happen to us are because others have caused them—deliberately or accidentally. Someone might have damaged your car on purpose, or in an accident, and it makes sense to blame them because they or their insurance company will then pay for the damage.

Many of the things we blame others for, however, are a result of our own choices. The line you are in is long because you picked it and chose to go to the store at that time. The traffic jam you are in is a result of you choosing a place to live and work and a particular time and way to travel. You don't deliberately choose to pick the longest line or search for the worst traffic jam. But the fact that you end up there is a result of other choices you have made before.

Whenever we blame someone, we try to pinpoint who else is 'responsible' for what has happened to us and who we can point to for solving it. I say 'responsible', because they are of course not responsible.

They may or may not be an important cause, but we are responsible for our future and for how we respond. In other words, even if others affect our lives (which they do), we have to solve our own shit. No one else can be held accountable for it and no one else will solve it for us.

Blaming has a lot to do with what scientists call our 'locus of control'. It refers to who or what we think controls our lives. Some people have an outspoken external locus of control. They think that everything important that happens to them, good or bad, is caused by others—politicians, CEOs, parents, gods, etc. They feel they have hardly any control over their lives and are the plaything in the games of others. Other people have a more internal locus of control. They feel they control their own lives and determine what they do with it.

To beat your bananas, it helps to have primarily an internal locus of control. After all, we can't get out of the banana mill if we blame others for our being in there. For developing a more internal locus of control, I draw again on Fred Luskin's book *Forgive for Good*. To illustrate the futility of blaming others, he uses the metaphor of a policeman with a broken-down car writing tickets for every speeding car that passes. Picture a police car, half-hidden on the side of the road with two policemen. One of them holds a speed camera and the other sits behind the steering wheel. Because their car has broken down, the only thing they can do once they catch someone speeding is write a ticket and wave with it. There is no way they can stop the speeding cars or fine the drivers. The drivers probably don't even know they were speeding in the first place. Do you see the picture and the frustration of the ticket-waving policemen?

This is a pretty accurate picture of what we do when we blame others. We wave with tickets for what they are doing wrong, but without any real effect. This brings us to the first thing you can do to reduce your amount of blaming. Whenever you find yourself blaming someone or something for your misfortune, create a picture in your mind of yourself waving a speeding ticket. Seeing yourself engaging in this useless waving should give you a sense of the futility of your blaming behavior. By creating this picture, you make yourself look a bit ridiculous. Maybe you can even laugh about yourself—which is an effective mechanism against bananas.

Another strategy to reduce your amount of blaming is to focus on your own role as part of the cause of your misfortune. As the examples of the line in the store and the traffic jam above show, you have ended up there as a result of choices you have made in the past. So, instead of blaming others, ask yourself: "What did or didn't I do that led to this situation?" or "What choices have I made or not made that led me to end up here?" Asking such questions helps you internalize your locus of control. This makes you less likely to blame others and go bananas about them. It even helps you find solutions that mean you don't end up in similar situations next time.

When you insist on blaming others and want a solution from them, you need to know when blaming others can be effective and when not. Blaming others when it can have an effect, can be useful. However, blaming others when it doesn't lead to anything is bananas and only feeds further banana behavior. So, how do you know? Blaming others can only work if all three of the following conditions are fulfilled:

1. If they are the cause of the problem and can do something about the solution. In other words, if they are *capable* of doing something.

2. If they can be convinced to act, for example, because they want it themselves, or through legal, social, or moral pressure. In other words, if they are *willing* to do something.

3. If they have the right or are otherwise permitted to do something about it. In other words, if they are *allowed* to do something.

If any of these conditions are not met, blaming is an act of ticket waving. You can blame them until eternity, but the other person or organization is not going to solve your problems if they are not capable, willing, or allowed to do something about it. So, whenever you find yourself blaming someone, check the three conditions. And if one of them is not met, let it go.

You can also reduce your amount of blaming (and the amount of frustration created by futile blaming which does not achieve anything) if you disconnect situations from people and look for solutions rather than explanations. As Roger Fisher and William Ury explain in their bestseller *Getting to Yes*, this is also the heart of effective negotiation.

"Negotiation?" you may ask, "What on earth has that to do with taking responsibility and not going bananas anymore?" A lot. Blaming is ineffective for the same reason that many negotiations are ineffective: they focus on the past, on defending one's own position, and on demanding the other to give in. On the other hand, effective negotiation, or 'principled' negotiation as Fisher and Ury call it, focuses on the future and on finding solutions.

The main thing that we can learn from their work is to separate the people from the problem. Yes, someone may have caused us a problem, but we don't gain anything by blaming them. The only thing we gain from is solving the problem—with or without the other.

Suppose your boss is not giving you the promotion you expected. Or suppose you feel mistreated by your parents because they didn't give you the love or appreciation you feel you deserved as a kid. Neither your boss nor your parents in these examples fulfill the three criteria above. Your boss is probably not willing or allowed to give you your promotion, and your parents are no longer capable of doing anything about the fact that you feel you missed something in your childhood. So, there is no added value whatsoever in blaming them because it isn't going to change the situation. It only creates bananas.

Instead, rather than blaming your boss, you can do better by focusing your energy on how to resolve your dissatisfaction, get promoted, or get a better job elsewhere. And instead of blaming your parents, it is more effective to focus on the love and appreciation you find elsewhere, or on finding out why you feel mistreated and do something about that feeling. So, instead of blaming people, focus on solving the problem—the actual problem, or how you feel about it. Accordingly:

Banana Remedy 3.2: Stop Blaming

Don't blame others for problems. This only works if they are capable, willing, and allowed to do something. In all other cases, blaming is waving tickets. Focus on your own role and on finding solutions.

Speak Out

Complaining and blaming are vocal ways of avoiding responsibility. We talk to people and tell them how much a victim we are of the behaviors of others, and how much they should feel sorry for us or solve our problems. But, we also victimize ourselves and skirt responsibility in the opposite way: by not speaking out and by keeping things for ourselves.

Don't take me wrong. This is not a plea for talking more. Just go back to Remedy 1.3 (Stop Babbling) and the entire first step to see how silence and calming down are an important starting point in ridding yourself of your bananas. In general, less talking helps. But there are cases when we need to talk more if we want to get rid of our bananas.

One such case is when we don't say anything because we don't want to face how we feel or don't dare to tell others. This happens when we walk away from facing a confrontation—with ourselves or someone else—rather than have the guts to deal with it. For example, we might not love or like someone anymore, but instead of telling them, we simply stop all communications and hide. While perhaps understandable for a five-year-old, that kind of behavior as an adult is just cowardly. And it creates bananas too because we know it is.

Another case is when we don't talk about a problem we have. Maybe you are nervous or anxious about something you need to do next week, or maybe you worry about something that you did or didn't do. Or maybe you feel insecure because of something someone said to you. Not talking about this kind of stuff creates the kind of internal vicious cycle I referred to earlier. It makes our mind run in circles and reiterate the issue. And often we are not even aware of it, except that we notice we can't think sharply and are more tired than we should be.

If we could keep our anxiety to ourselves by not talking about it, this would only create internal bananas. But it affects others too. While we may think we can keep it to ourselves, we can't. And the harder we try not to talk, the more others will probably notice it anyway.

I bet you know what I mean: people who are actively *not* saying something. You see it in the way they look, in their eyes and their strained facial expression, in the way their mouth moves, or in the small uncontrolled movements of their body. Or you notice it because they act overly energetic, happy or interested in something, sigh excessively, or babble about everything but the thing they are anxious about. Being in the same room with such a person for a while can create substantial tension and be a serious energy drain—another source of bananas.

Like blaming and complaining, not speaking out about the anxiety we feel means that we don't take responsibility. We know that talking about it is beneficial for us and for the other person, and we even want to talk about it. But instead, we sit and wait and want others to draw us out. We want them to ask us questions, give us attention and solve the issue for us. Or we hope the issue will magically disappear by itself.

This also applies to cases where we do mention the issue that we are anxious about but dump it over the fence so that the other person hopefully does something with it. I mean the kind of short, pity-begging, sad-faced and non-informative messages like "I feel bad" or "I don't know what to do." That is not speaking out. It is dumping our problems over the fence. This may make us feel better for two seconds, but the issue remains, and we are still shifting the responsibility to others.

Yet another form of not speaking out is not asking for help when you need it. At first sight, not asking for help seems a responsible thing to do. After all, it shows you are an autonomous, strong and self-sufficient individual. Rather than bothering anyone else with your problems, you solve them yourself.

Of course, trying to solve your own problems is generally a good thing to do. It means you are taking responsibility and not asking everything of someone else. But there is a point at which not asking for help becomes the irresponsible thing to do. No one can solve all their problems on their own. And when we don't ask for help in such cases, we are seeding bananas. Rather than solving the problems ourselves—which we can't—we run in circles looking for a way out instead of a real solution. Taking responsibility in such a case means asking someone for help.

There can be many reasons why we are not asking for help. Maybe we are ashamed that we can't solve the problem or that we have the problem in the first place. Or maybe we are too proud or afraid of losing face by asking someone. Whatever the reason, not asking for help when you need it is helping you and your environment go bananas.

The remedy again is as simple as it is hard: speak out. Talk about the issues that you are concerned about. Share your fears, anxieties, insecurities, and frustrations. And ask questions. Ask for help, for others' opinions and thoughts. Open up and let them help you. I am terrible at this and keep things far too long to myself. But I—and you—have to do it anyway if we want to get rid of our bananas.

There are three main requirements for effectively speaking out. The first is that it should be targeted at two-way interaction. Merely venting or dumping isn't helping. What you want is an actual dialogue where you talk with someone else about the issues you are concerned about. This means listening carefully to your own feelings, but also to what the other side has to say. You want to learn from their answers and do something with it, rather than only send out a signal.

The second requirement is that your dialogue should be aimed at collaborative problem-solving. You are speaking out because you have some sort of problem. And you involve the other person because you want it to be solved. So, when you talk to someone, don't take too personally the advice, questions or suggestions you get. They are meant to help you solve the problem, not to attack or offend you. See your dialogue with them as an act of collaborative problem-solving in which, together, you try to find a solution.

By 'solution', I don't mean just a practical solution. While those are sometimes helpful, often the real problem isn't the practical thing but how we deal with it emotionally. And mostly the actual issue can't be solved anymore anyway. We can't 'solve' that we have an important test tomorrow, that we made a mistake yesterday, or that we broke up our relationship recently. But we can solve how we deal with such events. And that is what the dialogue should be targeted at.

The point of speaking out is not that you immediately feel happy or that your problems evaporate. That is completely unrealistic and misses the point. The talking itself *is* the point. Even if you feel miserable, genuinely speaking out makes you feel better because you have shared your issue with someone and listened to what they have to say about it.

Therefore, the last requirement for effectively speaking out is that you see it as the start of a discovery process, not as the final conclusion that you have reached. This means you don't wait with speaking out until you have sorted out exactly what is wrong yourself. When you speak out, it is not necessary that you already know exactly what the problem is, let alone the solution. The whole point of speaking out is finding this out. You know some issue is bothering you, but what it is, is to be discovered through talking with others. Accordingly:

Banana Remedy 3.3: Speak Out

Talk about the things you are concerned about and ask for help when you need it. Take responsibility and engage in a dialogue with others so that they can help you discover and solve your issues.

Allow Feeling Bad

We live in a happiness society. Everyone is supposed to be happy all the time about everything. We are supposed to smile, laugh, and enjoy every aspect of life. And as soon as something negative pops up, we try to eliminate, avoid or ignore it so that it disappears. In this way, we try our utmost to do away with sadness, anger, fear, uncertainty, illness, pain, and death. The result, as observed in Chapter 2, is that we can't handle negatives anymore.

Not accepting the negatives in our lives is a great source of bananas. It makes us create and maintain fictitious stories about our fantastic lives and tell them to others and ourselves. This is tiring and creates a disconnect between our actual lives and how we allow ourselves to think and talk about it. Protecting ourselves against negatives also means that we quickly go bananas when something bad happens. We are not prepared anymore.

Life is easier, richer and more fun if we accept that some things suck. They do. But accepting that is easier said than done. The problem with accepting this is that it is so simple and mundane that it can be extremely hard. I suck at it. The perfectionist I am, I want everything in my life to be perfect. Pain, anxiety, disappointment and so on, don't fit in this picture. Therefore, I often choose to suppress or ignore them. But as it always turns out, this is not a good idea. It doesn't work. The 'bad' feelings are there anyway, and they stay until I admit they are there. So, to go to fewer bananas, allow feeling bad.

There are a couple of things you can do to get started. The first is to acknowledge that you are feeling bad in the first place. Before you can accept something, you need to be aware of it. A simple way to help yourself with this is saying aloud what you feel. It is not even necessary that you say it to someone else. So, if you are nervous about something, say something like "I am nervous about…" and if you are sad about something, say aloud "I feel sad because…" And so on. Language is a powerful tool. The mere act of expressing in words how you feel helps you acknowledge and accept the feeling. By hearing yourself, you get outside your internal thinking loop and enable yourself to reflect on what you feel. Maybe you feel a bit silly the first time you do it (I did), but once you have tried this a couple of times, you'll see it works.

A second thing to do is to come to terms with the feeling you have and find it okay. Eternal happiness doesn't even work in romcom movies. They'd be extremely boring. Feeling bad is part of life. This doesn't mean you have to be thrilled about it. It is just okay. Nothing happens when you feel bad, and for both you and everyone else it is okay to feel bad.

The simplest way to start realizing this is a follow-up to saying aloud how you feel. You simply add that you are okay with it. So, after you have said aloud how you feel, you say something like "I feel … and that is okay" or, "It is okay that I feel…" Saying this aloud helps you be less harsh on yourself. Instead of imposing the unrealistic expectation of feeling good all the time, you allow yourself to feel bad and feel okay about it. If it doesn't sink in the first time (which it never does), repeat saying it until you start believing it.

A third strategy is a variation of the first two. Instead of saying it aloud you can also write it down or draw a picture. Saying it aloud is usually more effective because you physically let the words get out of your body, but writing and drawing can work too. So, when you feel bad, write down or draw how you feel. Don't worry if you can't find the right words or pictures immediately. And don't worry at all about the quality of what you write or draw. That is irrelevant. Start and see what you write and draw. The point is that you trigger a flow of thoughts and so you discover what you are worried about.

A fourth thing you can do is to question your judgment that what you feel is actually bad. Yes, you feel nervous, sad or angry. But why is that a bad thing? It is only a bad thing because you label it as such. We tend to divide the world into good and bad, and the way we do this is pretty arbitrary. Take fear. It is not only bad. It is also a useful mechanism to protect us from problems. The same applies to grief, irritation, uncertainty, heartbreak, and any other emotion we have. They all have their uses. They help us deal with things that happened to us or prepare us for things that might happen in the future. What can help along these lines, is to separate observation and judgment; separate observing what you feel from telling yourself whether that is good and bad. After you have observed that you feel angry, sad or afraid, you need to stop your judgment. You just establish your feeling and observe it. That is it. No judgment, no good or bad, you are just feeling like that.

Fifth and finally, you can also help yourself feel bad effectively by focusing on the *positive* side of feeling bad. "The positive side of feeling bad? What kind of hippie nonsense is that?" you may think. "I feel terrible and it sucks!" Sure, but if you think about it, these 'negative' feelings have their beauty too. Most notably, they show that you *care* about things. Being nervous means that you care about doing a good job. Being sad has a certain melancholy and means that you care about someone or something. And being frustrated also means that you care about something that happened or didn't happen. Isn't that far better than being indifferent or apathetic?

All of the above strategies are again simple. And they are not hard to start with. The challenge is to persevere. They are unlikely to work the first time, or the second, or the tenth time. You might need to repeat them a thousand times or more to get them in your system and replace your perfectionistic futile quest for eternal happiness. But once you manage to allow yourself to feel bad, you will see that there is not so much to feel bad about. Because you are not recycling your feelings anymore in your own vicious thinking loop, you'll discover that there is not so much that really sucks and that you have a pretty nice life, about which you don't have to complain anymore. Therefore:

Banana Remedy 3.4: Allow Feeling Bad

Stop your quest for eternal happiness and face it that life sometimes sucks. Say it aloud when you feel bad, find it okay, and even see the beauty of it. This will make your life easier, richer and more fun.

Accept the Consequences

The last way to take responsibility in your battle against the bananas is accepting the consequences of what you do. Life is a big chain of causal if-then statements: if you do this, then that happens; if this happens, then that will be the result; if you don't do this, then that won't happen either, etc. Taking responsibility means accepting both sides of this causal logic: if A is what you do, then B is what you get; and if B is what you want, then A is what you need to do.

Everything you do and don't do has consequences. If you take a shower, you get wet. If you drink too much, you get a hangover. If you forget to press CTRL-S while typing, your document isn't saved. And if you postpone your work, it doesn't get finished. That's obvious.

Furthermore, everything you do that involves other people triggers a response. If I hit you, you might hit back. If I complain to my wife all the time, she might stop liking me. And if I am kind to you, you are more likely to be kind to me. That much is obvious.

Even though it is obvious that such consequences are a direct result from our behaviors, we are not always ready to accept them. Somehow, we want our deeds to be without consequences. We want to do as we like without thinking of the consequences this may have. We want our work to be done without doing it, and we want others to like us even if we are not kind to them. But that is not how life on this planet works. All our actions have consequences, whether we like it or not. So, we need to accept this simple fact if we want to get rid of our bananas.

Accepting the consequences of what we do also means that we follow through on something that we started. This doesn't mean blindly going on with everything we start. That would be bananas, since it would mean we can never change our mind or try out different things. What it means is not giving up too easily. Never finishing a thing, and always giving up after the first few attempts doesn't get you anywhere. If we want to achieve something, we need to accept that we also have to do things we don't like. It means committing ourselves to something. As we saw in Chapter 4, great people get great because of this, and it is also part of the Benedictine idea of *stabilitas*, which means not walking away from something you have committed yourself to.

This implies that we don't just accept the consequences of something, but also the prerequisites. If we want to achieve something great, taking responsibility means accepting that this requires hard work, dedication or pain. If we want to be healthy, we must eat and drink healthily and exercise enough. If we want a nicer job, we must quit the job we don't like. And if we want to get rid of our bananas, we must do something about it.

How? The previous four remedies already give you a head start. If you quit complaining, stop blaming, speak out and allow feeling bad, you have already made great steps in taking responsibility. But there are a couple of additional things you can do. The first is the usual thing: just do it. Behave like an adult, be realistic, and accept that actions have consequences. If you do A, you get B and if you want B you have to do A. It's as simple as that.

The second thing you can do is focus on the outcome of your behavior instead of the effort it requires. So, whenever you find yourself postponing, complaining or not doing something that you should, take a moment and ask why you were planning to do it. What were you trying to achieve, and what was the purpose of your actions? And why do you find that important? Assuming that this purpose is still something you want to achieve, focusing on that might help to motivate you to do what you need to do. This is the core idea of what scientists call 'expectancy theory': people are generally motivated by what they expect their actions will lead to.

It is also helpful if you focus on the cause-effect link between what you do and the outcome. As the same theory says, we are more likely to do something if we believe that it leads to the desired outcome. Suppose you don't want to go to the gym because you don't feel like it. Then think about the outcome you want to achieve: getting in better shape, feeling more energetic, eating without gaining weight, etc. And now think about how going to the gym is helping you achieve this outcome. You are using your muscles, you are increasing your heart rate, and you are burning fat and energy. After thinking about this, you might not immediately be thrilled and run to the gym, but your likelihood of going anyway has probably increased.

A third thing you can do is to spell out the options you have by either doing or not doing the thing that you wanted to do and then explicitly choosing the option you prefer. Using the same example, option A would be going to the gym, burning some fat and feeling more energetic. Option B would be sitting on your couch, adding some fat and feeling listless. Then you pick the option you like the most.

The advantage of presenting yourself with options is that you look at the whole package, at causes and consequences together. In this way, you are less tempted to try and get away with something. You can't choose to sit on your couch, burn fat and feel more energetic, because that is not one of the possible options.

What also can help you to take responsibility, especially to follow through on something you have started, is announcing publicly what you are planning to do. Continuing the same example, you can tell your friends (in real life or through social media) that you go to the gym twice a week, or want to lose 10 pounds in 10 weeks, etc. By announcing this publicly, you create some pressure for yourself to conform and realize your intentions. But of course, do make sure that you are not making yourself go bananas about it…

Finally, instead of focusing on the outcome and causal mechanism or creating external pressure, you can also try to like the effort itself. One reason to avoid things that you should do is that you don't like them. You like a clean kitchen, but you don't like cleaning. You like being good at golf, but you don't like practicing. You want an eight-pack and impressive biceps, but you don't like the pain it takes. And so on.

But now ask yourself whether you really don't like what you need to do, and try asking whether you can start liking it. Is cleaning the kitchen really that awful? Isn't it kind of giving you a good feeling too? And is practicing your golf swing really that terrible? Isn't it fun too? And is the pain in your muscles really that horrible? Isn't it also something to feel good about? So, like with the previous remedy, try recalibrating your judgment and like the things you think you don't like. Accordingly:

Banana Remedy 3.5: Accept the Consequences

Be realistic and accept that all actions have consequences, that others will react to what you do and that results require effort. Focus on the outcome you want to achieve, do what it takes, and accept the result.

Conclusion

After calming down and coming to your senses in the first step, and letting things go in the second step, this chapter has shown how taking responsibility is the third step on your journey out of Bananaland. Along with this, you have learned another five remedies:

3.1 Quit Complaining
3.2 Stop Blaming
3.3 Speak Out
3.4 Allow Feeling Bad
3.5 Accept the Consequences

Taking responsibility is about letting the child in yourself go. Not the creative one, but the small dependent child that we all have in us. The part that wants to run away or hide, and that wants to cry and get attention rather than face the world as it is. Taking responsibility is about behaving like an adult rather than hiding behind other people, the government, the economy, or fate.

It is important to master the basics of this third step before you proceed—especially because the next step is a nasty one. To succeed and persevere with your journey, you need to be convinced that you and only you can do something about your bananas. So long as you blame others, or engage in complaining or dreaming up unrealistic wishes, you can't succeed in getting rid of your bananas. But once you succeed in taking responsibility for your own life, you are ready for the next step: dethroning yourself.

8

Step 4: Dethrone Yourself

Great. You calmed down and came to your senses in Steps 1 and 2, and reactivated the responsible adult version of yourself in Step 3. Feels good, right? Now, let's do something about that great feeling and start dethroning yourself. This means kicking yourself off your carefully constructed golden throne and discovering that you are far less important than you may think you are. This may not be the nicest step and is probably the most confrontational. Speaking for myself, there was and still is a lot of resistance when going through this step, and it is one of the most challenging ones for me. But it is a necessary step if you want to get rid of your bananas. And, in the end, it is rewarding too. After this fourth step, you will realize that many of the things you (and others) are going bananas about are not worth it. They (and you) are too unimportant to worry about.

Control Your Emotions

We live in a time in which we are supposed to express our emotions. We should be 'authentic' and 'true to ourselves' and not hide anything.

We shouldn't suppress our feelings but let ourselves go. We should talk about our feelings and share them with others. We should be angry when we are angry. We should laugh. We should cry. We should be emotional and show it to each other and to the world.

The supposed reason behind this is that not showing our emotions would lead to internal tensions, stress and other problems. And this, in turn, could lead to greater problems such as obsession, aggression, and depression. Or to physical problems such as headaches, heartburn, and palpitations. And we don't want that. So we must be emotional.

Of course, there is some truth in this. We need to show some emotions. After all, we are human beings, not robots, and human beings have emotions. If we didn't show a basic level of emotions, we wouldn't be able to function properly in our interaction with others. We wouldn't be able to establish contact with them or have a relationship. Also, if we don't talk about our traumas, we can get into serious trouble along the lines of the problems listed above. It is for this reason that Remedy 3.1 (Speak Out) in the previous chapter proposed talking about the things that you are concerned about and asking for help when you need it.

This may seem contradictory advice. How can you speak out and also control your emotions? The answer is balance. Always controlling your emotions is as bad an idea as always speaking out. It means talking about the stuff that bothers you, and in a way that you allow others to help you. And at the same time, controlling your emotions enough so that you don't throw them over the fence in the hope somebody will pick them up.

There is no need to express all your emotions and it often isn't effective either. Even though expressing your emotions seems authentic, is that the case? If you loved something yesterday, hate it today and don't care about it tomorrow, are those feelings authentic? Is that how you 'truly' feel? And are they even feelings? Or, are they made-up 'feelings' because you feel you need to feel something? And what about mixed feelings? If you feel good and bad about something at the same time, which feeling do you express?

Drawing from extensive personal experience, I can say that we need to be highly suspicious about our feelings and 'feelings'. I have been wrong so often about them that I now know that they are not necessarily a good compass to follow. And I also know that many of the 'feelings'

I had—and still have—are constructed feelings based on what I think I should feel because that is what people are supposed to feel in this situation. Expressing such made-up 'feelings' doesn't help.

But even if your feelings are real, there is a reason not to show them. It often just isn't effective. It doesn't give you the result you want. If you feel angry about someone damaging your car, unleashing your anger on the other person doesn't gain anything. It doesn't get the other side to understand you, it doesn't get your car undamaged, and it doesn't get your insurance claim filled in. It doesn't even make you feel better. You only feel angrier and more frustrated.

The same applies to other feelings. If you feel uncertain, giving in and showing that uncertainty makes you feel more uncertain probably leads you to perform less well—making you even more uncertain. If you feel sad, losing yourself in the sadness makes you feel worse. And if you feel happy, overly sharing that with the world is going to annoy a lot of people, or they will counteract by even happier responses.

Paying too much attention to your emotions and showing them to others is an important cause of bananas. It adds fuel to the flames. As the examples above illustrate, showing your emotions often makes your emotions grow stronger and triggers a chain of responses by others. Rather than helping you, sharing emotions in this way makes you and others go bananas.

So, there is a lot to say for controlling our emotions a bit more. Instead of focusing on our 'authentic' self and what we 'truly' feel, it can be helpful to keep our feelings to ourselves. There is even a certain nobility, respectability or dignity in that. When we control our emotions, we show we are adults who have grown beyond giving infantile and purely emotional responses. It means we rise above the child in us and can look at the world as a mature, grown-up person.

There are a couple of things you can do. The first is the good old 'count to ten' rule. As a child, you were probably advised to count to ten if you were angry, frustrated or upset by something. This still works as an adult. Whenever you feel the urge to express your feelings, count to ten and you will see that the urge weakens. And probably the feeling you had as well. It doesn't matter whether you feel angry, happy, excited, surprised or envious. Count to ten and things suddenly lose a lot of their importance.

You can also try to Charlie-Chaplinize yourself. Picture Charlie Chaplin imitating you in your anger, frustration or despair. That should make it easy to stop taking yourself and your emotions too seriously. Of course, you can choose another comedian or funny person. But Charlie Chaplin is a good example, because you don't need to imagine any sound and because that is what he was good at: making fun of people and situations. If you don't know who Charlie Chaplin was, YouTube him.

Another strategy is acting. Instead of letting your emotions flow, you can also act as if you are not emotional. In case your emotions are self-constructed (because you think you should feel in a certain way), you were acting anyway. This means you can also act the other way around and pretend everything is fine with you. So, instead of being angry, upset or overly excited, act that you are calm. You will notice that this will make you calmer and thereby less likely to go bananas.

The technique of 'method acting' can be especially effective here. It is a technique in which actors do not merely play a certain emotion but try to evoke that emotion in themselves so that they actually feel it while acting. To do this, they go back to similar feelings they have had in the past. So, when they have to play someone who lost their child, they go back to a moment when they lost someone or something dear to them and use that emotion in their acting.

Even though most of us are not actors, we can use this technique to control our emotions. When, for example, you feel you are getting angry, you can try and act as if you are calm and confident. To do this, go back in your memory to moments when you were calm and confident and try experiencing that same feeling again. This should make you feel calmer and more confident in your current experience as well.

Calmness and confidence are feelings that can help you deal with virtually any other emotion. This is practical, because it means that your method-acting skills can be limited to playing only the you that is calm and confident. Whenever you feel upset, angry, uncertain, etc., your response can be the same: act as if you are calm and confident.

The last thing you can do to control your emotions is to distract yourself. Rather than focusing all your attention on your emotion, on enlarging it and expressing it, you can also focus your mind on something else. Instead of going bananas, you can go to the grocery store and get yourself some bananas. Or you can look around you and wonder why the sky is blue. Or you start counting the number of red things you see. Or…, etc. It doesn't matter what you focus on, so long as it distracts you from your feelings. Accordingly:

Banana Remedy 4.1: Control Your Emotions
Realize that emotions are often an unreliable and ineffective guide. Instead of letting them flow freely, control them. Don't take yourself too seriously, and act as if you were a calm and confident adult.

Stop Soul Searching

We are not only supposed to find and express our emotions. We are also supposed to find and express our 'true selves'. We need to find out who we 'really' are and what we 'really' want. And we go to great lengths for this. We read self-help books, we follow seminars, we hire coaches, we have our personal shrinks, we consult self-help gurus, we go on a trip to India or we backpack on our own in Australia, we try to re-experience our childhood and find out what went wrong, and so on and so forth.

The fact that so many of us engage in such activities suggests that we are totally confused about ourselves and that the only way out is discovering our true self. But is this so? Are we confused? And is knowing your true self the answer? Or are we getting more confused by this whole soul-searching activity? Who has found the answer and who has become a better, happier or more productive person from that? I haven't—despite my extensive attempts. And I don't know anyone personally who has.

The idea that you have a true inner self that serves as your compass for life is attractive. But, as Svend Brinkmann asks us nicely in his book *Stand Firm,* what if there is no such thing at all? Imagine the grave disappointment when, at the end of your soul-searching quest, you only find a black hole of nothingness. Or, after a life full of futile searching, you still haven't found your true self when you die. Think about what else you could have done with all the time and money you have spent on your search. And about how much better you would have felt if you were not constantly on the lookout for it.

Even if your true inner self does exist, we can ask why that should be the starting point for everything you do. Why should your actions be guided by what *you* want? That is just an assumption. Of course, you might say: "It is my life!" Sure, but is your purpose in life to 'self-actualize' as the famous Mr. Maslow called it? Is it your own needs that should dominate, or is it your purpose or duty to contribute and do things that others need?

Of course, there is no objective answer to this, but note that putting our own little self-actualization needs on top of the hierarchy is merely one of the options. And also note that, when approaching the end of his life, Maslow added 'self-transcendence' on top of his hierarchy. It concerns our ability to look beyond ourselves to our significant others, and to humanity and nature at large.

Again, the main remedy here is simple: stop soul searching. Just don't. Don't try to discover your 'true' self. Trying is pointless anyway and it diverts you from having the nice life you could otherwise have. This also means you quit the guided soul-searching activities you are engaged in. Sack your mental coach, stop your purpose-of-life training, put away your find-your-true-self books, and stop bothering your peers to discuss your quest for meaning. I can tell you from my own experience that this can be liberating.

This doesn't mean that you should put on blinders and go on mindlessly with what you are doing, without any reflection. That would be bananas again. On the contrary, you should remove your blinders so that your scope of vision expands beyond your own navel. Instead of gazing at your navel, you open your eyes and look around you to find out what you can mean and do for others.

By not putting yourself at the center of your quest for a meaningful life, you make yourself less important. You are not so worried anymore what you feel and think, or what you should do. Instead, you think of what others need. And, paradoxically, by making yourself less important to yourself, you make yourself more important to others. You are not spending your time on navel-gazing anymore, but you use it to do something that helps other people. That is the self-transcendence

Maslow was talking about—and it's far more satisfying than navel-gazing.

Next to 'just' stopping the soul searching and focusing on what you can contribute, a third thing you can do is lower the threshold for your quest. Instead of focusing on what you *really* like or *really* want and on finding your *true* self, you just do something you like or want. Nobel Laureate Herbert Simon coined the term 'satisficing' for this. It means that instead of looking for the ultimate solution, you look for the first thing that does the job. This also works as a remedy for soul-searching: explore a couple of different things and stick to the ones that you like.

A final thing you can do is learn to live with yourself. Accept yourself as you are, with all your peculiarities, weaknesses, demons and imperfections. Soul searching implies you want to be something else than you currently are. It even implies that you think you *are* something else than you currently are. Why else are you searching? This means soul searching is, in fact, a self-denying activity that leads you further away from your actual self. Accepting yourself, on the other hand, brings you truly to your true self. Who you are now is who you are: the person who doesn't have the big purpose in life, who doesn't know the meaning of life—and who is actually okay with that. There is nothing you need to do for that besides accept this. Isn't that great? Therefore:

Banana Remedy 4.2: Stop Soul Searching
Stop trying to find your 'true' self and what you 'really' want. You will never find it and it distracts you from having a nice life. Instead, focus on what you like and on how you can help others.

Enjoy Your Averageness

This is a painful one. For me at least. Accepting that I am an average person? Me, an exceptional, super-smart omnitalent with a special calling to save the world by helping everyone on the planet get rid of their bananas? How could I be average? How dare you compare me to you, ordinary people. And even more ridiculous: how could I *enjoy* being average? There is nothing to enjoy, is there?

I am really not good at this. But I can tell you that it is worth trying and that it most certainly helps as a remedy for bananas. As referred to in Chapter 2, many of us cry out to be special in some way. We want to be the best or unique in at least something. And if we can't excel at something, we want to be extremely bad at it so that we are at least somewhat unique. We want to be on either end of the bell-curve—the hero or the victim. As long as we aren't average, we are okay.

But that is the whole problem. We *are* average, at least for most of what we are and do. You may be exceptional in one or a few things, but for most of who you are, you are in the big belly of the bell curve. Maybe you have a very high IQ or are extremely allergic to cats. That makes you a bit special in those respects. But at the same time, you have an average height and weight, you live in an average house and drive an average car, you are average at sports or other hobbies, you have an average memory, and so on. So, if you look at yourself as a complete person, you are on average pretty average. And even for your very special IQ and cat allergy, there are millions of other people who have the same. Indeed, you—and I—are average people.

The fact that we are all average means that we mostly like the things that are ordinary. Whether we admit it or not, most of us want to settle down, have kids, a pet and a garden. And we do watch the TV shows that everyone watches, read the books everyone reads, wear the clothes everyone wears and eat what everyone eats. We live ordinary lives and that is how most of us want it. And it can't be different. The whole meaning of the word 'ordinary' is that it is what most people like. That and only that makes it ordinary, average or normal. So, plain logic means that it must be that most people are average and ordinary.

"But not me!" you might say, "I'm different!" Nope. You are not different, special or unique. Neither am I. And the fact that you think you are, means that you, like me, still have some hard work to do on your journey out of Bananaland. Of course, everyone is different in a sense. We are all individual human beings with our own peculiarities. But that doesn't make you special. In all your differences you are as average as anyone else. Therefore, you might want to start looking at the upside of being average. After all, only if you see the advantages of being average, can you enjoy being it.

Being average is great. The biggest advantage of realizing that you are average is that it takes away the big burden of specialness. Trying to be different, special and unique takes a lot of energy—especially if you are not. The whole time you have to search for your specialness, enlarge it, act accordingly and display it to the world. This is tiresome. It requires a 24/7 role-play pretending you are something or someone you are not.

Trying to be non-average is tiring in a second way as well. If we are all doing this, it creates a pointless rat race. Suppose we all tried to be extremely good at preparing cocktails, math or making money. The only thing we achieve with that is that we raise the bar for being non-average. Since being extremely good becomes the average, it only becomes harder to be even better than average at preparing cocktails, math or making money. The result is that we are still average, but that it takes us more energy. That doesn't sound overly smart to me.

So, what can you do? Enjoying your averageness requires two steps: accepting that you are average and learning to enjoy it. The importance of the first step is obvious. If you don't accept that you are average, there is no way this remedy can help you in your battle against the bananas. The second step is important too, though, since if you don't learn to enjoy it, your non-averageness will keep bothering you.

The issue of seeing yourself as an average person is all about mindset and self-image. And changing how you see yourself is hard for most people. You won't change your self-image by merely reading this chapter or after some exercises. It requires your continuous effort. But there are two practical things you can do to get started.

To begin accepting your own averageness, take a sheet of paper and draw three columns. Label the columns from left to right: 'Things I Am Very Bad At', 'Things I Am Average At' and 'Things I Am Very Good At'. Now you start populating the table by listing all possible things that apply to you. Make sure that in both the left and the right column, you only list things where you belong to the top 10% of people in the world. After all, if you don't even belong to the top 10% in something, you are not very unique or special in it.

When you are done, have a look at how the table looks. It doesn't matter what is in there. Just look at how much you have written in the three columns. I am sure the left and right columns will be mostly empty, while the middle column is almost or completely full. You have just created your own rudimentary upside-down bell curve. If you don't know what a bell curve is, Google it and look at one of the zillion examples. Now, if you put it upside down, you will see your table looks like that too.

This exercise shows you that most of the characteristics that make up you as a person are in the big belly in the middle of the bell curve. This means that, by and large, most of the characteristics that define you are the things you are average at. Probably about 90% to 99% of what defines you are average things. Knowing this and seeing this should help convince you that you are indeed average. Tip: to remind yourself of this, place the table somewhere where you see it regularly.

Now you are ready for the second step: learning to enjoy your averageness. We are going to create a second list for that. So, take another sheet of paper and label it 'Non-Bucket List', 'Not-to-Do List' or 'Things I Don't Have to Do Anymore Because I Am Average List'. As you may guess, this is going to be a list where you write down all the things that you don't have to expect any longer from yourself once you are average. That said, the biggest problem with pretending to be special is that it creates all kinds of requirements for you. It means that you have to perform and do stuff that you don't want to do. This second list should help you liberate yourself from this self-inflicted duty. To help you, here are some examples you could put on your list:

- I don't have to become rich and famous
- I don't have to make a world trip
- I don't have to get another promotion
- I don't have to be friends with everybody (or {insert name})
- I don't have to write a novel, children's book or self-help book
- I don't have to be the best in my team or be in the best team

Unlike with a bucket list or a to-do list, the point of this list is not to cross things out. No, the list should get longer and longer to liberate you from all the things you forced yourself to want so as to avoid being average. Put this list next to the other list and watch it with a smile. Thus:

Banana Remedy 4.3: Enjoy Your Averageness

Let go of the idea that you are special, unique or different. You are not and that is great. Accept that you are as average as everyone else and enjoy how this takes away your self-inflicted duties.

Embrace Your Unimportance

This one can be painful too. You are not only average, you are also unimportant. Ouch. Whatever you think, feel, say or do, in the end, it doesn't matter.

Of course, it matters to some people, some time. Who you are and what you think, feel, say and do, hopefully matters a great deal to your partner, children, parents, brothers and sisters, friends, colleagues or anyone else close to you. To them, you make a difference. And there is also this nice metaphor of moving a stone in a river. Once you have moved a single stone, the river never flows the same as before, anymore. This depicts the idea that, no matter how small our actions are, they can have significant and lasting effects.

Sure, in these ways we all matter. But so does the butterfly in the sky, the stone in the river, the grain of sand in the desert, the mosquito in your bedroom, and everything else in the universe. And exactly because everything matters, none of it matters when seen in the bigger scheme of things. I know personally how hard it can be to accept this simple truth. But, embracing your unimportance is worth it if you want to get rid of your bananas.

There is a typical cliché moment when we realize we are unimportant: lying on our backs gazing at the stars and telling our better half, yet-to-be-confirmed new love or best friends, in a melodramatic philosophical mood: "We are so tiny, aren't we!", "We are like grains of sand!", "Isn't it astonishing how enormous the universe is!", or "Imagine someone watching at us from over there!" etcetera.

But that is usually one of the very few moments when we feel small and unimportant. Mostly, we bluntly overestimate our own importance. Whether it is our jobs, our feelings, our kids, our problems, our worries, our achievements, our pensions, our wardrobe, or our ideas, we treat them as if they are the most important things in the world. They might be for us, but not for the world.

Have a look at the bigger picture. There are about 8 billion people in the world. You are one of them. This means you represent 0.000000000125 percent of the world's population. That is not very impressive. And assuming everyone else is as average as you, you are not exactly playing a lead role on the global stage.

Or look at it from a time perspective. Let's say you live 80 years, and compare that to the 4.5 billion years of our earth or the 300,000 years that homo sapiens has been around. 80 years compared to 300,000 years is similar to one second in the hour. It would mean that in a full two-hour movie about the history of homo sapiens, you would be visible for two seconds. And that is not even on your own, but together with the other 8 billion people currently populating our planet. Not impressive.

"Okay" you may say, "But that is a nonsense comparison. It is all about the people around me and the community I live in, and I matter greatly to those!" You have a point. But even there, how much does what we feel, think, say and do matter? Maybe a tiny fraction of it does, but most certainly not everything. And yes, most of us mean something to some other people. But keep in mind that you are also only one of the people that matters to them. I wouldn't go as far as saying that we are all as unimportant and easily replaceable as a light bulb, but we are not too far off either.

You may think you are an exception. Because of your job, background or calling, you are more important than others. "But I am a doctor and I save lives!" Sure, but a bus driver saves lives too by driving safely. "But I have invented a new and groundbreaking type of battery that will solve all the energy problems in the world!" Sure, but you have built upon what many others had already done before you. "But I am an author and write super-important books that can help people across the world stop going bananas!" Sure, but two million new books appear every year. If you still think you are more important than others, I gladly refer you back to the previous remedy: enjoy your averageness.

The conclusion is, that a tiny bit of what we think, feel, say and do matters for a tiny while to a tiny share of all the people that currently live on this tiny globe in the endless universe. And that is great. It is great because it means we don't have to go bananas about anything. Whether it is the stuff we like or the stuff we are worried about, in the end, they don't matter. Realize that is liberating.

This, by the way, is not an excuse for not doing something about problems such as global warming. Joined together, what we do does matter. And the only way to solve large and global problems is by acting collectively. Embracing your unimportance means that you don't focus on your own special position or contribution. What you do on your own has no significant effect, but as part of a large community, it has.

Like enjoying your averageness, embracing your unimportance is a matter of mindset. This can be hard to change. This one is especially challenging for me—why else write a book like this? Would I write it if I thought I was totally unimportant? Probably not. So, a bit of overestimating your own importance may lead to interesting outcomes—a book, a new medicine, a new technology and so on. Nothing wrong with a bit of dreaming. But how to avoid starting to take yourself too seriously?

The first thing is repeated reading of humbling texts. In Chapter 4, I referred to Benedictine monks as a source of inspiration for how to master the art of not going bananas. One of the techniques they use is what is called *lectio divina*, which means 'divine reading'. Originally, this referred to reading God's word. The core idea is that you read slowly and let sentences sink in one by one. Like a cow does with grass, you ruminate the words until you have digested them.

This same technique can work for embracing your unimportance, as well as for the other remedies in this book. You could, for example, slowly repeat reading this section and focus on one or two sentences that trigger something. You then chew on them until you feel your resistance drop and that there is indeed a point in embracing your unimportance. If you prefer to chew on something with more philosophical depth, try Milan Kundera's *The Unbearable Lightness of Being*, any of his other novels, or the works of Friedrich Nietzsche. There is more to ruminate there than in this book. Reading those gives you food for thought for many of the other remedies.

A second thing you can do is visualize how unimportant you are. You can, for example, take a sheet of paper and start filling it with eight billion dots to visualize how many of us there are. You will probably get the point after a hundred dots or so. Or, you can draw the timeline of humanity in which you mark your own tiny life (tip: use a very large sheet of paper and a very thin pencil).

You can also draw a social network picture of the most important person in your life (not yourself…). Put a firm dot in the middle of a sheet of paper and write this person's name there. Now add additional dots with names of the people who are important to this person. This probably includes family, friends, colleagues, etc. Put the most important names close to the dot in the middle. Your name (hopefully) is one of the many dots and (hopefully) somewhere close to the middle. This shows you are important, but also that you are only one of the many people who are important to this person.

You can also use visualizations made by others. Effective ones are the various zoom out videos that you can find on YouTube. They use Google Earth and some other imagery from Apollo and Voyager 1 to zoom from the world as we experience it out to the universe. Search for 'zoom out' or 'how small we are' on YouTube and you will find them. Like with the *lectio divina,* the point is not to only watch them briefly as a form of entertainment. Watch them again and again until you get a feeling for your own unimportance.

Like with the previous remedy, your goal is not only to accept that you are unimportant but also to embrace and enjoy it. Only then can you change your mindset and experience the liberating feeling that you need for ridding yourself of bananas. Being unimportant has tremendous advantages. It means you don't have to worry about your 'purpose' or 'calling' and that all your problems, thoughts, ideas, needs and wants are merely tiny little chemical or electric reactions in your brain.

Again, visualization can help. Whenever your thoughts or feelings keep you busy, or awake at night, close your eyes for a moment. Picture a sky with slowly moving clouds. Now, put your thoughts or feelings one by one on a cloud and see how it drifts away. For example, take your anxiety about the interview tomorrow, put it on a cloud and watch it disappear. This can be an effective way to get rid of some of the bananas in your head. Rather than having them control your mind, you make them less important by putting them on a cloud. This clears your head and should give you a feeling of relief.

Another way of embracing your unimportance is to try and see life as no more than a game that is there to enjoy. Forget about any bigger purpose, possible next life, judgment day, heaven, hell, or things that you think you have to achieve for a while. They are mostly mental constructs that we have been told and accepted to cherish. Put those on a cloud and try seeing life as a game with the sole purpose of enjoying it. After all, if you are not enjoying it, what is the point of living in the first place?

I don't mean the kind of 'devil-may-care' or 'after me the deluge' enjoyment. That only leads to excessive banana behavior—and you do have your responsibilities. I mean the kind of 'don't worry, be happy' enjoyment in which you try to appreciate things for what they are and not take yourself and your life too seriously. So, try to see the fun and futility of what you are doing.

One way of helping you realize this is to assume you are Truman Burbank in the *Truman Show* (the movie with Jim Carrey). Watch out of the window and imagine the sky is a projection screen. And imagine all the people around you are actors playing out a script and your sole purpose is to entertain viewers of the reality television show (and who says you are not...?). That makes everything you do, say, think and feel, less important. And it doesn't matter what you do or what the result is: whether you succeed or fail, viewers will like it anyway.

The last thing you can do, to learn to embrace your unimportance, is to ask yourself "Why?", "So what?", or "And then?" for everything you worry about. And ask it multiple times: "I have to finish this report by today." Why? "Because otherwise my boss will get mad at me." So what? "He will fire me." And then? "I will lose my job!" And then? "I won't have any money anymore to pay the rent and buy food." And then? "I will die of hunger." You'll find that your worries quickly lose significance if you do this. And, in the end, you will always conclude that you die. But as the next few pages will remind you, you will die anyway.

You may observe that the scenario that unfolds by asking these questions is similar to the basic banana mechanism described in Chapter 3. We are also going bananas by quickly reasoning from one thing to the other. But that is exactly why this remedy works. Instead of doing it in an uncontrolled way (and thereby going bananas), you go through the same steps in a controlled, slower and rational way, using the System 2 part of your brain. By doing so, the bananas disappear because, if you think about it, there is no way you can hold that it is true that you will die because you didn't finish a report today.

Let me close with a final note. Embracing your unimportance doesn't mean that your life is meaningless. Not at all. It is meant to get rid of your Big Self so that it no longer sits in the way of seeing others. Embracing your unimportance helps you liberate yourself from worrying about all your personal concerns. As such, it frees your mind so that you can pay more attention to others and thereby gain in meaning for them and the rest of the world. I return to this in Step 9. But for now:

Banana Remedy 4.4: Embrace Your Unimportance
Accept that nothing you do, say, think or feel, matters in the bigger picture. Enjoy the liberating feeling this creates, and live life in humble enjoyment rather than to realize a bigger purpose or calling.

Celebrate Your Temporality

As some would say, we are merely temporary guests on our tiny little earth. Cliché as this may sound, it is how it is. We are there for 80 years or so and then we are gone. We all die. I do and you do. Earth to earth, ashes to ashes, dust to dust, etc. And like our averageness and unimportance, this is something to celebrate.

Imagine you could live forever. Of course, there are people trying to. They take pills, undergo plastic surgery, or let themselves be preserved at minus 196 degrees Celsius until the problem of aging has been solved. Or they name buildings after themselves, produce art, or write books in the hope that at least their names never die. Or, they assume that after their body dies, their soul remains forever in heaven or returns back to earth in a different body.

That is all nice, but imagine living forever as the person you are—like the Elves in *Lord of the Rings*? Wouldn't that be terrible? If we never died, life would be one big repetition show that bored us to death. This is like watching *As the World Turns*—forever. Furthermore, if there is no risk of dying, what is the fun of living in the first place? If there is no risk whatsoever, what is worth doing? What is the point of 'adventure' sports, of buying lottery tickets, of a first date, of a relationship, of anything if there is no risk involved?

It is our whole temporality that makes life worth living in the first place. But we have a hard time accepting this. Today, we mostly deny that death is part of living. We pretend that we can fix all diseases and make every effort to prolong our lives by two seconds if we can. And the problem is that we have become good at it. Science and technology have developed so much that we can keep ourselves alive much longer than before. And through better food, education, medicine, etc., life expectancy has dramatically increased over recent decades.

Accepting death is a no-go area for many, let alone celebrating it. Given the inevitability of death, this is bananas. We all die, and there is no point in denying that. Whatever age you are, you can look up your average expected shelf life in the various 'life expectancy tables' that are available online. If you are female and live in Japan, you are expected to live 87 years. If you are male and live in the US and have just been born, you are expected to live 75 years, and your chance of dying within a year is 0.6 percent. And if you are a 65-year-old man living in the US, you are expected to live another 16 years and have a 16 percent chance of dying within a year.

For myself: based on the general statistics for men of my age in my country, I have an estimated 34 years to live and about 4 percent of men born in the same year as me have already died. And at the age of about 110, there will be an estimated zero survivors. Statistics are refreshing…

Of course, statistics have no real predictive value for individual cases. Based on these numbers you can't calculate an exact day of death and put it in your calendar. But these numbers make clear that we will die and give us an indication of when that will most likely be.

So, here is the first thing you can do to celebrate your temporality: estimate your remaining shelf life. If looking it up in tables is too complicated for you, or you want a slightly more precise estimation, you can also go to websites like fatefulday.eu, death-clock.org or deathclock.com to calculate your statistically expected day of dying. What these websites told me, respectively, is that I am supposed to die on Sunday October 1, 2045, Thursday December 9, 2049 or Thursday November 30, 2051. There is a bit of range, partly due to the different kind of questions that are asked. But the point, of course, is not to find an exact date. The point is to increase awareness of your own mortality. To make this even clearer, you can put this date in a count-down app on your phone and have a look at it every now and then. Picking the middle expectation above, I have about 31 years and 26 days left when writing this. Not enough time to be spending it on bananas.

Accepting your temporality doesn't mean you immediately become a fatalist or dogmatic religious fanatic resisting doing anything. That is the other side of the spectrum and equally bananas. Death is part of life, but it is not life itself. And the way we can to a large extent influence how we live it. Accepting your temporality means that you calculate death in as part of your daily life. You learn to live with it. So:

Banana Remedy 4.5: Celebrate Your Temporality
Accept that death is as much part of life as everything else and be happy about it. Realizing you will die anyway makes life more fun, and without death nothing would be worth living for in the first place.

Conclusion

After cleaning up your mental waste and putting on your adult jacket in the first three steps, you have embarked on one of the most difficult steps of your journey: dethroning yourself from your self-made pedestal. The following five remedies were put forward to help you with this:

4.1 Control Your Emotions
4.2 Stop Soul Searching
4.3 Enjoy Your Averageness
4.4 Embrace Your Unimportance
4.5 Celebrate Your Temporality

All these remedies have the same purpose: making you realize that whatever you feel, think, say or do is not important enough to pay a lot of attention to and certainly not to go bananas about.

When you have come as far as dethroning yourself, there is hope. In our self-centered, individualistic society of today, dethroning yourself is not easy. All forces are against us. Wherever we look around us, it is emphasized how important it is to know yourself, to find your true identity, to express it, and to construct a person who lives happily and successfully ever after. Going against these forces and breaking through the self-glorification trend isn't easy.

But it must be done if you want to get rid of your bananas. You don't go bananas about things that you don't find important. You only go bananas because you think that you—and everything that concerns you—is worth going bananas about. So, if you stop finding them important, you automatically are less likely to go bananas about them.

This fourth step echoes another important Benedictine lesson: be humble (*humilitas*). Don't think too highly of yourself. This doesn't mean you have to play at being humble or that you have to make yourself smaller than you think you are. That is false modesty, intended to get a particular response from someone else. It means being truly humble and seeing yourself as average, unimportant and temporary as everyone else. You know you are. Now learn to live with it without paying it too much attention.

9

Step 5: Build Character

As the first four steps show, getting seriously rid of your bananas takes guts. It means you have to be willing to challenge your thoughts, break with your habits, and take responsibility for the things you think, feel, say and do. That is not easy. But it is even more difficult if we take into account that it means you deviate from the people around you. We are all social animals that look at other people and try to blend in. Furthermore, we are biologically, psychologically, sociologically, technologically and economically conditioned to go bananas. As a result, going bananas has become the norm. Deviating from that norm requires courage. It requires character building. In this chapter, you will find five remedies that can help you do this.

Ignore Apps and Advice

We live on life support. We are so dependent on other people and technology that the mere thought of being autonomous individuals is a funny myth. For pretty much every aspect of our lives, we depend on them. We watch our clock to see if we are hungry, we check our weather app to see whether it is warm or cold, we look at rankings and ratings to determine whether a book/movie/song/game is worth buying, we ask others for their opinions to make a decision, we have coaches and therapists to solve our problems, we look to celebrities for inspiration about how to live, we look at food apps for what to eat, we let our running/Tabata/step counter apps tell us how much to exercise, etc.

Sure, a lot of this is convenient. But convenience is not necessarily the best criterion. Because we rely so much on others and technology, we almost forget that we are adult human beings who can make decisions and do things without the support of apps and advice. This makes us behave like infants who can't decide anything on their own. And if we can't make our own decisions, it is going to be hard to get rid of our bananas.

Therefore, to succeed in ridding yourself of your bananas, you need to be able to stand firm and ignore what the people and technology tell you. To learn and do it, it helps to rely less on apps and advice than you do now. Instead of relying on them, try making up your mind and making decisions yourself.

The first thing to do is to resist picking up your smartphone if you are not sure about something. Instead, figure it out for yourself without consulting an app or googling it. So, don't consult your weather app but look outside or open the door. Don't open your navigation app but try getting somewhere without it. Don't look up what others say about something but decide yourself. Don't Google it, but come up with the answer yourself. And so on.

Since picking up our smartphones is an automatism for many of us—including me—this can be hard. To get started, it can help to switch off your Wi-Fi and data connection so that you can at least not connect. The fact that you would have to switch it on again for getting the information you want may be enough to make you aware of your habit. Try this for as many days as possible, and you will find that there are many things for which you don't need apps. As a bonus, you will probably be even more satisfied or even a bit proud of yourself that you did without. And when you are ready for it, you can delete them.

To extend your independence of smart technology, try and do without anything with a sensor in it for a while. Sensors are great, they see, hear, smell, taste and feel for us, and are convenient. But we often don't really need them, and they reduce our ability to make our own judgments. So, avoid using, ignore, or switch off for a couple of days your parking assist, thermostat, automatic camera settings, light sensors, and other types of sensors you rely on. Instead, rely on your own evaluations, judgments and senses.

Another thing you can do is to sack your coach or therapist, or to visit them less regularly. This has already been suggested before as a way to stop soul searching. But it also helps to build character. Of course, I don't mean that you should stop seeing a therapist if you have serious mental issues or that you can't consult any coach anymore. Everyone may need that every now and then, and some for a long time. But the point is that your default mode should be to do without them. To live your life as a mature, adult human being.

The same for advice. Get less of it and rely more on your own judgments and intuitions. Being a consultant myself, that may sound strange or hypocritical. After all, don't I make my money giving advice to others? Not really. I rarely and barely give advice. Instead, I listen to what people are saying themselves and then summarize what I hear them saying and give this back. So, I am a mirror that projects their own thoughts and ideas back to them. Of course, I add my own perspective, but my advice is always primarily based on their own inputs.

And you may find it even stranger or hypocritical because this book is full of advice. Isn't the advice not to follow advice a contradiction in terms? Not really. This book does not contain any personal advice for you. It can't, because I have obviously no idea who you are and how bananas you are. The book contains a set of steps and remedies that have helped me and that I think can help other people to get rid of their bananas. But it is up to you to decide which of them to apply, how to apply them, and whether to do anything with the contents of this book in the first place. You decide.

And that is the point. Most of the time you know the answer. You don't always need opinions, expertise or advice from others. All you often need is the guts to rely on yourself. To trust your own ideas, opinions or judgments. How to do this? Just do it. You might want to start small. Maybe that means for you that you choose yourself which shirt to wear or what to eat. Or maybe it is something slightly bigger, such as choosing which phone to buy or which country to go to for a vacation. It doesn't matter what the subject is, so long as you get used to making up your own mind rather than relying on others.

This is in no way to suggest that you should refrain from relying on technology and advice that are vital for you. So, don't switch off your car safety systems and don't ignore all your accountant's advice. And, as suggested in Chapter 7 (Take Responsibility), do speak out and ask for advice and help when you need it. Not doing all of that is bananas. But, to help yourself build character, try limiting your dependence on apps and advice in those areas where your life or health aren't immediately at stake. Hence:

Banana Remedy 5.1: Ignore Apps and Advice

To build a banana-proof character that can withstand the collective lunacy, you want to be able to make decisions on your own. Therefore, reduce your reliance on technology and others in making decisions.

Deviate from the Herd

You can only become anywhere near banana-proof if you dare to deviate from what 'everyone' or your important peers are doing, saying, thinking and feeling. So long as you care and conform, you stay in the banana treadmill. You look at them, listen to them, imitate them, talk with them about the things you are supposed to talk about, anticipate what they will think of you, and so on. And this makes you go bananas.

Deviating from the herd is difficult. Because of our biological, psychological and sociological roots, and because of the technology and economy we are surrounded by, the pressures to conform are strong. Using the metaphors of a flock of birds, school of fish and herd of wildebeest throughout this book, it is clear that deviating from the herd is one of the most difficult things to do for many of us. But that is exactly why you need to do it. If you don't dare to deviate, you can't get rid of your bananas. Therefore, the second character-building remedy in this chapter is to practice exactly that: deviating from the herd.

The first thing you need to do is stop caring about what others say, think, feel and do. Or, as Mark Manson says it eloquently in his book, *The Subtle Art of Not Giving a F*ck*, you need to stop giving a fuck. Not about your close family and friends. You care about them and vice versa. I mean all the others. The people you barely know or have at best a loose relationship with. They make up the large majority of your Facebook friends, LinkedIn contacts, Instagram followers, colleagues and so forth. The sociologist Mark Granovetter calls these your weak ties. You know them, but your relationship with them is weak. Exactly because your relationship with them is weak, why would you care about what they think, feel, say and do?

If you think you have to, a helpful exercise is to put yourself in their shoes for a moment and ask whether you would care about you if you were them. If you were Facebook friend 347 of yourself, would you care about what you were posting? I don't think so. Most people around you don't care about how you behave, what you wear, what your opinion is, etc. They are so busy living their own lives that they hardly notice whatever you do, let alone care.

In fact, it is not them, but your self-centered imaginary version of them that cares. Because you are focused on yourself, you mistakenly assume that they are focused on you too. There is a mix here at play of what scientists call 'projection bias' and 'egocentric bias'. Projection bias means that we project our own thoughts, ideas, etc. on to others and assume they have them too. And egocentric bias refers to our tendency to rely too much on our own personal perspective. The result is that we think others care about what we do, say, think and feel. Because we worry about whether we say the right things or wear the right shoes, we assume others will also worry about whether we say the right things or wear the right shoes. But the truth of the matter is that they usually don't.

No longer caring about what your weak ties think of you is one thing you can do to make deviating from the herd easier. But there is also another side. Sometimes you do care, and you care deeply about what others think and feel. This is especially the case when it concerns close friends and, even more, with family. Granovetter calls those your strong ties. Because of your similar DNA, shared experiences or matching characters, you have a strong bond with them. And exactly because of that strong bond, you cannot simply not care.

For seeing how to deviate from your strong ties, let me zoom in on family because that's where the strongest ties are. Whatever we tell ourselves, we keep on caring what our parents, brothers, sisters or children think or would have thought. Even if they are not alive anymore, if we have expelled them from our lives or hate them furiously. Our biological bond with them is too strong not to care. And deviating from them can be painful. It hurts. Maybe in the background, but there always remains a bit of pain.

Telling yourself not to care isn't going to help you with this. But that doesn't mean you should conform. Okay, it hurts. But that is how it is and that is not a reason to conform (see also 'Allow Feeling Bad' and 'Accept the Consequences' in Chapter 7). Accepting the pain and willingly deviating is part of the never-ending process of growing up. It creates the kind of frictions we need to mature and develop. So, for those aspects of life where you can't stop giving a fuck, the trick is to do it your way anyway.

The main point of deviating from the people around you is that you learn that nothing bad happens if you do. The world will still turn and basically everything will go on as if nothing has changed. Only you are changing—and in a good way, because you are making yourself less banana sensitive.

To lower the threshold for starting to deviate and to get the most out of your deviant behavior, see it as an experiment: try something new and reflect on what happens—to you and to others around you. How do you feel? What do they do? And then try something else and reflect again. In this way, you will learn that you can deviate and that it makes you feel better if you do. And by doing so, every deviation experiment brings you a bit closer to a banana-proof character.

So, look around you and see what your first act of social disobedience will be and break a social rule. Wear pajamas all day and do nothing. Start your dinner with dessert. Decorate your house with lights in July instead of at Christmas. Walk barefoot when you go shopping. Give a 200% tip in the restaurant. Ask for ketchup at your Sushi bar. Visit the men's room if you are a woman (and vice versa). Celebrate that you live one billion seconds instead of X number of years.

Or do anything else that goes against the common conventions. There are so many unimportant social rules around us that you can break without any harm, that it must be easy to find some that fit you. And when you break them, enjoy the fun of it too. Accordingly:

Banana Remedy 5.2: Deviate from the Herd
Stop caring about and conforming to what you think others think you should do. They don't care, and even if they do you can still deviate. Show some social disobedience and break a few social rules.

Take a Risk

Deviating from the herd means taking a social risk. You risk being judged, hammered or expelled. Getting over that and finding out that life is rarely that harsh is one way of building character through taking risks. But taking risks in itself is another remedy for bananas. Fear is one of the great banana propellers. In the introductory chapter, I mentioned the fear of missing out, the fear of being left alone, the fear of failure and so on. Taking risks means facing your fears and acting anyway.

We are not used to taking risks anymore. In our comfortable lives, we do not like to take risks and we spend a great deal on avoiding, insuring, outsourcing or mitigating them. We try to construct a riskless society in which we all feel safe. But the result is the exact opposite. Because we are not used anymore to taking risks, we are more afraid than ever. And this fear makes us go bananas as soon as things might possibly get somewhat close to a little bit of being slightly risky.

The point of taking a risk is not to do things that people generally see as risky. You don't have to base jump, skydive or go on an ultimate survival tour carrying only your pocket knife. What 'people' find risky is not relevant. The point is that you do something that *you* find risky. And this shouldn't even be the things that you find very risky. There is no need to go on a suicidal mountain climbing trip if fear of heights is your biggest fear. No, you can focus on the things that are slightly out of your comfort zone. That helps to become a bit bolder than you currently are.

Some examples. Suppose you are afraid of speaking in public. Then find yourself an occasion where you give a short talk for a small group of people. Lead a training session for your kid's hockey team, give a photo presentation of your fantastic holiday to your friends, or organize a wine tasting session in which you introduce the wines. Prepare well, deliver, and experience that it is not as bad as you thought it was. Maybe it was even fun.

Or suppose you are afraid of driving at night (and have a driver's license). Then ask someone that you trust and who you know and who stays calm under whatever conditions to accompany you. First, let them drive to a well-lit and quiet industrial zone. Then you switch seats and you start driving. And then, step-by-step, you drive to increasingly crowded and less well-lit roads and areas.

In this way, there are many things that you find risky that you can try out by starting small. But sometimes this is hard or impossible. It is a bit of a challenge, for example, to quit your job hour by hour, to gradually break up a relationship, or to incrementally move to another city or country. Those are more all-or-nothing decisions, and your fears are keeping you from taking the jump.

In such cases, a more analytical approach may be helpful. Again, you can take a sheet of paper for this. Divide it into four quadrants and write down the pros and cons of doing something and not doing it. So you create two columns that you label 'pros' and 'cons' and then create two rows, which you label 'doing it' and 'not doing it'. Now you populate all four quadrants to see whether the risk is worth taking or not. Since it is something you are seriously thinking about doing, I bet that the pros of doing it will outweigh the cons and that the cons of not doing it will outweigh the pros. By making this explicit, you can persuade yourself to take the risk, because it is worth it.

Another thing you can do, is take another sheet of paper and list all the possible negative consequences associated with the risk and evaluate the likelihood that they will happen on a scale from 1 (very unlikely) to 5 (very likely). If you are afraid of driving at night, for example, you list all the possible things that could happen, like being unable to see the road, bumping into others that you didn't see, being blinded by the lights, etc. When you then rate the likelihood of such things happening, you will see that they are very low.

If you are not convinced yet to take the risk, you can also add, for every possible consequence, reasons why it will not happen. So, for the risk of being blinded by lights, you argue that it will not happen because a) cars are designed not to blind you, b) no one else is being blinded, c) you can always look slightly away from the light, etc. This should convince you that your fears are not rational and therefore unnecessary.

As you may observe, in many of the suggested remedies, the emphasis is on using your ability to think rationally to beat your bananas. I know that many fears aren't rational and that a rational approach is not always the solution. Some fears go deep and can be traced back to various things that have happened to you in the past. They require professional therapy, and it might not even be possible to get over them. But those are the exceptions. Many of our fears today are pseudo-fears. They aren't real fears but reflect the fact that we are a bit cowardly and afraid of the unknown. For those fears, a rational approach can be very effective. Furthermore, because the whole point of this book is to help you behave more sensibly while being surrounded by bananas, a rational approach is what you need anyway to overcome your bananas.

The good thing about taking risks is that there is no downside. Of course, this refers only to the risks that you can bear. This doesn't include the things that can get you in serious trouble, such as jumping off a cliff, or investing all your savings in bitcoins. But for the kinds of risks talked about above, there is no real downside. If you take the plunge and things work out, that is great. Then you will be glad you took the risk and immediately reap the benefits. But when things don't work out as expected, you still reap the benefits. It is not merely the cliché that you learned something from it. On top of that, the mere fact that you took the plunge means you have built character. This should make you less fearful the next time and for other risks too. Accordingly:

Banana Remedy 5.3: Take a Risk
Step over your fears and take a risk. Realize that most of them reflect a fear of the unknown and aren't real. Focus on the upside and go for it. If it works, great. And if it doesn't, you build character.

Guard Your Boundaries

Building the character that is needed to withstand the bananas around us doesn't only happen through saying and doing things that cross social norms and your own risk appetite. It also happens by doing the opposite: guarding your boundaries and resisting the pressure put on you to cross them. You may be pushed to do, say, think and feel things that don't fit you. Guarding your boundaries means that you are clear about how far you will go and how far others can go in relation to you.

We all have plenty of boundaries. Anatomically, our skin marks the boundary between us and the rest of the world. Energetically, it is our personal space that tells us how close people can come. Physiologically, it is our heartbeat, lungs and muscles that tell us how fast and long we can run. Mentally, it is how much stress we can bear. Timewise, it is how much time we have in a day, week or year to do something. Financially, we can't spend more money than we earn. And so on and so forth.

These boundaries aren't fixed. Your skin is flexible enough to expand when you gain weight, the size of your personal space can vary a bit over time and between people, you can improve your condition and stress-coping skills, and you can plan things differently so that you have more or less time for something or someone. But they are boundaries. And these boundaries determine to a large extent who you are and what you can do.

Guarding these boundaries is important. It makes sure that you don't get ahead of yourself and that you don't let your life be determined by external factors. Guarding your boundaries makes you less likely to go bananas. When you are exhausted, when you let other people come too close—literally and figuratively—or when you work yourself into a burnout, your chance of going bananas increases exponentially.

The main way to guard your boundaries is to learn to say no. To others and to yourself. Saying no means that you clearly indicate where your boundary is: up to here and no further. When someone asks you something that you really don't want or that you are really not able to do, say no. It doesn't matter who it is. Whether it is your boss, partner, children, friends, neighbors, colleagues, or anyone else, you have boundaries that they should respect—and vice versa.

Saying no is not easy. Of course, uttering the word is easily done. But effectively saying no to a request that you get is hard. At least, I find it hard. We don't want to be the spoilsport. We don't want to disappoint the other party. We are afraid of them getting angry at us or not liking us anymore. And so on. At heart, our fear of being left alone is taking over when we don't say no. Being the social animals we are, we don't want to be expelled from the pack. So we say yes more often than is healthy for us.

To learn to say no more often, it helps to see the benefits of saying no. The clearest and most obvious benefit is for yourself. When you say no, you have effectively guarded your boundaries and stayed close to yourself. You have time to do other stuff, you feel less exhausted, you have less stress, etc. This feels good and is good for you. This in itself should be enough already to convince you to say no more often.

Another benefit for yourself is that saying no breaks people's assumption that you always say yes. If you say yes to any request, people will give you more requests. After all, they think, you are the kind of person who will respond positively to every request. So, by saying yes to too many requests, you attract even more requests. If that is what you want, that is fine, but if you don't, this creates a lot of stress. So, say no more often to show people that you are not a boundary-less 'yes person'.

A big part of the problem of not saying no enough is our social fear of being excluded. You are supposed to be sociable and say yes to everything. Otherwise, you aren't a good friend, spouse, colleague or neighbor. But that is nonsense. In the long run, everyone benefits if you guard your boundaries. By saying no to one thing, you can perform and enjoy another thing more. And by saying no, you make sure that you can keep on delivering in the future. If you are exhausted, you can't do anything for other people. Saying no helps you avoid getting exhausted, and so you can mean more to others.

Saying no to guard your boundaries also makes you a more dependable and respected person. Because the pressure on all of us to say yes is so great, people secretly respect you if you dare to say no. Maybe they act disappointed or agitated in the first place, but behind it is often a bit of jealousy and respect for you: they see that you say no while they said yes again. When you clearly guard your boundaries, people know what you stand for and what they can ask you and what not. They appreciate this, because it creates a sense of stability in the collective madness.

This makes it obvious what you can do to guard your boundaries: say no more often. As with many of the remedies given before, it is a remedy of the just-do-it kind. Just say no to the next boundary-crossing request that you get. Say no to a party invitation you don't want to go to, an extra assignment your boss wants to give you, your kid's request for the newest pair of sneakers, a ringing phone or an 'urgent' email request. And enjoy doing it.

You can only seriously guard your own boundaries if you take into account the boundaries of others too. Thus, as you learn to say no, you also have to respect other people when they say no. This means openly and willingly accepting their no in answer to your request. It also means not asking them something which you already know they aren't able or willing to do. By asking them anyway, you put unnecessary pressure on them. If you put out fewer boundary-crossing requests to others, you can expect to get less boundary-crossing requests yourself, too.

The last, and paradoxical thing you can do, is to say yes more often. The point of saying no is not saying no for the sake of saying no. It is to guard your boundaries. And there will be quite a few things that you are asked to do that you might not be thrilled about but that are safely within your own boundaries. Saying yes to those requests means you help other people or do them a favor.

Being kind like that is nice anyway, but it also makes it easier to say no at other times. If you say something no-ish all the time—like saying yes but in a grumpy way—you slowly build a feeling of guilt and dissatisfaction, piling up to make you go bananas. After all, you want to say yes, and by not saying it convincingly it feels the same as saying no. If you say a loud and clear yes to those requests within your boundaries, you will feel more confident to say no at other times. Therefore:

Banana Remedy 5.4: Guard Your Boundaries

Know how far you can and want to go, and say no when something seems to be going to cross that boundary. Realize that guarding your boundaries is not only good for you, it is also good for others.

Adopt a Work-Rest Rhythm

This is one that took me a while to learn. If you are in a traditional nine-to-five job, where you and your colleagues take breaks and have lunch every day at exactly the same time and where you leave the office exactly at 5pm, you factually have a clear work-rest rhythm. Even though this may look old-fashioned nowadays, or even claustrophobic, there is a lot to say for it.

I have always considered my freedom to decide when and where I do things, about the most important thing there is on earth. I don't like others telling me what to do, and I don't like sticking to the schedules others have thought up. And I like to blend my working and private lives because I can't tell the difference anyway. This is why I quit my full-time job as a university professor and became an independent trainer/consultant/writer.

But there is a downside to this freedom. Or better, a challenge. As it turns out, having a rather strict work-rest rhythm like in a traditional job has its merits. I learned this from the Benedictine monks I referred to before. Monastery life is regulated extremely precisely in terms of time. In the monastery where I have been a guest on a couple of occasions, the schedule was like this: 5.45 get up, 6.15 first service, 6.45 breakfast, 7.30 second service, 8.15 reading, 9.30 third service, 10.15 study and work, 12.15 fourth service, 12.30 lunch, 13.00 dishes, 13.30 study and work, 17.00 fifth service, 17.30 meditation and prayer, 19.00 dinner, 19.30 dishes, 20.30 sixth and last service. Every day, throughout the year, including the weekends.

When being a guest there, I tried to blend in and follow the same work-rest rhythm as the monks. This wasn't mandatory, but appreciated and well within my boundaries, so why not join them? Aside from skipping a service or two per day (admittedly, I never made it to the first…), I managed to do this fairly easily. And it was not only easy, it was also a relief. The most surprising thing was that I got a lot of work done during the work hours—being in part the writing of this book. I got much more done than I would have accomplished during a 'normal' working day, despite having less time because of all the services.

Thinking about why this would be and doing a bit of research on it, there are two things that stand out: take rest and force yourself into a rhythm. The taking rest part is obvious. We all are most productive if we take enough rest. It makes us more productive during the hours that we do work. This was certainly the case for me. During the working hours, I could fully concentrate and work hard, and during the service times I focused on something else, thereby resting and letting my subconscious process the things I had been working on. Then, after service, I could start working immediately again, with enough energy and focus. So, the implication is: take more rest to get more done.

The rhythm part may sound less obvious, at least it was for me. Why impose a rigid work-rest rhythm on yourself if that is what you wanted to get rid of by quitting your job in the first place? Furthermore, who doesn't know the feeling of being in a flow and working on longer, or the idea of first finishing a task before you take a break? Isn't it more productive to continue working on a task so long as you have the motivation, energy and focus to do it? Surprisingly, it isn't.

The main advantage of adopting a rather rigid work-rest rhythm, is that it teaches you how to start and stop working on something. Learning to stop is important. As referred to in the previous section, you have your boundaries and you should guard them. Once you are in the flow of working it is too easy to cross your boundary. Forcing yourself to stop for a coffee break, lunch, walk in the forest or whatever at a predefined time, helps you learn to stop working. And once you get used to that, it will also be easier to stop at a time when you want.

Adopting a work-rest rhythm also teaches you how to start something. I assume we all know the feeling of not wanting to do something. We know we have to do it, but we procrastinate. Or we don't know how to start and therefore first spend hours on unproductive pondering, smartphoning or Googling. A work-rest rhythm helps you cut through this. Because you have taken a rest, and because the clock tells you it is working time, you will have less difficulty getting started.

Furthermore, the very fact that you *didn't* finish a task first makes it easier to start again. Before you took a rest, you were in the middle of something. Picking up that something is easier than starting something new. So, by taking a rest before you have finished a task, or by starting a task shortly before you take a rest, you lower the threshold of starting again. That may sound counterintuitive, but it works. It is one of the reasons why this book was finished.

Of course, you shouldn't necessarily adopt the monks' schedule. You have to develop your own. One that is feasible and works for you. For me, it is: get up at 6.45 and have breakfast, start working at 7.30, have a coffee break at 9.30, work from 10.00-12.00, have lunch at 12.00, start working again at 13.00, have a coffee break at 14.30, work from 15.00-17.30, cook and have dinner, and then try not to work the rest of the evening. Looks like a traditional working day, no? Of course, I can't stick to this schedule every day. I also have to teach, visit clients, have meetings, etc. But whenever possible, I try to stay as close as possible to this schedule. And it works. I get done more in a day than before. You can develop a similar schedule that works for you.

How does this help you survive in Bananaland? In two ways. First, it creates a sense of calmness in your days. Rather than jumping on every trigger, crossing your boundaries by working too long, or procrastinating about your work, you have a steady rhythm that helps you calm down. As such, adopting a work-rest rhythm supports Step 1. But it also helps you build character. Instead of letting others or the amount of work you have determine when and how much you work, you let your clock dictate you. And that means you are deciding yourself when and how much to work. After all, it is you who sets the clock. Accordingly:

Banana Remedy 5.5: Adopt a Work-Rest Rhythm

Get control of your daily agenda by adopting a rigid-as-possible work-rest rhythm. Define upfront when you work and when you take rest. This makes you feel more in control and you get done more.

Conclusion

The first four steps were primarily aimed at deconstructing the banana version of yourself. They help you cut out the noise, get rid of your mini-me and rid yourself of a too-large ego and made-up feelings and thoughts. The remedies in this fifth step should help you to start constructing the confident, strong and grounded non-banana version of yourself. They are:

5.1 Ignore Apps and Advice
5.2 Deviate from the Herd
5.3 Take a Risk
5.4 Guard Your Boundaries
5.5 Adopt a Work-Rest Rhythm

These remedies should help you develop the character that is needed to withstand the collective madness around you. They help you to stand firm and become a stronger person. This is needed, because the banana forces are strong. And they might even get stronger as soon as people find out that you are not playing the banana game anymore. They might push you even more to join them on their banana journey.

As explained in Chapter 1, the main thesis of this book is that, in this postmodern society, we have abandoned all but one of our pillars of certainty—The Other—and, as a result, we have lost our individuality and go bananas. That is precisely what this fifth step is aiming at: reclaiming your individuality so that you do, say, think and feel the things that fit you. Not because others are doing, saying, thinking or feeling the same, but because you, as an adult individual, want it.

When you master this fifth step, the hardest part is done. There are still four steps left but these are generally less confrontational than the previous three. Rather than focusing on deconstructing and constructing yourself, they focus on the more practical aspects of surviving Bananaland. This starts with detoxing yourself.

10

Step 6: Detox Yourself

The first five steps have helped you create the right conditions for ridding yourself of your bananas. You have cut out the noise and controlled things that made sensible thinking impossible in Steps 1 and 2, and you have worked on creating a stronger you in Steps 3 through 5. In that way, you have equipped yourself to avoid too many new bananas coming in and have developed the working mindset that is needed to withstand the collective madness. Now it is time for a cleanup. Therefore, your next step is detoxing yourself from many of the bananas already in you—especially the ones that you have been carrying with you for a long time.

Challenge Your Beliefs

There are a lot of things that we believe are true but are not. I am not referring here to checking the correctness of information or the truthfulness of what people say. I will return to that in Step 8. What I refer to here, are your beliefs and convictions about yourself. The things that you hold true about yourself but that may not be true after all.

Challenging your beliefs implies an attempt to get to know yourself a bit better. 'Know thyself' was an ancient Greek maxim used by great minds such as Socrates and Plato. As you might infer from Chapter 8, knowing yourself doesn't refer to an endless search for your own true inner self. It also doesn't mean that this should lead to some sort of set-in-stone picture of who you are. What it refers to is the idea that you first need to understand yourself a bit before you can try to understand other things. And this 'understanding yourself' is a never-ending process, because you, as well as everything around you, keeps on changing all the time.

Challenging your beliefs and understanding yourself is about getting rid of the beliefs that aren't yours, the made-up beliefs. The kind of beliefs where you think you believe something, but you don't. You only believe so because your parents did or because your friends do, or because the media and 'everyone else' does.

For example, you think you like arthouse movies, psychedelic post-rock music, modern abstract art, or complex multi-layered philosophical novels. But if you are honest with yourself, you don't like them at all. You find them confusing, unnecessarily complicated and intellectual, or you don't get what people like about them. You only made yourself believe you like them because you think it makes you look more interesting or intelligent. Fooling yourself like this makes for some fertile banana soil.

Challenging your beliefs is also about the things about you that were true in the past but are not anymore because you have changed. When you were younger, it perhaps made sense to believe that bullying was the only way not to get bullied, or to believe everything your parents told you about yourself was true, or that you don't like brussels sprouts, or that you can only sleep with at least some light on. But now that you are older, you have changed. And, as a result, these beliefs about yourself may not be true anymore. So rather than sticking to these old beliefs, it makes sense to challenge them.

Sticking to incorrect beliefs is bananas in and of itself. After all, why stick to beliefs if they are wrong? But, it also leads to more bananas. Mistaking misbeliefs for beliefs is a great source of frustration. It leads to internal stress-causing inconsistencies between what you think and say you believe and what you actually believe.

For example, suppose you made yourself believe that you are a morning person. You convinced yourself that you like to get up early in the morning and that you prefer to start the day energetically with some hard work. In reality, though, you are not a morning person at all. And you are also not an evening person or afternoon person. You just don't mind. Sometimes you get up early, sometimes you like working until late, and sometimes you perform best after lunch. If that is what you are like, then sticking to the belief that you are a morning person creates inner conflict. Every day when getting up, you impose some stress on yourself by acting according to your own made-up beliefs.

Another example. Suppose you made yourself believe that you are a hypersensitive person. That is all fine if you actually are. But if you are not, you have to pretend to keep the image alive—not only for the outside world but also for yourself. You must be interested in what other people say, think, do and feel, and focus all your energy on trying to pick up their signals. And then you must make out that you are overwhelmed by all the sensory stimuli around you. Being truly hypersensitive can be tiring, but pretending that you are maybe even more so. Trying to maintain such inconsistencies costs a lot of energy.

As you can infer from the title of this section, the remedy is not so much that you try to find out what you truly believe and thereby replace your current mistaken beliefs. Instead, the focus is on challenging your current beliefs. So, the idea is not to embark on a quest for self-discovery but to deconstruct the main misbeliefs about yourself. This is more practical because it makes you focus on the present and what is available, on what you believe now, instead of on some distant self-image that you might or might not discover.

So, what can you do? There are two main routes here. The first starts with examining your beliefs and the second with examining some internal strain or tensions that you experience. For the first route, you put on your scientific hat and start analyzing your beliefs one by one. For any suspicious belief, you try to gather evidence that you are right and evidence that you are wrong and then draw a conclusion. A belief is suspicious when it resembles closely what your parents, better half, friends or 'everyone else' believes, or when you have had it since childhood. Those beliefs are most likely to be invalid today because most beliefs are not universal or eternal.

An easy way to analyze such beliefs is to take a sheet of paper and divide it into two columns. On top of the paper, you write down the belief in the form "I Believe That…" Then, you label the two columns "Signs That I Am Right" and "Signs That I Am Wrong". Then you try to find as much evidence as possible for both sides and list it in both columns. When you are done listing, you look at both sides and draw your conclusion.

The second route is not to start with your beliefs but with identifying your feelings of stress. If you observe yourself with a bit more attention than usual, you can discover which misbeliefs are causing stress. To find them, you need to examine your bodily response when saying or doing things (or have someone observe you). If you find yourself making small uncontrolled movements with your face, head or the rest of the body when acting in line with your belief, there is a big chance it is a made-up belief. And that is the kind of belief that deserves to be evaluated in the way suggested above.

Another way of discovering potential misbeliefs is, as soon as you have identified a candidate in one of the ways above, you say it out loud to yourself. So, if you think your belief that you are a morning person is wrong, say out loud "I am a morning person!" And when you think that you don't like modern art as much as you made yourself believe, you say "I like modern art!" If these sentences come out naturally and convincingly, then you are probably right. But if you feel some hesitation or internal strain, you have most likely discovered a misbelief. If you are not sure, also say out loud something that you are 100% sure of, like "I am a man!" or "I am 41 years old!" and compare how that feels. If it feels different, the belief you said out loud before is probably not true.

The difficulty here is not so much in identifying the misbeliefs and certainly not in making the analysis. It is in admitting you were wrong and then acting upon it. If you are honest with yourself and rationally analyze your beliefs in this way, I bet you find out soon that a belief is wrong— maybe even before you have drawn the two columns on the paper. Admitting it is the hard thing, though. After all, that means that you have stuck with a wrong belief for a while and that you aren't the person that you thought you were. But after the previous steps and especially Step 3, you can deal with that. So, quit complaining, allow feeling bad, accept the consequences, control your emotions, and so on. Accordingly:

Banana Remedy 6.1: Challenge Your Beliefs
Get rid of the things that you believe about yourself that aren't true.
You have copied them from others or stuck to them from your past,
but they hinder you today. Challenge them and admit you were wrong.

Rethink Your Aspirations

Once you have started challenging your beliefs, you can continue your
detoxing journey by rethinking your aspirations. There is a great chance
that you have not only created various misbeliefs about yourself but also
that some of your goals, wishes and ambitions aren't yours. And like the
misbeliefs, you have them because you are supposed to have them,
because others have them or because you had them in the past.

It is obvious that aspirations can change. You no longer want to be
the pilot, fireman or nurse that you wanted to be when you were four-
years-old. Your goal is no longer to get drunk at the weekend or to
spend as much time as possible hanging out with your friends. And you
no longer want to rebel against the authorities—if you ever wanted this
in the first place. But, despite that, we often insist on aspirations that
may not be ours anymore or were never ours in the first place. Instead,
we adopted them because others (seem to) have them too. And if others
have them, our tendency to worship the other makes us hold them as
true for ourselves as well. They are, in a sense, imposed on us by the
social and cultural pressures around us that we can't withstand.

Some of our fictitious aspirations are very specific. They developed
by our interacting with the people close to us. We have them because of
the way we grew up and the particular parents, family, friends, and
colleagues we had or still have. They comprised our own little micro-
cosmos in which certain things are expected from us. A typical example
is that you think you aspire to be a doctor, lawyer or bus driver because
one of your parents aspired to that. Or you think you aspire to be an
entrepreneur because most of your friends do too.

In addition, there are also more widely shared, general aspirations
that have become part of our culture. In today's world—at least in the

country I live in—we are supposed to have all kinds of aspirations. Here are 15 examples that are widely spread:

1. We aspire to be successful.
2. We aspire to grow old.
3. We aspire to have children.
4. We aspire to earn a lot of money.
5. We aspire to own a big house with a garden.
6. We aspire to have the newest phone.
7. We aspire to travel abroad.
8. We aspire to go on vacation three times a year.
9. We aspire to retire early.
10. We aspire to have a higher level of education.
11. We aspire to be slim and muscular.
12. We aspire to be funny.
13. We aspire to make the best of ourselves.
14. We aspire to be different.
15. We aspire to have aspirations.

Of course, not all of them may apply to you. They are merely a list. But the point is that, in every culture, there are widely shared aspirations that people have and therefore you also are supposed to have. But do you? Are aspirations like these your aspirations? Or are they what everyone else says they want because that is what everyone else says they want? Do you want a bigger house and newer phone, or do you prefer a smaller one and to keep your current one? Do you want a great career or to retire early, or do you prefer keeping your fun, not-so-challenging job as long as possible? Do you want to improve and work on yourself all the time or are you happy as you are? And do you have clear aspirations in the first place?

Sticking to your fictitious aspirations may seem the easiest thing to do. By not deviating from the herd, you blend in and reduce the chances of being called strange by the people around you. And adopting their aspirations means you conveniently don't have to think about your own. So, on the surface, there seems to be a lot to be said for conforming.

But this is not as much a low-risk strategy as it seems. After a while, the misalignments between what you aspire to and what you tell yourself to aspire to, build up and cause tensions and stress. The same for pretending that you aspire to something while you are not really aspiring to anything. It creates stress. And, one day or the other, this will make you go bananas.

This means there is room for some detoxing here as well. The remedies are the same as for challenging your beliefs. Like with the beliefs, you focus your attention on the misaspirations, on what you wrongly hold yourself to aspire to, not on what you would or 'truly aspire' to or 'really want'. That only creates an endless navel-gazing quest for something that might not even exist.

And, along the way, you can identify your inauthentic aspirations by evaluating the suspicious ones (the ones that everyone has or the ones you have had for a long time) or you focus on the feelings of distress you may have. The two-column exercise works here as well: you analyze your aspirations one by one and list the signs that you are right or wrong about them and draw your conclusions.

Another simple exercise you could do is to list the main aspirations that you are supposed to have in your culture and ask yourself whether you really aspire to them. As a start, you could use the list of 15 aspirations above and replace the word "We" with "Do I really" and end the sentence with a question mark: "Do I really aspire to be successful?" or "Do I really aspire to grow old?" etc. Any "Don't know" or "No" could be a sign that you have to rethink your aspirations.

The last thing that you can do is to challenge the whole idea that you have important aspirations in the first place. I know we are supposed to be ambitious and aspirational, but what if you are not? What if you are happy the way things are? When we focus on our aspirations, we focus on being something that we currently aren't. So, we focus on what we are *not*. You can also turn it around. Instead of focusing on what you are not, you can also focus on what you are and what you have.

In addition to the Non-Bucket List referred to (the list of things you don't want to do anymore), it can be useful to also create a 'Pocket List'. This is a list of the things already in the pocket; that you have achieved, and that you are happy or satisfied with. By creating this list, you take stock of your current life and help remind yourself to appreciate it. And by focusing on that, you might be able to cross off a few more of your misaspirations and further reduce your inclination to go bananas.

Finally, like with your beliefs, the main challenge is not identifying your aspirations or evaluating whether they are real or made-up aspirations. If you think about them in a clear-headed moment of reflection, you can easily identify that. The main challenge is accepting that you were wrong and acting accordingly. Therefore:

Banana Remedy 6.2: Rethink Your Aspirations

Don't think you aspire to something just because everyone else aspires to it. Identify which aspirations aren't yours, let them go, and be happy about the fact that there is one less thing to aspire to.

Question Your Habits

As you know by now, there are strong biological, psychological and sociological forces that make us always look at the other for what to do, say, think and feel. This applies to our beliefs and our aspirations, where both of them are largely shaped by aping others. And it also applies to our habits, the things we do without thinking about them. You may have developed quite a few that don't fit you anymore or never fit you in the first place.

Some of our habits are a result of the culture we live in (plus a substantial dose of commercial pressure). A clear example is how we celebrate Christmas. In Chapter 2, I already described the collective desire that pops up somewhere in November or early December to decorate our houses with trees, lights, and red and green decorations. We can add to that the sudden urge to listen to Mariah Carey, Wham!, Band Aid or Bing Crosby all day, and the need to get together, give each other presents and eat too much. Why? Because that is what we are supposed to do for Christmas because everyone else does it too.

This applies not only to Christmas but also to other public holidays. Take New Year. Why count down from 10 to 1, drink champagne and light fireworks? Or Easter. Why the sudden preference for eggs, rabbits, light yellow and other pastel colors? Or Carnival. Why, somewhere in February or March every year, do we wear costumes and masks for a couple of days and go bananas as if it is our last week on earth? Whatever culture you are from, I am sure you can name similar types of public holiday with their accompanying habits.

Don't get me wrong, it is not Christmas, Easter, Eid al-Fitr, New Year, or whatever holiday or habit itself that is the problem. And most certainly it is not the underlying holy day or event that is celebrated. It is the way and extent to which we celebrate, and how this has lost any connection with the original event that makes collective rituals like these bananas. Exactly because, for many people, there is hardly any connection anymore with the original events, which have lost their purpose to such extent that people don't even know anymore what is being celebrated in the first place.

Next to public habits like these, there are also more individual habits that were formed in the course of our lives and by interacting with our families, friends, neighbors and colleagues. I am particularly referring here to the habits that make us go bananas: the habit of grabbing your smartphone every two seconds, or using Facebook, WhatsApp or any other type of social media, of complaining about things, gathering more stuff and information, worshipping the other, making ourselves more special than we are, loathing ourselves for something we did, and so on so forth. I mean all the banana habits referred to in Chapter 2.

And I also mean the habits that make us go bananas indirectly: the habits we keep because we were raised like that, or because others around us have them but that are not ours. An example is the habit of having lunch at noon because that is what you have always done, even though you don't like having lunch at noon. Or the habit of celebrating birthdays even though you dislike celebrating birthdays. Or the habit of partying all night long on Saturdays when you don't like to party. And so on. Of course, the point is not to get rid of all your habits. If they make you happy, keep them. But if they cause some kind of tension or stress, because they aren't in sync with how you would like to behave, then changing them makes a lot of sense.

To get rid of such habits, it helps to understand what habits are and how they are formed. According to science, habits are the things we do that are triggered automatically in response to some specific cues and that we associate with some sort of desired result. You wash your hands after visiting the toilet, you say "How are you?" when someone says,

"How are you?" You put on your seatbelt when you start driving, etc. You do these things without thinking. You have experienced, or were taught somewhere in the past, that these behaviors caused a desired result (hygiene, friendliness, safety, etc.) and that is why you keep on doing them.

Habits are formed primarily by repetition. The mere fact that we do something time after time turns it into a habit. Of course, there are other factors at play such as how much you enjoy what you are doing: the habit of eating a donut every morning can develop quicker than the habit of doing 100 sit-ups. But it is repetition and routine that turn the things you do from something intentional to something habitual.

This means that the main mechanism to change your habits is repetition as well. You can change your habits by replacing the behavior that you want to get rid of with something else, and repeat that something else for a while—until that has become your new habit. So, if you have the habit of grabbing your smartphone as soon as you have ten seconds of spare time, try replacing it with something else—counting to ten, watching things around you, thinking about how lucky you are, breathing slowly, or anything else. And then repeat, repeat, repeat, until you have got rid of your old habit.

Or if you have the habit of complaining or talking about the weather whenever you speak to someone, force yourself not to talk about the weather but about something else and repeat, repeat, repeat. Or if you have the impulsive habit of buying more clothes every time you see a fashion store, force yourself not to buy clothes for a while. Walk around the shops again and again without buying anything. You can make it even easier on yourself by not carrying a wallet and phone the first couple of times so that it is impossible for you to buy something.

Whatever habit you are trying to change, don't worry if you fall back to your old habit. That is perfectly normal. It is the whole reason why so much repetition is needed. It takes a while before an old habit is gone or replaced by a new one. How long 'a while' is, is hard to tell. Some say three weeks, others say two months (or 66 days, to be more precise), others say 21 days for changing it and another 90 days to make the change stick. For me, a good six weeks seems to be the amount of time it takes to make a change. So, I guess somewhere between a month and six weeks seems to be a realistic period.

You can also go cold turkey. When you try to change habits through repetition, you focus on changing the habit itself, your behavior. But you can also change the underlying belief. And if you succeed in doing that, you may be able to change your habit from one moment to the next.

Take the habit of celebrating birthdays. You may do it because you believe you have to do it. Everyone else does it, so you are expected to do it too. And you believe that your family and friends will pick on you or abandon you if you don't celebrate your and their birthdays. But is this so? Or is it merely something you believe? As soon as you realize that this may not necessarily be true, you can replace your belief by the belief that birthdays don't matter. And if people would really rebuff you because you don't eat cake or drink a beer with them on particular dates, they might not be worth visiting in the first place.

Or take the habits of complaining and blaming. You may have them because you believe that they are effective mechanisms to connect with others. They make it seem that you always have something to talk about, and they put you in a nice victim position where you believe the other will give you the kind of attention that you long for. But once you realize that complaining and blaming don't produce the right kind of attention and that what you really want is a true conversation with other people, you might be able to drop this habit from one day to the next. You might still make the occasional, or more than occasional, slip, but once your belief has changed your habit will most likely change soon too.

Whether it is the belief you focus on, or the habitual behavior itself, sometimes you first need to believe that changing your habit is possible in the first place. One big barrier to changing habits is that you believe they can't be changed. "I have always done it like that", "I am too old for changing that", or "It is simply how I am" are oft-heard excuses. In those cases, you first need to prove to yourself that change is possible.

An effective way to do this is by doing the opposite of your habitual behavior. So, instead of confirming the habit again, you break through the habit by doing something very different. These don't need to be radical things. Many of our habits consist of small things anyway, so the opposite or different thing can be small too. If, for example, you always have breakfast first thing in the morning, try starting the day with an hour of work or exercise before breakfast for a couple of days. Or, if you always watch TV in the evening, force yourself to read a book instead for a couple of days. Doing such opposite things can help you realize that change is possible and that your habit is indeed just a habit.

Changing habits on your own can be hard. Even recognizing that you have habits that cause internal tensions and that make you go bananas can be hard. This is why the AA works with group therapy and everyone there has a buddy: getting rid of a drinking habit is less tough when done together. The same applies to changing your banana habits. That is also easier when done together.

I am not suggesting group therapy or even any therapy. But joining a group of people who don't share your habit can be helpful. After all, we are social animals who like to conform to the group. This means that, if we have people around us who don't look on their smartphones all the time, who don't care about birthdays or who don't buy new clothes all the time, we will start showing less of such behaviors as well. So, if you want to get rid of a particular habit, join people who don't have that habit.

It can also be useful to have a buddy who helps you dispose of your banana habits. This should be someone who you see often and who can confront you with your habits, or keep you to your own intention to get rid of a habit. Most naturally, and if you have one, this could be your better half. After all, it is your *better* half, so he or she knows better than you anyway. And assuming you trust each other and see each other frequently, he or she is your ideal habit-breaking buddy. In my case, she most certainly is. If you don't have a partner like that, a close friend could be your buddy too. Accordingly:

Banana Remedy 6.3: Question Your Habits
You may have various habits that aren't yours and that make you go bananas. Get rid of them. Replace them with different behaviors and beliefs. Find yourself a buddy to help and repeat, repeat, repeat.

Filter Your Words

As already suggested in Chapter 5, reducing your amount of babbling is an effective mechanism for calming down. When you speak less, there is more room for silence, reflection and nothingness. As such, talking less helps you go less bananas than you would otherwise do. Rethinking what you are saying is helpful for an additional reason as well. It also helps you detox yourself.

What I refer to here are the things you say, but that aren't the things you want to say. These are the things that make you go bananas. They cause a similar kind of internal conflict as keeping beliefs, aspirations and habits that don't fit you anymore. The same goes for saying things that you don't want to say. That also creates an internal conflict that causes stress and thereby makes you go bananas.

The remedy is not talking less in general. That is mere volume and helps you create the silence you need for ridding yourself of your bananas. Here it is about talking less bullshit by filtering what you say. So, it is about what you say and not how much you say. Bullshit is the kind of stuff you say but that you don't really believe or think is important. If you are interested in learning more about the philosophical underpinnings of bullshit, I can recommend reading *On Bullshit* from Harry Frankfurt.

And oh boy, we talk a lot of bullshit. When you think about it for a moment, do you want to spend your time talking about the weather, joking around trying to be the funniest, bragging about your achievements, polishing your experiences to make them sound more impressive, gossiping about others or pretending that you know what others (and you) are talking about? I don't, and I hate it when I do.

We bullshit for various reasons. We do it to stay part of the group. We want to conform and therefore join the conversation, to make sure that others keep liking us. We also do it to hide the fact that we don't know or care what others are talking about. We don't want to be caught being ignorant or not interested in something others are engaged in. We do it to hide our own insecurity and to make ourselves look bigger and more confident than we are. Or we do it to convince ourselves of something that is not true.

An example of the latter: you may find yourself keep on telling others how happy you are or how much you like something. You do it to convince yourself that you are happy ("I should because all the circumstances are right!") or that you like something ("I should because everyone likes it!"). It is clear bullshit though, since you are trying to ignore the fact that you aren't so happy after all, or that you don't really like the thing at all that you say you like so much.

We are surrounded by bullshit. Everyone does it, and whole industries or jobs are built around it. Think about the last few commercials or advertisements you have seen (especially for laundry detergents, cosmetics or telecom products). Or think about some of the self-help and business books at the airport that tell you how to become happy and successful in a few simple steps. Or think about all the quizzes, competitions and real-life soaps on TV—especially the ones featuring celebrities. It is truly remarkable the amount of bullshit we face every day. And this makes it hard not to go bananas.

I want to single out a specific case of bullshitting: the apparently irresistible drive to express our so-called opinion. In today's world, we are supposed to have an opinion about everything. And preferably a strong one for or against something. We must say we are for or against Brexit, we must have an opinion about the Kardashians, we must have a favorite color, and we must love or hate sushi. We can't be neutral or indifferent. And if we say we don't know or care, we are told to try harder or be honest.

But let's face it. About a lot of things, you don't really have an opinion, and certainly not a strong one. I don't, even though I often make myself believe I have it. Fabricating an opinion in that case just creates friction. You invent a made-up opinion and enforce it upon yourself by expressing it loudly. And since you first need to convince yourself, you probably overdo it. This means there is a substantial disconnect between what you say ("I love sushi and it is the best invention ever!") and what you feel ("Mwah, not bad. Tastes like fish"). This creates stress and is yet another trigger for going bananas. So don't.

And that is immediately the remedy for bullshitting. Just don't. Again, no special skills or talent is needed. Everyone has the capability to not bullshit. You just need to find it back and use it more often. The main challenge is probably resisting the urge to join the bullshit game.

Whenever you are in a conversation with others, the chances are big that bullshit will be dominating what is being talked about. It takes a bit of guts not to join in and instead stay silent or say something serious. After all, you don't want to be the banana breaker.

Or do you? If you are serious about ridding yourself of your bananas, being the spoilsport is part of the game. But maybe that is not the place to start. There are plenty of occasions where you can filter your own words without spoiling the bullshitting fun that people may have. The best starting point is to focus on the things that you are saying about yourself but that aren't true. Discovering, analyzing and resolving those things works exactly the same as the earlier remedies in this chapter: you focus on the tensions you feel when saying something and you analyze whether what you say makes sense. In this way, you find out whether what you say is what you want to say or not. And then you stop saying it and say what you want to say. Therefore:

Banana Remedy 6.4: Filter Your Words

Talk less bullshit. We are already confronted with too much of it, and it creates tensions to say stuff you don't want to say. Listen to what you are saying, analyze, and then filter out the bananas.

Change Your Yardsticks

The last remedy for detoxing yourself is to change what you are comparing yourself to. The previous four remedies focused on what you hold for true, on what you long for, on what you do, and on what you say. In all of that, you often compare yourself to some yardstick that tells you how well or how much of something you should be doing. Along these lines, the yardsticks are telling you what you are supposed to hold true, long for, do and say. But the yardsticks we pick don't always make sense. Often, they don't make sense at all. And, as a result, they form yet another source of bananas. So, now is the time to change them.

We have many yardsticks. An important and banana-causing one is perfection. Unlike everyone else, we should be perfect (I most certainly should, or at least I often make myself believe…). We should be good at everything and rather better than others, or preferably: the best. And we aren't allowed to make any mistakes, or to hesitate, because that makes us less than perfect. Once we fail to meet this yardstick, we get frustrated, feel helpless, punish ourselves, and tell ourselves to do better next time.

Perfection is the perfect banana yardstick. It is so perfect because it is both fully made-up by yourself and never achievable. Even though you may not like to think so, your definition of perfection is completely subjective. Because what is perfect? Why would making no mistakes, for example, be perfect? You could also say that making no mistakes means that you went the easy way by not trying to stretch your own abilities. And why would something going exactly according to plan be perfect? It also could mean that you have failed to embrace any new opportunities along the way. And so on.

Next to being subjective, measures of perfection are also impossible to achieve. You don't want to make a mistake once. No, you should never make mistakes. And everything should go according to plan always. No one can live up to such expectations. And that is the whole point of perfection yardsticks. You create them to give yourself a feeling of failure. And with that failure, you keep your self-image of a victimized hero alive.

One effective remedy for perfection as a yardstick you have already seen in Chapter 8: dethroning yourself. You aren't perfect and will never be. Like everyone else, you are an average, unimportant and temporary person—and that is great. So, if you still think you need to be perfect, revisit that chapter until you don't anymore.

In addition, you should keep on reminding yourself that your definition of perfection is merely one out of many. To help yourself with that, you can take a sheet of paper on which you write as many definitions of perfection as you can come up with. Not general ones, but related to the specific thing you should be perfect in.

Suppose you have created a yardstick that, in your job, you should always be the first to finish a task. Write that definition down in the following format: "My current definition of perfection in my job is that I always should be the first to finish a task." Probably the mere fact of writing this down already gives you a sense of how idiotic this yardstick is. Then, underneath that definition, you write alternative definitions. You start with "Alternative definitions of perfection in my job would be…" and then you list a couple of alternative definitions such as "Being a good co-worker for my colleagues", "Having the most satisfied customers", or "Having most fun in my job". This exercise shows how subjective your yardstick is and thereby help you relax it.

Another exercise you could do is listing the advantages and disadvantages of keeping the yardstick alive. So, pick another sheet of paper, write down on top your current definition in the same format above. And then, underneath this, divide the sheet into two columns, which you label "Advantages of keeping this yardstick" and "Disadvantages of keeping this yardstick". When you populate the list, you will see that the list of disadvantages is substantially longer than the list of advantages. Then you draw your conclusions and change or lower your perfection yardstick.

Next to perfection, we use plenty of other yardsticks that aren't useful either. Parents are a great source of banana-inducing yardsticks. And then not even our real parents, but our imagined parents: the made-up version of the parents in our head that still tell us how we should behave, even though we have passed the threshold of becoming adults ourselves long ago. Who doesn't know these voices somewhere in the back of our head that say you are not doing the right thing? Sure, keeping yourself to their norms and values was mostly useful when you were a child. But maybe not anymore when you are thirty, forty or fifty.

Another source of banana yardsticks is our friends, family, neighbors and co-workers. We tell ourselves we should perform at least as well as they do in everything they do. If they buy a bigger car, then we should buy one as well. If they organize a party, we should organize a party. If they mow their lawn, we should mow our lawn. If they give their kids expensive presents, we should give our kids expensive presents. Etcetera. And if we can't live up to that self-induced yardstick, it makes us feel we are underperforming.

None of that makes sense. Of course, it makes sense in the light of our biological, psychological and sociological heritages. We are wired to compare ourselves to others and take their behavior as a yardstick. Remember the school of fish, flock of birds, and herd of wildebeest I keep on referring to. That kind of behavior is a result of us looking at what others do and trying to do the same. So, we can *explain* why we behave bananas.

But that doesn't mean it makes sense. It doesn't. Why would our (imagined) parents, families, friends, neighbors or co-workers be the right or even a useful yardstick? If what they want coincides with what you want, then it is okay. But a great deal of the time, that is not the case. They are they, you are you. And they have their norms, values, hopes and dreams, and you have yours. All of this means that, if you want to get rid of some more bananas, it makes more sense to pick your own yardsticks rather than use perfection or borrow them from others.

How to do this? You could start using the two sheets of paper described above. On one you write your definition of the yardstick and list alternative ones; and on the other, you list the pros and cons of trying to live up to the yardstick. These two exercises work equally well for using perfection as a yardstick as for using yardsticks from others.

In addition, you can ask yourself a couple of times whether what you think you have to do is really what you want to do. So, instead of pre-ordering your next bigger car because your neighbor has one, you ask whether you really want it or whether you want it because he has one. It can help to use another sheet of paper for this. You start again with writing down your yardstick, but this time in the "I think I should because..." form: "I think I should buy a new car because...", "I think I should work harder because...", "I think I should eat healthier because..." etc. And then you list the various reasons why you think you should do this: "Because my neighbor has one too", "Because everyone talks about how hard they work". "Because that is what you see on TV" etc. Look at the reasons you write down and draw your conclusions. I bet there are many yardsticks that can be traced back to other people rather than to what you want yourself. Accordingly:

Banana Remedy 6.5: Change Your Yardsticks
Much of what we think we should do can be traced back to using unproductive yardsticks. Get rid of those where perfection, your parents or others are the source, and create your own instead.

Conclusion

With the detoxing remedies outlined in this chapter, you have started to actively work on disposing of your bananas. Since we all carry a load of bananas with us, this is another crucial step in making yourself banana-proof. To facilitate your banana cleanup, you have been advised to:

6.1 Challenge Your Beliefs
6.2 Rethink Your Aspirations
6.3 Question Your Habits
6.4 Filter Your Words
6.5 Change Your Yardsticks

You probably know the principle of physical detoxing from alternative medicine, your personal dietitian, glossies, or hearsay. The idea there, is that you stop taking in food for a given period or only eat or drink particular kinds of food during that period. As a result, your body starts cleaning itself by getting rid of the toxic substances it carries.

While the science is not entirely clear about whether physical detoxing works, or whether it is even harmful, there is no doubt that mental detoxing helps. Getting rid of made-up beliefs, aspirations and habits, or stories and yardsticks enlightens your mind. It makes life easier, more fun and more real.

The main reason that mental detoxing works is that it helps you get rid of your bananas in a structured way. Unlike a physical detox, your aim is to get rid of your banana ideas forever, not merely until the next detoxing round. Of course, repetition may be required, but all the remedies in this chapter are aimed at helping you get rid of the bananas that you are carrying with you and never want to carry again. And the other steps on your journey out of Bananaland will help you not to gather too many new bananas.

11

Step 7: Get Organized

Now you have cleaned up your mental bananas in the previous steps and grown your ability to withstand the bananas around you, it is time to get rid of the bananas in your day-to-day activities. This chapter, therefore, focuses on how you can get more organized by removing some of the important banana traps that you might fall into every day. This will make it easier for you to stay banana-free. Thus, while the previous chapter was concerned with how you think and who you are, the current chapter focuses on what you do and don't do. The last remedy of Chapter 9— Adopt a Work-Rest Rhythm—already got you started. Now we will explore another five remedies for getting more organized.

Clean Up Your Stuff

Clutter is fertile soil for bananas. Your bananas grow easier, faster and larger in environments which are full of unorganized stuff. To think clearly—which is what bananalessness is about—you need a clear environment. Or at least a reasonably clear one. If you are surrounded by piles of stuff, your mind gets easily stuffed as well.

You might argue against this and say that having a full desk is how you like to work. Or that a packed house or office is cozy and comfy. Or that you need to be surrounded by stuff because otherwise you feel alone or incomplete. Maybe. Maybe that is indeed how you think you feel. It has been how I felt for a long time—especially about my desk. But maybe it is habit, laziness, or some sort of fear that keeps you from cleaning up your stuff.

Because you should. Across the globe, numerous studies have been conducted on the cognitive, emotional and physical effects of clutter. And the results are clear: clutter is bad. It increases cortisol levels and thereby stress. It gets you stuck, sometimes literally, in that it is hard to navigate or find something in a house full of stuff. It leads to feelings of shame or inadequacy (because you feel you should clean up, but you don't). It makes it harder to focus because you are distracted. It makes you forget things because out of sight is out of mind. It makes you eat unhealthily. It makes you feel dissatisfied. It makes your thinking less efficient. It decreases productivity. It isolates you because people don't want to be in places that have been stuffed by others. And so on. The list of negative effects is endless and goes in one direction: bananas.

But, despite the negative effects, we keep on gathering more stuff. A key cause is our omni-obesity, multiplied by our tendency to do as others do; everyone gathers stuff, so we do it as well. And maybe for some of us, it is also an instance of compensating behavior by which we gather stuff to fill another type of gap in our lives. Maybe we feel we miss out on a loving partner or on attention from particular people. Or maybe we don't have the power or capabilities that we wish we had. And we compensate by collecting more stuff.

Once we have gathered it, the clutter stays because we also have a hard time disposing of stuff. Some stuff we keep because we have become emotionally attached to it, other stuff because we think we might still need it somewhere in the future, and still other stuff because we like the mere idea of 'having' it. A personal example (and another confession): I recently bought a plastic trombone for fun, even though I play the trumpet and know I will never really use the trombone. But it was cheap and having it seemed fun! Unless you are a fanatic minimalist, I'm sure you have stuff like that in your house as well.

The last reason why we keep the stuff we gather is that we don't feel like cleaning up. Call it laziness, call it being busy, call it procrastination, but I'm sure there is stuff lying on your desk, in your drawer, in your attic or wherever which you just haven't taken the initiative to get rid of. But you should get rid of such stuff. Science tells you. And you know it too. You experience how clutter clutters your mind. Or you apologize for the mess when people visit you. Or you feel secretly ashamed for all the stuff you pile up.

If you want to get rid of your bananas, it is time for a cleanup. Obviously, you want to clean your home so that there is no rubbish, dust or other filthy stuff lying around. But on top of that, you want to get rid of all the stuff that you don't use. And with getting rid of it, I mean getting rid of it—Marie Kondo style. You shouldn't move it from the desk to the drawer or from the living room to the attic. That is relocating the problem and that helps only a tiny little bit. The clutter is not in sight anymore, but it is still in your home and therefore still in your mind. It is still renting space and feeding your bananas.

This means that you have to dispose of stuff. But where to start? A practical rule of thumb that I use is to throw away everything I didn't wear or use over the last year. You can also take two years if one year is too harsh a threshold for you. Or you can use Marie Kondo's "Does it spark joy?" as the guiding question, and evaluate all your stuff, category by category, and throw away the stuff that doesn't make you feel better. While the precise criterion is not so relevant, the fact that you use a clear criterion is important. It makes you more systematic in evaluating your stuff and thereby throwing away more.

Incidentally, with 'throwing away' I don't mean putting it with the garbage. Wherever possible, give your stuff a second life with people who need it more. The nice side-effect is that it makes you feel even better: you have cleared both your mind and your conscience.

If throwing away your stuff in this way is too radical, you could also gather the stuff you think you can throw away and stack it in a place where you can hardly access it: the back corner of your attic, a storage box far away, or something else like that. But don't let this be an excuse to keep the stuff. You should agree with yourself that, after you haven't touched the stuff lying there for another half year or so (and probably have forgotten about it anyway), you will still throw it away. So, you introduce an in-between step. This is like putting files in the trash bin on your computer: you can still recover them until you empty it.

Since most of us will keep gathering more stuff over time, you need your cleanup to be a regular thing if you want it to be effective. Therefore, once every three or six months, for example, you explore your home looking for unused stuff and throw or give it away. I do this, and it always amazes me how much stuff there is every time that can be thrown away. Or let me say it correctly: *we* do this after my wife takes the initiative. I'm still too much of a gatherer to take the initiative myself.

If you are successful and manage to keep your home structurally free from unused stuff, you may find out that it is bigger than it needs to be. As soon as your house is no longer a warehouse to stack stuff in, but a home to live in, there is free space in it. You can use this space for things other than stacking stuff. Or you can move to a smaller place. I have done that twice now and can recommend it to anyone. Having less stuff and space around me makes me more focused and have fewer bananas. And I even save money by cutting down on my mortgage.

If you are not convinced about the advantages of throwing away stuff, and if you are the 'in case' kind of collector, think about the last thing I said. You keep stuff because you might need it somewhere in the future. And keeping it is cheaper than buying it again, you think. But maybe not. There are a lot of 'in cases', and keeping stuff for all of them eats a lot of space. Think about the costs of occupying that space. Count the number of square or cubic meters your stuff is occupying, divide it by the total surface or volume of your home and multiply that by your monthly housing expenses. That is about how much it costs you to keep all the stuff in your house. And then decide what is cheaper: keeping all your stuff and living in a warehouse or living smaller with less stuff? So, whatever reason counts most for you, cleaning up your stuff is a sensible thing to do. Therefore:

Banana Remedy 7.1: Clean Up Your Stuff

Clutter is an important cause of bananas. Therefore, get rid of all the unused stuff lying in your home or office. Create cognitive, emotional and physical space to enable clear thinking.

Get Rid of Work

To free your mind from bananas and give space to sensible thinking, you shouldn't only clean up the stuff around you. You also need to clean up the things that you do. This means getting rid of tasks, work, or activities that you are doing—at home, at work, at the hockey club or wherever—but that you shouldn't be doing. It also means getting rid of 'responsibilities' that you feel obliged to have but that aren't necessarily yours. There are many things in your life that are not necessarily *your* responsibility, and maybe they need not be done at all. Not doing them or leaving them to others can help get rid of some more bananas.

Timothy Ferriss's *The 4-Hour Workweek* is an inspiring book to get you started. One of the key messages of this book is that there are so many things we do that can be eliminated, outsourced or automated, that we should be able to reduce our workweek to half a day—and still make a living. Even if your goal is not necessarily reducing your working time from 60, 40, or 20 hours per week to four, the way of thinking that the book reflects is helpful. It shows how to get rid of work and thereby free time for other things.

While our goal is not necessarily to become more efficient and productive per se, getting rid of unnecessary work is a great remedy for bananas. Many of us feel busy and stressed, and we feel pressured by the expectations that we put on ourselves and that we think others have of us. We don't want to be called lazy, inattentive or spoilsports. So, we do as much as we can and more. We have jobs and hobbies, we spend time with families and friends, we go to parties, we produce birthday treats for our kids, we cook, we clean, we maintain our garden, we renovate our house, we repair our bicycle, and so on.

Why? Maybe all the work that you do is needed and nobody else can do it. Maybe you have no other choice. Maybe you lack the money to hire others to do some of the work. Or maybe you feel great by doing all of that. But my bet is that you wouldn't then be reading this book and you would spend your money on something else. And while outsourcing some tasks to others will indeed cost money, there are plenty of free ways to clean your calendar.

The solution is in three simple questions: "Does it really need to be done?", "Am I the one who should be doing it?", and "Does it really require this amount of effort and time?" The first question helps you to get rid of activities that you do but that do not have to be done in the first place. The second question helps you leave some of the remaining activities to others. And the third question means that, if you have to do something, you do it in no more time than is necessary.

The hard part in the first question is to distinguish between the stuff that needs to be done and the stuff that you *think* needs to be done. For some things this is obvious. You need to eat, sleep and brush your teeth. Equally obvious, you don't need to wash your windows every day, cook a five-course dinner, or go on a three-week holiday to Hawaii. But for many of the things we do, deciding whether or not we should do them is less obvious. Take visiting a friend on Friday evening, or going to a meeting at work. Should we really do this?

To help you make this decision, you can use two criteria. The first is: does doing this bring me something? If you like an activity, for example, that is enough reason to do it, because if you like something, it will make you feel better and give you energy. So, if you like visiting your friend or going to a meeting at work, then do so. Also, if it makes your boss feel better and if that makes you feel better too, then show up at the meeting. The last addition is important. If you do something out of guilt, a feeling of duty, or simply 'because', then don't. It won't bring you anything, and therefore, at the end of the day, it won't bring others anything either.

The second criterion is: do I suffer when I don't do it? If there are serious repercussions if you don't do something, then that is a reason to do it. After all, you don't want to suffer. But only do it if the consequences are real. Often, we think we will get a terrible response or that the consequences will be disastrous. But are they? Will we really be shunned by our friends or fired by our boss if we don't show up? And if that is the case, is it worth showing up in the first place?

These criteria don't only apply to activities involving others. You can ask the same for the things you do on your own. Does watching television the entire evening bring you something and do you suffer if you don't? Do you benefit from cooking a five-course dinner and do you suffer if you don't? Do you gain something when you wait in line and fight for a bargain on Black Friday and do you suffer if you don't?

Do you like cleaning your toilet and will you suffer if you don't? For all nos, you have identified possible activities to eliminate.

The two criteria may sound self-serving. In one sense they are. By using them, you are putting yourself first. But remember, this step comes after the previous steps, including taking responsibility and dethroning yourself. So, if you went successfully through the previous steps in the suggested order, your ego has already significantly shrunk. Furthermore, in the last, ninth step, 'Pay Attention', you will be invited to pay serious attention to others. In that light, there is nothing wrong with a bit of self-centeredness in this phase of your journey.

Furthermore, in the long run, the criteria are just as much other-serving as self-serving. Their point is that you reduce your workload to a level at which you are not going bananas anymore. If you go bananas, not only you, but also others, suffer. Therefore, whatever you can do to reduce your bananas will ultimately help them too.

Sometimes the answer to the two criteria is yes. For example, you do benefit from cleaning the toilet and you suffer if you don't (at least I would). In those cases, you move to the second question: am I the one who should be doing it? So, ask yourself: are *you* the one who should be cleaning the toilet (and the rest of the house)? Should *you* file your own taxes? Should *you* do the gardening? Should *you* be typing out the interviews you did? And so on. Again, your answer should be real: should you do it, or do you *think* you should do it?

This also applies to the 'voluntary' work you do for others. I don't mean the voluntary work that fulfills you because you help others. I mean the 'voluntary' work you do because you are 'supposed' to do it because it is 'normal' or because 'everyone does it'. Things like organizing a birthday party, being on the boards of both your son's soccer club as well as your own hockey club, helping at your kid's school, and so on. Sure, this stuff needs to be done, but should it be you who is doing it?

Again, this is not an invitation to an egocentric way of life. The point is that, if these things make you go bananas, then you are not helping anyone. Therefore, first make sure you rid yourself of bananas and then you can see whether you can do more work.

Even though it is common practice in organizations, we are not so used to delegating and outsourcing activities to others in our private lives. Outsourcing and delegating are presumed to be exclusively for the rich and famous who can afford a full-time butler or large staff running around. And if we, ordinary people, hire someone to do stuff for us, we are being lazy or snobbish because we supposedly feel superior to others and are too good to do our own stuff.

But why not? Why not hire someone to clean your home, do your laundry, maintain your garden, do your paperwork, take care of your bills, write complaint letters, get or order your groceries, answer (most of) your emails or plan your meetings? Really. Why not?

I am going to assume that money is just a minor reason. Yes, it costs something, and if you are already living on a shoestring and merely making enough to live a comfortable enough life, or you are having to save money for any other-than-primary expense, you might not have this luxury. But, if you bought this book, you have at least some money left to spend on other-than-primary needs. And you'd be surprised how much can be done for, let's say, a hundred bucks per month.

If you don't have that money spare, and if you don't have the luxury of being able to put it aside either, then outsourcing work may not be an option for you. But if you have a slightly higher income, you can look at your expenses and see whether you can make some changes to spare the money. If you spend your money on going abroad on holiday more than once a year, or on buying the newest flagship smartphone, for example, you could decide to skip a holiday or stay closer to home, or buy a less expensive phone or skip one model and wait for the next one.

At the end of the day, it is a simple cost-benefit analysis. What gives you more value for money: paying someone to clean your house, do your laundry or maintain your garden, for example, or buying that new iPhone or going to the Bahamas? Or what do you value more: having someone do your paperwork, or buying that new but expensive shirt, bag and pair of shoes? This is a matter of priorities. What is worth more to you: time, or experiences and stuff?

Outsourcing things is not always immediately possible. You might have made yourself so seemingly unmissable that it is hard to withdraw from an activity from one day to the next. If this is the case, you need to start making yourself missable first. This means redesigning your work in such a way that it can be done without your involvement.

To do this, you can start tracking all the activities that you spend time on during a week or so. A simple way to do this is to take a piece of paper and divide it into two columns. On the left, you write for each day what things you did. And on the right, you write how much time you spent on each of them. Or, alternatively, in the left column you write the times, and in the right column, you write what you did.

After this simple time-keeping exercise, you have an overview of everything you did during the past week. The next thing you do is mark those activities that only you can do because they absolutely require your unique and special skills. That is your *core*. All the rest could basically be outsourced to others. So, think about it and decide whether there are already things that you can outsource or delegate.

If you want to go one step further, you can look at this core and see whether there are any activities that you can split up. For example, if shopping for clothes is on your list, you might be the only one able to make the choice for which t-shirt you want to buy. But the rest can be done by someone else. Or maybe you are the only one able to come up with brilliant ideas for how to improve a product or process at work. But doing research on that idea and writing that idea down can probably be done by others. And so on. By scrutinizing your list of activities in this way, you get to your *absolute core*—the few things that only you can do. You'd be surprised how small this list is and how little time you spend on your absolute core. All the rest could be outsourced or delegated. So, if you want to clear your calendar, start outsourcing the stuff that you don't need to do and don't like doing either.

Outsourcing stuff to others requires making careful instructions and agreements. After all, you want other people to do the stuff in a way that you like. This takes some extra time initially and requires some finetuning the first couple of times. For example, someone may initially not make your bed as you like it, cook your spaghetti the way you prefer, or plan your calendar in the way that suits you, but if you tell them how you like it, you will get there after a couple of iterations. And, once set, you can enjoy the spare time you have created and spend it on something else—or on nothing. How great is that?

For outsourcing activities in this way, you might need to overcome a psychological hurdle first. You need to start seeing that hiring people or telling them how we want things done does not make us more or better, and it does not make them less and worse. Because it doesn't. People generally like it when they know that what they do makes others happy or satisfied. How disappointing is it to find that after five years of cooking spaghetti, cleaning beds, or maintaining someone's garden, you find out that the person you are doing it for likes it differently? Careful instructions avoid such disappointments.

Furthermore, it also helps if you realize that, by outsourcing things to others, you generate income for them. Of course, hiring someone to do stuff for you doesn't immediately make you a generous and life-saving do-gooder. But the fact is that you take some of your income and use it to provide them with paid work—instead of spending that same money on flying to the Bahamas, buying speakers you don't need or having an exorbitant 3-star dinner. If you see it this way, which of the two is more snobbish or self-serving, hiring or not hiring someone?

Okay, after going through the first two questions, you have eliminated those activities that don't need to be done in the first place and outsourced activities that *you* don't need to do. Now it is time to move on to the last question: can it be done using less effort and time?

We often confuse the amount of time and effort spent on activities with the results these activities produce. We implicitly assume that spending more time and effort on something will make it better. But this is a false assumption.

It is false for two reasons. The first concerns the result itself. What others find better doesn't necessarily coincide with what you think is better. And if you produce something for others—which is often the case—what matters is their view of what is good and better, not yours. So, while you may think that perfecting that report makes it better, your boss or client may find that the report is too long and complicated and that it takes you too long to produce it. This means that spending less effort and time could have made the report better: simpler, and delivered faster.

The second reason why this assumption is false is that it is based on a false idea of cause and effect. Why would spending more time and effort make something better? In my own work, I have experienced that this relationship is often not linear, but more shaped like a bell curve. Initially quality goes up when you put more time and effort into something. But, after a while, the slope of the curve flattens and eventually goes down: quality decreases if you put in still more effort. The trick is to find out for yourself where the top of the curve is and how far before the top you can stop because what you produce already fulfills the requirements.

Equipped with this awareness, you can now look at the various things you do and see whether you can spend less time and effort on them without losing quality, or with gaining in quality. So, does it make the report better if you spend another night on it? Does it make your boss happier if you work harder? Does it make the design of that logo better if you tweak it for another four hours? Does it make your spaghetti better if you try harder? Probably not. This means you would be better off saving the time. Oh, and one more remark: don't use the freed-up time to fill it with work again. Keep it free, do nothing and get bored. So:

Banana Remedy 7.2: Get Rid of Work

Do less. Have a careful look at all the stuff you do and assess which activities you can eliminate, outsource or do more efficiently. Change your perspective on what you should do, what counts as quality.

Stop Procrastinating

Like gathering and keeping stuff and doing things you shouldn't be doing, procrastination is another source of clutter. When you procrastinate, it means you do things later than you think you should do them. The result is that these things keep on circulating in your mind until you have done them. This is like a juggler adding additional balls all the time, without getting rid of some. Every extra task that you postpone is an extra ball. It is easy to see how this makes juggling—and doing the stuff you do—increasingly hard, energy-consuming, and prone to mistakes. You can easily drop a ball or two.

The extra problem with procrastination is that the things that you delay usually become bigger and bigger in your head. What started as a small task that you needed to do, ends up eating more and more space in your head until the actual small task has turned into some imaginary huge thing. Once you execute it—or if you had executed it immediately—you find out that it was just a bit of work and not even as bad as you thought it would be. So, procrastination means that you both have to keep more balls in the air, and the balls become larger and larger while you are juggling.

As research shows, the costs of procrastination resemble those of cluttering your home. By procrastinating, you lose time that you could have used otherwise—including doing nothing and enjoying it. It makes you less productive. It makes you feel less satisfied. It lowers your self-esteem. It decreases the quality of your work since you have to rush it at the end. It can put your reputation at stake. It creates stress and health problems. So, the science is clear: procrastination is bad for you.

"Hey, but I can't help it, I am a born procrastinator!" you may say. And you could have a bit of a point because the tendency to procrastinate is indeed moderately heritable. There is something that we could call a 'procrastination gene'. It is the same gene that also causes impulsive behavior. So, if you are both impulsive and a procrastinator, this may be partly caused by your gene set.

But that is no reason to stick with it. You can do something about it. A lot. And it doesn't require any special or supernatural skills. Of course, it is up to you whether you put any effort into trying to get rid of your bananas. But the same applies to procrastination: you can do something about it, and it doesn't require any special skills. And if you are serious about getting rid of your bananas, you also should *want* to do something about it because the disadvantages are clear.

There are multiple types of procrastinators: thrill-seekers, avoiders, and indecisive perfectionists. Thrill-seekers procrastinate because of the positive stress they experience when being close to a deadline. Avoiders do it to avoid making decisions or to run away from the discomfort of doing an unpleasant task. And indecisive perfectionists do it out of insecurity and to perfect what they are working on.

I'm the avoider-indecisive kind of procrastinator. On the outside, and as far as it concerns major activities, I do not procrastinate much. People who know me might even find me a good planner, well-prepared, always on time, fast responder and always delivering according to schedule. At the same time, though, I find myself procrastinating about the things that I don't like doing or am uncertain about. I know it is bananas, and I do suffer the consequences of unnecessary stress and wasting my time, but I find it nevertheless very hard to get rid of this banana habit.

There is a fourth type of procrastinator that I'd like to add: the pretender. These are the people who procrastinate so they always look busy, because that is one of their status symbols. By procrastinating, they keep their to-do list filled so that they can always tell others that they are busy. And by keeping their to-do list populated, they also keep themselves away from their fear of nothingness. For some people, having nothing to do is about the scariest thing on earth. And by procrastinating, you can make sure there is always something to do.

The main remedy for procrastination is as simple as it can be: don't procrastinate, and do stuff at the time you can and should do it. The benefit is immediate because you feel better once something is done. Plus, you'll save time by not wasting it on procrastinating. The problem is of course that, even though we know this, we still procrastinate. Therefore, you may need some tricks to help you.

There are many. Some you have already seen before. Adopting a work-rest rhythm, for example, is a great remedy for procrastination. By adopting such a rhythm, you learn to start and stop with something, making you procrastinate less. Also, some of the remedies of Step 1 will help. By switching off notifications, consuming less information and seeking silence, it is easier for you to concentrate on a particular task and execute it because there is less distraction.

An additional thing you can do is to break down large tasks into smaller tasks. Especially if you are an avoider-indecisive type of procrastinator like me, it can help to lower the threshold for doing something by dividing it into smaller chunks. So, rather than putting 'writing a book on bananas' on my to-do list and estimating that it will take an infinite number of hours, I can divide the tasks into chapters, sections, etc. to make it smaller. You can do the same for your tasks.

Another thing you can do to reduce your tendency to procrastinate is to get used to starting the day with the task you find hardest or are dreading most. If you postpone them to the end of the day, these tasks keep you concerned all day. But if you do them immediately, they are out of your system, making the rest of the day more fun and productive.

The same for the week or month: do the stuff you dislike most first, to get it over with. I need to keep on telling myself this, but every time I succeed, it does make me feel much more relaxed.

The last remedy is that it can help to think in versions of what you are doing. Especially if you are a perfectionist, this can help. If you focus on the final, perfect version of something, the threshold of starting is huge and you will keep on refining, improving and amending the thing all the time until it never gets done. If you think in terms of first, second and third drafts (like with reports), or in alpha, beta and gamma versions (like with software), the threshold is lower. Your goal then is not to produce the final report or market-ready version of something, but a first full version. This means your goal is to get something finished rather than finalized. While doing that, you will probably discover that your first version is not so bad after all and that improving it further is not so much work. This means that the threshold for finalizing it has become lower too. Accordingly:

Banana Remedy 7.3: Stop Procrastinating
Stop postponing the things that you should do but don't. Lower the threshold of doing them by dividing them into smaller chunks and versioning them. And start with the things you dislike most.

Multitask Sequentially

"I am a true multitasker" and "I love doing many things at the same time because otherwise I get bored", you may say. I thought so too. But we are lousy multitaskers. And this doesn't only apply to men. As science tells us, women are lousy multitaskers too. As human beings, we are not wired to do more than one thing at the same time.

Of course, we can breathe, see, hear, smell and bake pancakes at the same time. That is because a large part of our body and brain works on autopilot. Those things we can multitask. But when it concerns activities that require our attention—such as talking, writing, exercising or baking pancakes—we can't. We can only pay attention to and concentrate on one thing at a time because that is how our minds work.

The problem with multitasking is that you constantly have to switch your attention from one thing to the other. Our brain is like a TV. We can only put on one channel at a time. As soon as we want to watch another channel in parallel, we get into trouble. We can't follow the news and enjoy watching a movie at the same time. And if we try, we find ourselves constantly switching and neither getting the news nor enjoying the movie. The result is that rather than having watched two things, we haven't really seen either one of them.

The same happens with every other type of multitasking that we try. If we answer emails while at the same time working on a report, neither gets the attention it needs. And if we are driving and at the same time texting our colleagues that we are late, we don't give enough attention to either. Because we constantly have to switch between the two, our brain constantly has to start and stop a task. This costs time and energy, making trying to multitask inefficient and ineffective. And if you nevertheless insist on doing it, it makes you go bananas.

The standard advice against this is to focus on one thing at a time. That is excellent advice. And factually, that is what our brain does anyway, so why not stick to it? The problem, though, is that in practice, we often don't have the luxury of focusing on one thing only. Going through the previous steps, you might already have improved your conditions greatly so there is more opportunity for concentrated single-tasking. But you might still find a need to multitask because there are various things that are expected from you.

As a compromise, the remedy is to multitask sequentially. This means that you don't necessarily work on one task until it is finished before you go to the next task, but that you work with time slots during which you work on different tasks. For example, you work half an hour on task A, then an hour on B, then 15 minutes again on A, half an hour on C, an hour again on B, etc. etc. In this way, during about half a working day, you have worked on three tasks more or less in parallel.

The advantage of this compromise is that you are focusing long enough on a single task to avoid the constant switching associated with multitasking and, at the same time, are flexible enough to switch quickly between tasks. I have practiced this kind of sequential multitasking for a couple of years now and it has become my preferred way of working.

This works especially well if you can combine tasks requiring different degrees of mental or physical effort. If tasks A, B and C all require the same mental or physical effort, sequential multitasking is okay. But if, for example, tasks A requires a lot of mental effort, task B just a little bit and task C asks for physical effort, then this way of working can be even more productive than single-tasking. After all, after two hours of A, you might be so tired that you can't do B and C anymore. But by switching between A, B and C, you have enough energy to complete all three.

The main reason why multitasking sequentially works is that it is a variation of the work-rest rhythm referred to earlier. Instead of fully resting, you let one part of your brain or body rest while you are engaged on another task. As such, it is one more way to make yourself less prone to going bananas. Therefore:

Banana Remedy 7.4: Multitask Sequentially

You can only pay attention to one thing at a time. To still work on different things in parallel, divide your day into time slots during which you work interchangeably on different things at the 'same' time.

Plan for Uncertainty

Plan for uncertainty. That probably sounds like an oxymoron. How can you plan if things are uncertain? How do you know what to do when things are unpredictable and changing at a fast rate? You can't. But that doesn't mean that you can't plan. Even if things are very uncertain and are changing all the time, planning is useful. Even more, especially because things are uncertain and change all the time, planning is useful.

A significant portion of our bananas are caused by a feeling that we are not in control. We feel that circumstances or others determine our lives and that we are primarily responding to their requests and needs. As referred to in Chapter 6, this reflects an external 'locus of control': we feel the external world is controlling us. And that makes us go bananas because we feel like we have to conform rather than do as we like. What we want, and also need to be banana proof, is a more internal locus of control so that it is us instead of them who determines our calendar.

And that is where planning for uncertainty comes in. There are many things that we can't predict or control. They happen to us. We can't tell our car or oven not to suddenly break down, we can't tell our customers or kids not to change their minds, we can't avoid the train being delayed, we can't plan not to get ill or break a leg, and we can't tell when someone close to us needs our help. These things happen and are largely out of our control.

But we can factor in that they *might* happen, and we can take steps to ensure that things like this do not immediately get us into big trouble. Of course, you can't think about every possible thing that might happen to you and factor it in. That would be impossible, and merely trying to run all the scenarios would fill your entire agenda. But you can make sure that there is a bit of slack in your calendar so that you have time, should something unexpected happen.

You plan for uncertainty by deliberately and explicitly planning spare time, by not filling your entire calendar with other activities. How much time you need to reserve depends on how unpredictable your life is. Some people have a pretty good idea of what their schedule looks like for the next 30 years. They, for example, have a stable job, live in a home where they want to stay for the rest of their lives, and every week looks more or less the same. Others, though, don't even know what their agenda could be next week or tomorrow. They work from one assignment to the other, like to move and travel a lot, and make spontaneous decisions from one moment to the next. This makes their lives certainly less predictable.

But in all cases, there is uncertainty. Unpredictable things can and will always happen. This means that, whatever your life looks like, it makes sense to schedule in some idle time. A simple rule of thumb would be to reserve about 20% of your time for unexpected things. If your total working time is ten hours a day, this means reserving about two hours for unexpected things. This will usually give you enough time to adjust your schedule and adapt to unexpected changes.

This rule is rather rough, and it doesn't factor in that your life is more predictable in the short-term than in the long-term. Usually, you can be pretty certain about your calendar and the things that could happen today, but far less so about next week or next month. To adjust for this, a more refined rule of thumb would be to reserve 10% of your time today, 20% of your time this week, and 40% of your time this month for unexpected things. This means that, for today, you can pretty much fill your calendar, but don't do this for the whole week or month.

"But I don't have this luxury!" you may argue, "I need every minute and more!" and "I already have too little time for all the things I have to do!" If that is how you feel, then it is time to stop seeing idle time as a luxury. Because it isn't. It is absolutely essential if you don't want to go bananas. Furthermore, it makes you more productive and responsive. Instead of being stressed all the time, you are in control and can be a better employee, father, sister, neighbor, etc. Plus, it allows you to seize promising opportunities that you would otherwise have no time for.

You can always make time. Always. No matter how busy you think you are, there is always room in a day for idle time. If you currently feel you don't have that time, then throughout this chapter and the entire book, you can find many things you can do to empty your calendar. You can spend less time on consuming information (1.2) and on babbling (1.3), you can stop soul-searching (4.2), you can guard your boundaries better (5.4), you can clean up your stuff (7.1), get rid of unnecessary work (7.2), and so on and so forth. Implement those and then plan for uncertainty.

Planning for uncertainty is advantageous either way. If something unexpected and important pops up, you have the time to do it and do it well. If you plan for uncertainty, you will have time for the important unexpected things rather than try to ignore them, rush them, or squeeze them in. This helps you get a feeling of control and makes sure you can do the things you need to do, well enough. And if nothing unexpected happens, you have extra time. You can spend this time on something else that you would like to do or should do. Or—even better—on doing nothing and enjoying that.

That last thing is a real challenge for me. I do plan for uncertainty by making sure I don't completely fill my daily and weekly calendar. And I have become pretty effective at that. However, as soon as some idle time appears daunting, I mostly start putting extra stuff on my to-do list so that it is filled again. My logic is: if I do it today, then I have more spare time tomorrow. But if I am honest, that is complete nonsense. Because tomorrow I will do the same. It is my own fear of nothingness that is causing this, and my self-created feeling that I need to be busy and efficient. And even though I know this is bananas, I find it very hard to let it go. Let's call it work in progress. Anyway, planning for uncertainty helps to get organized. Therefore:

Banana Remedy 7.5: Plan for Uncertainty
Don't fill your calendar 100% with things you should do. Plan in idle time so that you can respond to unexpected things and have the time to do stuff that pops up, without going bananas.

Conclusion

After having worked on who you are and how you think and feel in the previous steps, this seventh step is a bit more practical. It aims primarily at improving how you work, at doing stuff in such a way that you minimize the chance of going bananas. The following five remedies should help you achieve this:

7.1 Clean Up Your Stuff
7.2 Get Rid of Work
7.3 Stop Procrastinating
7.4 Multitask Sequentially
7.5 Plan for Uncertainty

Together, these five remedies should help you to get more control of your own calendar. They help you create more idle time so that, whenever something unexpected happens—and it will—you are prepared and can do it without going bananas.

Getting organized is definitely an issue many people have difficulty with. We find it hard to throw away stuff, to stop doing stuff, or to delegate things to other people. There are plenty of companies making a living out of organizing people's lives. Whether it is paperwork, interior design, throwing stuff away, time management or planning a birthday, there is always a specialized company that we can hire for it.

Without suggesting these companies should all be out of business, there is a lot to say for being able to organize stuff yourself. Of course, delegating stuff to others can be a way to save time (see remedy 7.2: Get Rid of Work) above. But organizing is in itself a skill we need for not going bananas. If you try to outsource that too, getting rid of your bananas is going to be more difficult. The main reason is that, when you outsource it, it still isn't you who is in control. And that is what you need: the feeling that you are in control. Not them.

Many people find it hard to deliberately keep their calendar partly empty. After all, we ought to be busy and efficient and wasting time on nothingness is a sin. Or so we think. It should be evident by now that it isn't. On the contrary, reserving time in your calendar for doing nothing is an absolute must if you want to get free, and stay free, from bananas.

A key point made in this chapter is that there is a huge difference between working more or harder and working smarter. Working more and harder is an excellent breeding ground for going bananas. You don't think about what you do and how you do it. You run around like a headless chicken. You go and put more time and energy into it. As a result, you become tired and go progressively bananas.

The remedies in this chapter should help you work smarter. Working smarter means that you put your head back on top of your body and think about what you are doing. When you apply the five remedies effectively, you will find that they even help you work *less* and with *less* effort—and at the same time achieve *more*. Who doesn't want that?

12

Step 8: Think Sensibly

By going through the previous seven steps, you have removed a great share of your bananas. You have done all the groundwork now for making sure you don't go bananas. In the last two steps, we will work on how to use your senses in a practical way. So, rather than working against bananas, we change our focus to grounded, practical thinking and doing. In this chapter, we focus on how to make sensible judgments and decisions based on the information around us. And in the next chapter, we focus on the ultimate step: taking in new and extra information and processing it with care and attention.

Assess Importance

Thinking sensibly starts with distinguishing between what is important enough to think about and what isn't. There is so much stuff we think and worry about that isn't worth thinking and worrying about. Take decorating our homes. How important is it which door handles we have, or which precise shade of white the power sockets are? Or take others' opinions. How important is it what they think about the jacket we are wearing or whether we put on make-up or not? Or take the news. How important is it to know that some guy living on another continent dresses his cat like Elvis?

Of course, if you find this stuff interesting, important or fun, that's great. It means you can spend hours on it and enjoy it. In that way, it gives you energy rather than making you go bananas. But, we often spend hours on stuff like this even when we don't find it interesting, important or fun. This means we are using one of our most precious resources—brain power—and wasting it on stuff that is not important to us. It really is a waste, because our conscious brain power is limited. We can only concentrate on one thing at a time. This means that every minute we concentrate on something trivial, we are unable to use the conscious part of our brain for something more important, interesting or fun.

Using our brain to think, talk and worry about trivial things produces bananas. The process of using our brain is like any process: garbage in, garbage out. Or, better said, bananas in, bananas out. So, if we use our brain to think, talk or worry about bananas, it produces more bananas. The more brain time we give to door handles, power sockets, other people's opinions and unimportant news messages, the more 'important' we make them for ourselves and the people around us. After all, the fact that we and our peers think, talk and worry about these things must mean that they are important, right? You see the vicious banana cycle here?

So, how do you assess whether something is important enough to spend your brain power on it? There are two aspects to take into account. The first is rather obvious. It is how substantial the outcome or effect is of something. The more that is at stake, the greater the consequences or the more money you, for example, spend on something, the more important it is and the more sense it makes to spend your brain power on it.

A well-known tool that can help you focus on what is important is the Eisenhower Matrix—after a quote by Dwight D. Eisenhower, who reportedly said: "I have two kinds of problems, the urgent and the important. The urgent are not important, and the important are never urgent." It is a simple two-by-two matrix with urgency on one axis and importance on the other axis. This creates four cells to categorize the world in things that are both important and urgent, that are either important or urgent, and that are not important or urgent.

The point of this matrix is that it helps you decide what to pay attention to. In line with Eisenhower's quote, you should only pay attention to things that are important, urgent, or both. More precisely, it suggests that you *do* the things that are both urgent and important, that you *plan* the things that are important but not urgent, that you *delegate* the things that are urgent but not important, and that you *eliminate* the things that are neither important nor urgent. So, whenever you face something, think about whether it is urgent and important, and act accordingly. In this way, you help yourself only to spend brain power on things that matter.

The second aspect that you want to keep in mind when deciding what to spend your brain power on is less obvious, and we often forget it. It is how different the outcome will be depending on what we decide. There is an interesting paradox here. The more the outcomes resemble each other, the less important a decision is. After all, if both outcomes are equally desirable, it doesn't really matter which choice we make. Yet, it is this kind of decision that we spend most brain power and time on. Along these lines, paradoxically, we spend most brain power and time on the decisions that matter least.

Let me illustrate this with two scenarios about choosing between two pairs of jeans. Scenario A: one pair is ugly, expensive and doesn't fit, and the other is affordable and perfect for you. This is a no-brainer, and you probably decide in a split second without hesitation. Now take scenario B: you like both pairs of jeans, they both fit, they cost about the same, but have a slightly different color and fitting. The differences are so small that you keep on comparing them and can't make a decision.

If we compare the two scenarios, it is obvious that you spend more brain power and time on scenario B. Yet, in that scenario, the outcome of your decision hardly matters. The fact that you can't choose between the two pairs of jeans means that they are equally good. So, whatever choice you make, it will be the right choice. Instead of pondering about it, you could equally well flip a coin or decide in a split second. On the other hand, in scenario A, the 'stakes' are higher. Choosing the wrong pair of jeans there would mean you end up spending money on something that is useless to you. The very fact that the differences are important means that you can decide in a split second.

Of course, not all decisions are as straightforward and unimportant as choosing between two pairs of jeans. However, the basic principle that, the smaller the differences are, the more brain power we spend on it, applies broader. In order to think more sensibly, you always need to ask yourself, whenever you find yourself pondering something, whether it is worth pondering about. When you find yourself being unable to decide or choose, remind yourself that it could very well mean that either choice is good and that the very fact that you are pondering means that it doesn't matter which choice you make.

What this shows is that the importance of a decision not only depends on how big the outcome is, but also on how big the differences between possible outcomes are. Of course, you spend more brain power on choosing between two houses to buy than on choosing between two types of beer to drink. But the point is to only spend this brain power on differences that matter. If you can't make a choice between house A and house B, and have to start inventing criteria to enforce a choice, it might also mean that it doesn't really matter. You will be happy either way. When you apply this principle, you are likely to find out that many of the seemingly hard and big decisions are easy to make—even the ones about houses, jobs, children and the like that have a substantial impact on your life. Accordingly:

Banana Remedy 8.1: Assess Importance

You only have limited brain power. Therefore, spend it on the things that matter. Think about how important and urgent something is and spend your brain power on the differences that make a difference.

Check Facts

Your first filter in thinking sensibly was to focus only on things that matter. By applying that filter, you should be able to free your brain a bit. And you can now use this extra brain power to think more sensibly about the things that you do choose to think about. After all, the fact that you have to think about fewer things at a time means that you can think about them a bit more carefully.

The first thing to do with your freed-up brain power is to develop banana detection mechanisms. With all the information that is thrown at you, you want to be able to distinguish truths from non-truths, fact from fiction. As already referred to in Chapter 2 in the section 'We Don't Really Care About the Truth', we are surrounded by so much nonsense, 'fake news' and 'alternative facts' that it is no wonder we go bananas. And as a result, we seem not to care so much about the truth as we used to do. And that is a problem.

Of course, philosophically, the notion of 'truth' is an extremely complex and unanswerable issue. Philosophers have tried for centuries to solve the puzzle of what is truth and how we can discover it—and they still disagree. But that is not our concern here. Whether something is ultimately, universally and undeniably true is not so important. What matters is knowing whether something is based on enough facts to assume it is true, or whether it is nonsense. To find this out, it is helpful to make a distinction between five categories of statements: facts, interpretations, opinions, lies, and bullshit:

- **Facts** are statements for which there is evidence. Often, they are based on research or our experience that has shown that something is true. Global warming is such a fact: a long period of measurement shows that the world is increasing in temperature.

- **Interpretations** are the meanings we give to facts. They express what we think something means. Usually, this involves combining various facts and then drawing a conclusion. The fact that temperatures increase and the human-induced carbon emissions have increased may lead to the interpretation that humans are causing the increase in temperature.

- **Opinions** are personal viewpoints. They express how we think about something, what we find important, and what we like and don't like. We may have the opinion, for example, that global warming is a good thing or a bad thing and may have the belief that we can or can't do something about it. This opinion may be based on the facts and interpretations we see but could also originate somewhere else—as a result of what other people say, for example.

- **Lies** are statements that knowingly go against facts. To express a lie, you need to know what is true and then deny it. For example, you forgot your friend's birthday (fact) but you tell her you wanted to surprise her by calling a day later (lie). So, with a lie you do respect the truth, but decide to deny it.

- **Bullshit** are statements in which you don't care about the truth at all. You just say something, not even caring whether it is true, false or relevant. You bluff, pretend and produce hot air. The fact that bullshitters don't even find the truth relevant anymore makes bullshit an even greater enemy of truth than lies.

Being aware of these five categories of statements can help you filter the bananas from the other fruit. Whenever you read or hear something, think about what it is that you read or hear. Is it a fact, an interpretation, an opinion, a lie, or bullshit? This helps you discover how close to the truth it is or whether something is correct or not. Of course, doing this is not flawless, and you often may lack the knowledge to make a proper assessment. However, the mere fact of being actively aware of these categories should already help you be more sensitive to bananas.

There are more things you can do. You can put on your researcher's hat and start looking for empirical evidence. If someone is saying something, try looking for any credible evidence. Are there any facts they report that can be checked? Is it based on legitimate information? Is there any research that supports their claims? If that is not the case, you are most likely facing an opinion, lie or bullshit instead of a fact or well-founded interpretation.

Keeping on your researcher's hat, you can also try and refute what is being said. Scientists call this 'falsification'. Rather than trying to find support for a particular claim, you look for counter-evidence. The harder you try and the less counter-evidence you find, the more likely a statement is to be true. So, if, for example, someone is telling you that investing in cryptocurrency is the best thing you can do, don't only look for the evidence he is presenting. Also look for counter-evidence that can refute this claim. This may save you some money.

Often, it is hard to find out whether there is evidence for something that is said. Thoroughly checking may require too much effort and may be beyond our capabilities. This means that a lot of the stuff we hear, see and read, we have to take at face value. We don't have the time, resources or capabilities to check all the facts. This doesn't render all of the above useless, though. The five categories are still helpful in such a case. Even with limited information and time, we can always make a quick judgment on whether something is a fact, an interpretation, an opinion, a lie or bullshit. Of course, we won't be right all the time, but it does give us an indicator of how likely it is that some statement is true or not.

We can also look at *how* people say something. Part of this is looking at them to find clues about whether they are telling the truth or not. Well-trained police investigators and psychiatrists can detect this in people's voices, eye movements, facial expressions, and body language. While I would be thrilled to have such advanced skills, I am a lousy lie detector and can't say much of any value about it. But anyway, watching these physical details will give you additional indicators.

You can also listen and look carefully at the language people use. To discover bananas, there are five things to look for. The first is how often people emphasize that something is true, that it is based on facts and that you just have to believe them. The more people feel the need to say things like "It is true", "It is a fact" or "Believe me", the less likely it is that they are telling the truth. People who know they are talking about facts usually don't feel the need to emphasize the point. They are confident and let the facts speak for themselves.

The second thing to look for is overly difficult or specialized language. As soon as people start using difficult words such as 'idiosyncratic', 'disposition', or 'intentionalist' or foreign (usually Greek or Latin) words such as *habitus* or *modus operandi*, this is often an indicator that they are making things bigger than they are. By using such words, they hide that, at the bottom-line, there is not much substance in what they are saying. Of course, there are exceptions. Some people who use such language are really saying something important and new. But often, people are pretending—including pretending that they know what these words mean in the first place.

This brings us to a third kind of language to look for: meaningless jargon. My professional field especially—management—is developing and embracing jargon big time. Some examples: 'game changer', 'moving the needle', 'in the driver's seat', 'window of opportunity', 'low hanging fruit', 'bang for the buck', 'deep dive', 'growth hacking', 'outside the box', 'push the envelope', 'leverage', 'client-centric' and 'the new normal'. Yikes. To be honest, I find myself using some of this language as well, and I hate it if I do. Apparently, if people around you are using such jargon, you are almost automatically sucked into it as well. This is why I have to keep my internal bullshit detector active at all times.

A fourth thing to look for is the use of repetitive arguments. Instead of bringing new facts or ideas to the table, we often just rephrase the same message in different words and say it two, three, or five times to convince the other side. Here is an example: "I should get these new shoes because they are the most popular ones. Everyone else has them and they are the best-selling shoes of the last year. What's more, all my friends have them, and at school, I would be the only one not having them. Also, you see them everywhere on TV and every shop is selling them. Why should I be the odd one out?" Despite the length of this argument, the only thing it says is: "I should get these shoes because everyone else has them." The rest is repetition.

The last thing to look at is irrelevant examples or facts. Some people are good at convincing you by bringing in 'evidence' that might be true but is completely irrelevant. In this way, they make you focus on the facts but distract you from the fact that these facts have nothing to do with what they are saying. Here are some examples: "You should buy this phone/computer/car because the technology used is new", "You have to listen to me because I am older", or "This is impossible because the system doesn't allow it". Yes, the technology is new, I am older and the system doesn't allow it. Those are facts. But that doesn't mean that you should, therefore, buy the phone/computer/car, listen to me, or not circumvent the system. So check the relevance of the evidence that people bring in.

You can't challenge everything you hear and read. That is so tiring that it makes you go bananas as well. But, within practical limits, it can help you a lot if you develop a habit of challenging what you see and hear along the lines of the remedies above. It makes you less tempted to follow the rest and respond to what is presented to you. Accordingly:

Banana Remedy 8.2: Check Facts

Don't take things for granted. Challenge what you hear and read and know whether it is facts, interpretations, opinions, lies or bullshit. Put on your researcher's hat and analyze what people say, and how.

Question the Source

Fact checking doesn't stop at assessing what is said and how it is said. It also involves being aware and taking into account who is saying it and why they are saying it. Of course, you know this. There is a difference between a respected professor saying something and your kid saying something. And there is a difference between one politician saying something, and another politician saying exactly the same. And there is also a difference between a company telling you something about their product and the Consumers' Association telling you the same. So the source matters.

There are two important things to know about a source: their expertise, and their interests. Expertise concerns whether people can know and do know what they are talking about. The world is full of people expressing their opinions about everything. To filter the bananas from the truth, it helps to pay attention to whether people know what they are talking about.

The mere fact that someone is famous or an expert in one domain doesn't make them an expert in other domains. This applies to music celebrities and sports heroes but also, for example, to professors. Even though we can assume (and hope) that professors have a certain level of intelligence, they are usually experts in one, often narrow domain. The fact that they are smart and know a lot about one thing doesn't mean they also know about everything else. So, whenever you read or hear someone talk about something, check whether they know what they are talking about. If you do, don't check only their profession. They could have built up expertise in their private lives as well.

Sometimes, people don't have the expertise themselves. A country's president, for example, or a newscaster, has to talk about so many things that they cannot possibly be an expert in all those areas. In that case, the question is whether the person saying something is surrounded by people who know what they are talking about. This means it is not only the person speaking but the organization or network around them that you have to look at.

Often you can't know. You can't call them and extensively test their knowledge about the subject matter. You can't trace back their careers and everything they have done. And you can't scrutinize people's networks and the people they work with. But you can make a quick assessment of whether they or the people with whom they work have relevant expertise about the thing they talk about.

The second thing to look at is people's interests. To assess the extent to which someone is speaking the truth, it is helpful to know their stakes; how they benefit or suffer from the thing they talk about. This is most obvious in advertisements. Companies want you to buy their products. This means that the information in their ads does not always speak the truth, the whole truth, and nothing but the truth.

But this is not limited to advertisements. Everything said is said for a reason. No one and nothing is neutral and objective. We are all people, which means that our stakes, interests, wishes, and intentions always play a role. Even if we are not aware of them. Generally, we say stuff to improve our lives in one way or the other. And that is perfectly normal. We aren't robots, and if we didn't say things to make our lives better, what is the point of saying them in the first place? This is why I told you on the very first page of this book what my intentions were when writing this book.

To identify bananas and harness yourself against them, it is therefore important to pay attention to why people are saying what they are saying. What do they want to achieve? What do they want from you? Why do they say one thing and not the other? How do they gain from one piece of information and lose from another piece of information? Asking yourself these questions helps you find out which information to pay most attention to and how to interpret it. Accordingly:

Banana Remedy 8.3: Question the Source
Note which person or organization is saying or writing something.
Assess their expertise and interests. Who are they, and how is this
influencing the truthfulness of what is being said?

Explore Perspectives

There are always multiple sides to a story. We make use of this wisdom
all the time. We have been told this already when we were kids. When
we went to our parents, crying after a fight with our brother, our mother
or father knew we had a part in the fight too and, if possible, got both
of us there to hear both sides of the story. Or maybe you have engaged
in a debating exercise at school in which you were supposed to take one
side and defend it while debating with someone defending the other
side. Also, in making important decisions, we almost automatically
compare the pros and cons, or we ask other people's advice. And
increasingly, we are getting '360-degree' feedback from our peers at
work and at school. So, we are used to looking at things from more than
one perspective.

That is good, because considering multiple perspectives makes the
world a better place. As research shows, heterogonous groups with
people of different backgrounds develop better ideas and make better
decisions than homogenous groups. Furthermore, the principle of
exploring arguments and counter-arguments has been used as a way to
discover the truth since the ancient Greeks. Socrates, Plato, and
Aristotle all used the so-called 'dialectical method' to come closer to the
truth. And more recently, the German philosopher Hegel achieved fame
with his 'thesis-antithesis-synthesis' approach. The idea is that you give
one viewpoint (the thesis), then explore an opposing viewpoint (the
antithesis) and then contrast these two to get your answer (the
synthesis). So, throughout history, both scientists and philosophers have
emphasized how considering multiple perspectives takes us further.

Considering other perspectives also makes us more empathetic and
understanding, thereby improving social cohesion in society. When we

explore another perspective, we put ourselves in the shoes of others and try seeing things their way. This makes us understand their world and way of thinking better, and thereby increases our understanding and appreciation of who they are and why they think differently to us. This means that both intellectually and socially, it is beneficial to look at things from more than one perspective.

Even though we know this, we live increasingly in isolated bubbles where we only receive information that matches how we already think. Social media is infamous for this. Through its personalization algorithms, for example, Facebook prioritizes messages based on their fit with our own profile. This means that we primarily see stuff that is similar to the other stuff that we see. Other digital services, such as Google, LinkedIn, Spotify and news apps do the same. They all use your profile and past online behavior in their algorithms to present you personalized stuff that matches what you have seen before.

It is not only the digital world that creates the bubbles. We have always lived in bubbles. Based on our tribe, genes, income, religion, country of origin, political preferences and hobbies, we have always clumped together with people like us. And this automatically meant that we primarily saw and heard stuff that fitted our own way of thinking. The digital world has just magnified this bubble behavior.

To some extent, that is great. The advancement in algorithms means that you get suggestions that are sometimes surprisingly accurate— spookily even. And how comfortable is it, to get your own world view confirmed and confirmed again! It makes you feel more confident, liked and supported in your preferences. After all, if 'everybody' talks about the same things as you, you must be doing, thinking, saying and feeling the right things, right?

But, the digital world also has substantial downsides. Even though it may make us feel comfortable, it increasingly distorts our world views. If we don't see enough and different enough other perspectives than our own, we get an exceedingly distorted picture of reality. And it is hard to think sensibly based on a one-sided, distorted image of what the world looks like. It leads to ignorance, misunderstanding, fear and hostility between people in different bubbles—and thus to bananas.

The good news is that the same technology that causes the 'filter bubbles', can also be used to explore other perspectives. Even though

Google is increasingly narrowing our scope by presenting us with personalized results that their algorithms assume are most relevant for us, the Internet still offers us an amazing window to almost any part of the world and topic we can think of. But you have to put in some effort.

A simple thing that you can do is to use search engines that don't track you or store data. Startpage.com is an example. It uses Google's search engine but through a smart anonymized interface that doesn't store any data. So, you're still benefiting from Google's algorithms but without sharing information with them. The disadvantage is that it may produce somewhat less accurate results (especially when you look for something local). Next to protecting your privacy though, the advantage is that it makes your search less sensitive to a filter bubble and thereby more open to surprises and 'objective' results.

Another thing you can do to avoid the bubble is to deliberately look for alternative perspectives. If you are a white, male, young and rich person, deepen your knowledge of black, female, old and poor people— and vice versa. And if you love soccer, beer and rock music, then explore ballet, wine and classical music—and vice versa. Read the others' blogs and magazines, watch their vlogs, listen to their podcasts, visit their events. Or talk to them. You'd be surprised how ignorant you are about the subcultures other people live in, even nearby to you.

You can also explore multiple perspectives by bringing up a person in your mind who is the inverse of you every time you have to make a judgment or think about something. Maybe you know someone who is the exact opposite of you in almost everything. Suppose this is Mike. Now, every time you have to make a judgment about something, you ask your internal Mike: "Hey Mike, what is your take on this?" Given that Mike is your opposite, he will always give you a different perspective than your own.

If you don't have a real Mike, you can also create your own imaginary Mike. Imagine someone who is your complete opposite and describe him or her in some detail. It helps to draw a picture and write down a couple of things to create a realistic as possible Mike. In this way, you can create an entire 'persona': a rich description of a particular type of person. And now, like with the real Mike, whenever an issue comes up, you ask your imaginary Mike (or Myra, Saleem, Ying, Erko, or whatever name you pick) how he or she thinks or feels about it.

The key point of these exercises is the same: explore multiple perspectives. And like many of the remedies before, this isn't difficult. Once you realize you are biased and look at things from one viewpoint, everyone can do it. But it starts with being aware of that. This requires disabling your automatic bubble response and stepping back for a second.

An easy way to start is to ask yourself whenever you find yourself making a judgment: "Why would I be wrong?" Invoking real or imaginary Mikes requires more effort because you need to bring in alternatives to your own viewpoint. When you start by asking why you are wrong, you don't have to worry about that. You focus on your own viewpoint and try to refute it. Doing that, I can tell from my own experience, can help you be less opinionated, dogmatic and frustrated. So:

Banana Remedy 8.4: Explore Perspectives

There never is only one viewpoint. Make better decisions and improve your appreciation of others by always trying to see things from more than one side. Challenge your views and see it their way.

See the Bigger Picture

A final way to think more sensibly is to look at the bigger picture. To some extent, that is already what you will do by applying the previous remedies. When you assess the importance of something, check facts, question the source and explore perspectives, you automatically take into account a bigger perspective than the one thing you hear, read, say or think. But you can also look at the bigger scheme of things in a more targeted way.

In fact, we are all tiny little ants being busy with our tiny little lives and 'problems'. So long as we keep our ant perspective, it is easy to go bananas. Our 'problems' become 'real' problems and our world becomes 'the' world. Everything seems so big and important. But when we zoom out and see the bigger picture, the importance of what we do, say, think and feel reduces dramatically. This in itself makes it immediately less likely that we will go bananas.

When we look at our own 'problems' and compare them to the bigger problems around us, this makes it harder to go bananas about our 'problems'. How, for example, can you go bananas about your phone freezing when you think about starvation, war, and child abuse at the same time. Putting things in perspective like this is a great way of relativizing the things we worry about.

But seeing things in the bigger picture also works as medicine for bananas in another way. When we look at how we fit in the bigger picture, we start looking at the connections between what we do and how this affects others. It makes us see, for example, that if we step on our brakes late on a busy road or change lanes all the time, we are contributing to a traffic jam behind us. It also makes us see that, if we buy cheap stuff, this is because someone on the other side of the world has produced it while being paid a fraction of what we earn. And it also makes us see that, if we continue eating meat as much as we do, we contribute to global warming.

Of course, unless you are a radical idealist, we can't think like this all the time. We are human beings with our own shortsightedness and blindness. We are bad at looking at the long-term and the bigger picture because they are outside our immediate experience. But this doesn't mean we can't try. And if it is not for idealistic reasons, there is a clear self-serving reason as well: considering the bigger picture makes you less likely to go bananas.

There are several things you can do to see the bigger picture. The cheap and cheesy way would be to ask yourself: "But what would I worry about if I look at it in the greater scheme of things!", "There is always someone with bigger problems!" or "This is nothing compared to the suffering of the starving kids in Africa!" Even though cheap and cheesy, this might work, because it does make you think of the bigger picture.

A more down to earth remedy is to think about who else is involved or affected by what you are doing. We are good at thinking about ourselves and our close friends and family. However, we also have the skills to look at others. If we think about who else is affected by our decisions and who else is involved in what we do, this opens our mind and enlarges our view. If you teach a class, for example, you can think about how this affects your students and how your course is part of a larger curriculum. If you sell cars, you can think about how this affects your clients and how you are part of your organization, or the entire car industry. Creating that perspective helps you see how you are part of a bigger, tightly connected ecosystem.

Another way of doing the same is to look at causes and effects. Everything you do, say, think or feel is partly caused by something else. And everything you do, say, think or feel is also causing something else. In this way, everything is connected through cause-effect linkages. You start thinking more sensibly if you are aware of this.

To create this awareness, you can take a sheet of paper and draw a causal map. At the center, you write down the particular thing that you are focusing on. This can be a decision you need to make, something you have done, something you said, etc. Suppose you consider firing one of your employees, for example, Mike. You then write down at the center of the paper "Fire Mike". On the right side, you write down the consequences ("Finding a replacement", "Mike out of a job", "No tiring arguments anymore", etc.) and draw an arrow from "Fire Mike" to those consequences. You do the same on the left of "Fire Mike" but now you list those things that cause this decision ("Late all the time", "Sarah pushing me to fire him", "Decreasing budget", etc.). Now, looking at the whole picture, you can decide whether or not to fire Mike. And if you are not sure yet, you can also draw a similar picture for "Don't fire Mike" and compare the two. Accordingly:

Banana Remedy 8.5: See the Bigger Picture

You are part of a bigger system. Whatever you say, think, feel or do, it is always connected to others. Look who is affected or involved and think about the causes and effects of your decisions and actions.

Conclusion

Thinking sensibly is a key remedy for bananas because of the simple fact that going bananas means that you don't think sensibly anymore. The previous seven steps were needed to get you there. They helped you create the conditions that allow and enable you to think sensibly. On top of that, in this eighth step, you have seen five remedies that directly aim at making you think more sensibly:

8.1 Assess the Importance
8.2 Check Facts
8.3 Question the Source
8.4 Explore Perspectives
8.5 See the Bigger Picture

Altogether, these five remedies reflect a call back to rational thinking. They stimulate you to let your rationality guide what you do rather than your primary animal instincts. This is so great about being a human being. We can be rational. We can see the bigger picture. We can put ourselves in the shoes of others. We can assess whether something is true or not. We can decide not to go bananas anymore. So, even though we are equipped to go bananas and are immersed in a world that seems to be built to go bananas, we have the brain power to beat these bananas.

We discovered this during the Age of Enlightenment—covering about the entire 18th century. During that age, the main ideas about science, reason and truth that we still have today were developed. And this has brought the world tremendous progress. Of course, this same Enlightenment has caused problems too. It has been one of the key drivers of technological development, thereby contributing to industrialization, war, pollution, and basically every problem we see around us. But, without the Enlightenment, it would have been completely impossible to inhabit a world with eight billion people at the level of comfort most of us are living today.

Despite the problems, if you want to beat your bananas, the verdict is clear. There is no alternative that provides a stronger remedy for bananas than sensible thinking. As soon as you start thinking about things, you can't go bananas about them anymore. And also, if you look back at the previous seven steps, it is your ability to think sensibly that is making them possible. It is by analyzing your own behavior, thoughts, words and feelings—and reflecting on them—that you can help yourself calm down, let things go, take responsibility, dethrone yourself, build character, detox yourself, and get organized. Now, with that powerful skill, let's move to the last step: Pay Attention.

13

Step 9: Pay Attention

In Steps 1 and 2, we started our journey out of Bananaland by limiting our distractions and letting go of some of our bananas. The main reason was that getting rid of your bananas requires free space in your brain so that you can start thinking and behaving more sensibly. In the six subsequent steps, we worked our way towards being responsible, down-to-earth people with the character and skills to stand strong against the bananas around us. This means we are now ready for the final step: taking in new information, attentively and in a non-banana way. This is important. After all, our goal was not to end up as disconnected hermits who withdraw from any interaction with others. Not at all. Our goal is to function as full human beings with both feet in reality and in society. This includes paying attention to the things and people that matter to us.

Welcome the Unexpected

There is a nice saying that goes "When life gives you lemons, make lemonade." This saying reflects the core of the first remedy, helping you to pay attention. It tells you to welcome the unexpected things in life, even if they are sour, and try to make the best of them. So, instead of trying to stick to your plans and avoid or ignore the unexpected things happening to you, you embrace them.

John Lennon said something similar in his song "Beautiful Boy": "Life is what happens to you, while you are busy making other plans." (This line, totally irrelevant but nevertheless fun to know, can be traced back to a 1957 Reader's Digest article).

The point of bringing in these quotes is that they emphasize how important it is to keep our minds open and embrace the things that we didn't predict or plan, but that are nevertheless worthwhile paying attention to. The same applies to the things that deviate and are different from what we are used to. Embracing them makes our lives not only more interesting but also more productive. And I would even say more efficient. The reason is, that welcoming the unexpected doesn't require any effort but at the same time can bring you a lot.

The previous steps were mostly aimed at getting more control of your brain and your life. That was important because going bananas is the ultimate sign that you are not in control anymore. By getting control of yourself again, you can beat and dispel a great many bananas from your life. And now that you are in control of yourself, it is time in this final step to let go of your attempts to control the world around you and start welcoming and appreciating the unexpected.

But how can you prepare for something you don't know? You can't actively seek it because you don't know what it is and where to start. And you certainly can't create it yourself because then it is not exactly unexpected anymore. But you can prepare. To bring in another quote, this time from the Roman philosopher Seneca: "Luck is what happens when preparation meets opportunity." Opportunity is the unexpected, but preparation is what you can do to meet opportunity.

This starts with your attitude. In Chapter 6, we already focused on letting things go. That is also exactly what you need to do as the first step to welcome the unexpected. Instead of focusing on your own plans and ideas, you open up and allow yourself to welcome the unexpected. Be curious and try seeing the deviant and the unexpected as potentially interesting opportunities rather than as threats to your plan.

It helps to tell yourself that you don't *have* to act upon the deviant and unexpected things on your path. See them as mere suggestions. You could accept them, but you could also choose to ignore them. So, rather than immediately putting them aside, you give them a chance. Of course, this doesn't mean you have to say yes to everything that pops up. But it does mean that your answer isn't a default "No." Therefore, rather than immediately saying yes or no, try "Maybe" or "I'll consider it" or "Why not?" as your first answer to the deviant and unexpected thing that you are facing. If it helps, you can write the thing on an ideas list or opportunity list and let it rest for a couple of minutes, hours or days. And then decide whether or not embracing it is a good idea.

I like the "Why not?" best as a primary response to develop. It has a positive intention but leaves it still open whether you embrace the opportunity or not. If you can come up with good reasons not to embrace it, you have made a conscious and explicit decision rather than an automatic and implicit one. And if you can't come up with good reasons, you have opened the door for something new and unexpected.

Another thing you can do is to reserve time for the unexpected. If you followed the suggestions in Chapter 11 on planning for uncertainty, you are already doing that. As argued there, it makes life more relaxed and with fewer bananas if you plan free time in your agenda. And this free time is exactly what you need to seize the opportunities that you stumble upon. After all, you can only act upon something unexpected if you have the time to do so. If your calendar is completely filled, you are less likely to embrace new opportunities. After all, everything on your to-do list needs to be completed first. Therefore, reserve spare time. Not only for those cases in which the work took longer than expected or in which you got more work, but also for those cases when something interesting pops up so that you can embrace it. Accordingly:

<table>
<tr><td>

Banana Remedy 9.1: Welcome the Unexpected
Be open to the unexpected things in your life. They might turn out to be great opportunities. Approach them with a simple "Why not?" and reserve time in your calendar to embrace them.

</td></tr>
</table>

Listen and Respond

With your head stuffed with bananas, it is hard to pay real attention. You are too busy with all the trivia circulating in your brain and with responding to every external trigger. But paying attention is an essential part of life. In fact, it may even be the one thing that makes life worthwhile in the first place: paying attention to the things that matter to you. If you don't pay attention to them, what is the point? You would be merely running on autopilot jumping from one banana to the other.

Having rid yourself of most of your bananas in the previous steps, you should be able to start paying real attention. By cutting out the noise, you can now hear the signals that matter. The main way of doing that is through careful listening and responding to what you hear.

I mean this both literally and metaphorically. Literally in the sense that you *really* listen to what people are saying. You don't nod or uh-huh them while your mind is elsewhere—on your phone, your to-do list or some banana you are worrying about. Also, you don't look over their shoulder to see whether there is something or someone more interesting around (the well-known 'reception look' to be found at business receptions). And you also don't interrupt them after two seconds with all the important things you have to say and with your wise and insightful counsel and advice. No, you listen.

I find this hard. It means sitting back, being patient, and putting the other person at the center instead of my own thoughts and impulses. And I am not so good at that. But I try, and it is definitely the right thing to do. Obviously, it is good for the other side, because how great an experience is it when someone listens and pays attention to what you are saying? But also for yourself. It is more relaxing and rewarding to truly listen than to engage in some word battle, fighting for who can claim the largest share of the conversation. As such, listening itself keeps your bananas at a distance. And in the long run, it leads to better and more interesting relationships as well.

Attentive listening implies that you also respond. If you don't respond at all, the other person could equally well speak to an empty room, a table, or a donkey. So it is important that you do respond. But not with immediate words or deeds. Trying to come up with immediate advice or solutions doesn't work. That leads to practical discussions about how to change a situation. What the other side wants first, though, is your attention and confirmation that you are there for them. Resolving the situation is a later concern. The only thing you need to do is show the other person that you are indeed listening. A well-meant "Yes I see" or asking questions like "And then?" or "How do you feel now?" does the job.

It is often suggested that the above interaction is a typical man-woman thing: women want you to listen and men want to come up with practical solutions. I have my doubts. My own experience and observations are different. We are all simply human beings with a need to be seen and receive undivided attention by others. And that is what listening and responding is about.

Next to its literal meaning, I also mean listening and responding metaphorically. I mean paying attention in a broader sense—to being receptive to the things you hear and see around you that require your attention. This could be other people, but also the garbage can that needs to be emptied, the clock that needs to be repaired, an envelope that needs to be opened, or an email that needs to be answered. In that sense, listening and responding equals paying attention in general, and, in particular, to details.

Like paying attention to other people, also paying attention to details helps you rid yourself of some further bananas. In all the examples above, not explicitly paying attention and responding means that you implicitly pay attention to it anyway. You know the garbage can needs to be emptied. You know the clock needs to be repaired. You know the envelope needs to be opened. And you know the email needs to be answered. These things are in your head already. And until you respond to them, they will stay in your head, creating bananas.

Listening and responding to people and situations that require attention is exactly what Benedictus' principle of *obedientia* that I mentioned in Chapter 4 is all about. It means being 'obedient' to the people and things around you. Not obedience in a slavish sense, but obedience in the sense of being attentive and thereby giving the other person and the situation priority over your own concerns.

In that sense, listening and responding is an exercise in modesty. As referred to in Chapter 8 (Dethrone Yourself), many of our bananas are caused by making ourselves too important. In that chapter, we worked on making ourselves less important by controlling our emotions, stopping our soul-searching, and enjoying our averageness, unimportance and temporality. Succeeding in that should make it easier now to listen attentively and respond. If we don't put ourselves on a pedestal anymore, we can listen and respond to what our environment asks for. Accordingly:

Banana Remedy 9.2: Listen and Respond

Pay careful attention to what others and your environment ask for. Don't overload others with your advice and solutions but listen and pay attention. And take care of the details that need your attention too.

Monitor Yourself

You shouldn't only pay attention to the calls of the people and things around you. You should also pay attention to yourself. Obviously, I don't mean the kind of soul-searching attention referred to in Chapter 8, or the cry-for-specialness attention of Chapter 2. I mean the more reflective and conscious attention through which you can look at yourself from a bit of a distance and monitor how you are doing.

When you are in banana mode, you lose your ability to think sensibly about yourself—as well as about everything else. You are too occupied with worrying about trivial stuff. I know all too well how this feels. Your animal brain is at work and you respond based on impulse rather than on what you think or want. Remember the jumpy school of fish, flock of birds and herd of wildebeest? The previous steps have all helped you rid yourself of bananas and mean that you operate less frequently and less deeply in banana mode than before. As a result, you can think more clearly and sensibly. You can now use that regained ability to also monitor yourself.

Monitoring yourself is helpful. It means that you listen to your own needs and take responsibility for changing things if needed. It also means that you try to learn from what you do and improve so that you make less banana 'mistakes' in the future. Again, we can draw from

Benedict's work here. In addition to the *obedientia* principle, I also referred in Chapter 4 to *stabilitas* (perseverance) and *conversation morum* (loosely translated as continuous improvement). That is what monitoring yourself is about: perseverance and continuous improvement. And Benedict's recommended basic attitude—always feel a novice—works here too. It makes us aware that we are never there yet and can always continue improving.

The basis of self-monitoring is that you become aware of what you are doing, and consciously decide whether you continue doing that or change something. You can apply it to everything you do habitually. Whether it is eating, working, watching TV, playing computer games, drinking, talking, complaining, or any other habit you can have, you can monitor yourself and decide whether you go on with it or not.

The problem with doing things habitually is that you aren't aware of them. This means that there usually isn't a natural moment when you will monitor what you do. You go on without thinking about it for a second. This means that you can best start with self-monitoring by scheduling it in your agenda on a regular basis. A good time is at the end of the day. Before or after dinner, for example, you can reserve five minutes for some reflection. You ask yourself two simple questions: "What went well?" and "What did not go so well?" Think about these questions, list your answers, and then formulate one or two things you can do better next time. That's it. The nice extra effect is that you become more aware of the good things each day, so you can appreciate them.

Once you have turned this way of monitoring into a habit, you can also do it more often, throughout the day. Every time you have a minute or two you can briefly look back and identify what went well and not so well over the past hour and learn from that. In this way, step-by-step, you make monitoring yourself part of your everyday mode of living. This will significantly reduce your chance of going bananas because it means you are more aware than before of the things you do.

What I have described so far is the mental part of monitoring yourself. But monitoring yourself also means that you pay attention to the physical signals that your body gives you. Your body is a great early warning system. It often knows things much earlier than your conscious brain wants to admit, and it puts a lot of effort into telling you things, to the extent that it starts shouting until you no longer ignore the signals.

There are many ways in which your body tells you that something is not okay in the way you work and do things. You have headaches. Your shoulders are tense. Your back hurts. Your neck hurts. Your eyes hurt. Your stomach hurts. You are constipated. You have diarrhea. You lose your appetite. You lose your libido. You sweat. You have heartburn. You get acne. Your heart skips a few beats or beats rapidly. You have a cold all the time. You breathe with your chest rather than your stomach. Your feet or hands sleep. You can't sleep. You wake up at 3 am. And so on. How many more signals do you need?

Monitoring yourself means that you pay attention to these signals and take care of yourself. Most of us—yep, including me—are stars at ignoring the signals and just get on with our work. After all, we are busy, and everything we do is so important that it needs to be finished, no matter what. And that little ache in your neck/shoulders/head/stomach? Nothing serious and it will disappear automatically if we carry on. We don't have the time to rest and can't afford to pay attention to such banal bodily discomforts. Until you realize you should. So:

Banana Remedy 9.3: Monitor Yourself

Pay attention to what your mind and body are telling you. Throughout the day, take a couple of moments to step back and evaluate what went well and what not so well. And listen to your body.

Read and Repeat

There is another way in which paying attention helps you rid yourself of bananas: reading. Not the quick and dirty reading that you do with a magazine, a news app, or a message on the various forms of social media. But the serious and attentive reading that occurs when you are completely absorbed in a book and are hardly aware of time and the things happening around you. Attentive reading helps. And the interesting thing is that this applies both to fiction and non-fiction, but in a different manner and for different reasons.

"Why reading?" you may ask, and "Why not watch a movie or documentary instead?" After all, they contain roughly the same information, right? Yes, but there is a key difference. With reading it is you who sets the pace and creates the images in your mind. You decide how fast to read and which parts you read more carefully. And it is you who can stop for a while, put the book away and pick it up again. In a movie and documentary, the flow and images are produced by someone else. It is this difference which makes reading a very different experience to watching. And it is this difference that means that reading helps against bananas, while watching often creates bananas.

As far as fiction is concerned, there is first the direct, short-term effect. It is mentally impossible to be fully immersed in a novel and at the same time go bananas. Reading a novel that you enjoy helps you forget your day-to-day troubles and lets your imagination take flight. And during that time, you can't worry about Facebook, your next holiday or other carefully crafted problems. This means that the more time you spend on attentively reading fiction, the less you can go bananas.

But reading novels also has more profound and long-term effects. Various studies have shown that attentive reading of a novel improves some of our brain functions. Being immersed in a work of fiction increases blood flow to your brain and improves connectivity between various parts of the brain. It particularly affects the left temporal cortex (the place in your brain that is associated with your receptivity for language) as well as the primary sensory and motor parts of the brain (the part responsible for sensing stuff and movement… even while it is not you, but the protagonist in the book that senses things and moves!). One result, as it has been found, is that it improves our ability to put ourselves in the shoes of others. And all of that just by reading novels.

I could imagine there is some difference in terms of effect between reading, for example, Tolstoy and E.L. James. However, the bottom-line is more about *how* you read than about *what* you read. The main point is that what you read should get you immersed so that it absorbs your attention and your imagination is put to work. And if that happens with *Fifty Shades of Grey* rather than *War and Peace*, then the first is probably the better alternative for you. This gives you a nice excuse to read every book you want, even if it is no high-class five-star literature. As long as it gets you immersed, reading fiction improves your brain.

Reading non-fiction can help too. Not so much recipe books, instruction manuals or phone books, but preferably books that have some serious lessons baked into them. Think the Bible, Koran or any other big religious or philosophical work that is meant to contain important lessons. Or think a book with around nine steps and 45 remedies for going bananas. Just a suggestion.

Like with novels, it is again more about how you read than what you read. It is all about careful and repeated reading so that whatever you read gets the chance to sink in. As the saying goes, "Repetition is the mother of learning." This doesn't only apply to practicing in order to master a skill. It also applies to reading something repeatedly until it changes how you think.

As referred to in Chapter 8, many monks practice this kind of repeated reading every day. As explained there, Benedict called it *lectio divina* ('divine reading'). Its core idea is that you read slowly and ruminate the words so that you let sentences sink in one by one. Not all sentences, but especially those that trigger something in you. Read them, repeat them and absorb them. From this, you can learn from these texts in a way that can produce a lasting change in how you think and feel and what you say and do. Accordingly:

Banana Remedy 9.4: Read and Repeat

Develop a habit of reading, both fiction and non-fiction. Read attentively and let yourself get immersed in what you read. Repeat and reflect upon what you read until it changes how you think and feel.

Use Your Senses

You are there: the very last remedy of the very last step on your journey out of Bananaland. When starting this journey, the focus was on reducing your information intake and on creating silence in your head. This allowed you to think more sensibly and individually rather than mindlessly following the herd. But now it is time to open up again and use all your senses to take in information in a rich and attentive way.

As observed, we are living in a visual society. We rely so much more on our vision than on our other senses that it sometimes seems to be the only thing that counts. But of course, we can do more than just see. We can hear, feel, smell and taste too. Therefore, to complete our journey out of Bananaland, we need to use those senses as well. Only then can we really pay attention to what is happening in our environment, to the people around us and to ourselves.

Throughout the past chapters, I haven't ignored those senses. Above, for example, I have talked about listening and monitoring yourself and, in Chapter 6, we saw some physical exercises you can do. Furthermore, relying on your own senses is what reducing your app and technology use was all about in Chapter 9. Instead of relying on technology, you rely on what you hear, see, feel, smell and taste.

But it is worthwhile emphasizing the importance of all your senses again in this final step. The main reason is that using your senses helps to get you out of your head. We mostly go bananas because we only use our heads. We see things, look at what others do and act. And it is by staying in our heads that we develop the vicious cycles mentioned in Chapter 5. But when we use all our senses, it is harder to stay in our head and go bananas.

So what can you do? Given the dominance of our vision, a first simple thing you can do is close your eyes. It is no coincidence that closing your eyes was part of various of the remedies discussed above. It takes away many of the visual distractions that you would otherwise be looking at. Closing your eyes not only calms you down, it also automatically makes you pay more attention to your other senses. You start hearing and feeling things that you would ignore with your eyes open. So, whenever there is a good opportunity, or whenever you go seriously bananas, close your eyes and pay attention to your other senses.

You can also deliberately use the other senses. Listen to what you hear now, wherever you are. Outside, inside, the sounds you make yourself, and so on. I am doing that right now, while sitting at a Starbucks in Amsterdam and writing these lines. Even though there is a lot of noise, focusing on active listening helps me calm down rather than being too much immersed in my writing. So listen attentively and you will find that you calm down too. Maybe not when you are listening to some aggressive death metal or fast techno, or when your neighbor is drilling holes or cutting down trees. But generally, listening attentively to the sounds around you has a contra-banana effect.

The same applies to your other senses. Attentively feeling whatever you touch, attentively smelling the scents around you, and attentively tasting whatever you eat and drink have the same effect. Try it and you will see that it calms you down. This is why it is also one of the key elements of mindfulness: that you do the things you do in a mindful way, with attention, rather than on autopilot. It doesn't matter what you do, so long as you do it mindfully, using your senses consciously. Therefore, as a final remedy for going bananas:

Banana Remedy 9.5: Use Your Senses
Use all your senses and use them attentively. Listen, feel, smell and taste things with focused attention. This will get you out of your head and make your bananas disappear.

Conclusion

While we started by disconnecting ourselves from the world through an information detox in Step 1, the point of this last step was to get back in touch with the world, but in a more relaxed and sensible non-banana way. To support you in that, the last five remedies of this book are:

9.1 Welcome the Unexpected
9.2 Listen and Respond
9.3 Monitor Yourself
9.4 Read and Repeat
9.5 Use Your Senses

With these last five remedies, you have completed your journey out of Bananaland. This means you should be ready to join the herd again but stay yourself rather than join the collective craze.

Of course, the journey is not literally completed. Like me, you probably have to go back to each of the steps all the time. Because ridding yourself of bananas is a lifetime activity. You will become better at it, and be able to lower your average number of bananas over time, but they will keep on coming. We are too much wired to go bananas, and all the circumstances are right for going bananas.

No More Bananas!

Everything that needed to be said has been said. So, let me merely draw a quick conclusion. First of all, you now know *what* to do to say goodbye to your bananas. Divided into nine steps, Chapters 5 through 13 offer you no less than 45 possible remedies to do this. When applying them in practice, the Table of Contents may come in handy. Whenever you find yourself swamped in bananas, have a look at it and see which step and which remedy would be most helpful for you at that moment.

Second, you also know *how* to do it. As emphasized in Chapter 4, the road out of Bananaland is a bumpy, winding, and never-ending road. As emphasized there and repeatedly afterward, it requires a novice attitude and a lot of perseverance to start, continue, and restart your journey continuously. And while doing that, you may be going through various phases including denial, hopelessness and euphoria. Hold on and take one step at a time.

Third, you also know *why* to do it. You probably knew before you started reading this book, because you will have had your own reasons to obtain it. In addition, Chapter 2 illustrated how deeply the bananas have invaded what we think, feel, do and say. Furthermore, Chapter 3 gave you a peek into the science of bananas, thereby showing you how natural and self-evident it is that we go bananas.

The bottom-line of all of this is staying grounded and keeping a cool head in the collective madness that surrounds you. The idea is that you want to discover, enhance and celebrate your individuality and your human capacity to think sensibly instead of mindlessly following the herd. Overall, the nine steps and 45 remedies comprise one big journey towards becoming that more conscious and sensible person.

This is hard work. Getting rid of your bananas is challenging, and you will always keep on creating and gathering new bananas. I do. And I am nowhere near an endpoint. Despite all my efforts, I go bananas about something at least once every day and usually more often. And I find myself going back to all the steps all the time. But still, I am making progress. The number and size of bananas occupying my head have significantly dropped. And I hope the same will happen to you.

Because the payoff is great. Even though you will never reach an endpoint, every banana you can get rid of helps in making progress. And it is worth it for at least three super-important reasons:

1. **It makes you feel better.** With fewer bananas, you feel more relaxed, more confident, and more in control of your life.

2. **It makes you more effective.** With fewer bananas, you get more done and you do it better with less effort.

3. **It makes you a nicer person.** With fewer bananas, you are nicer and kinder to others, giving them the attention they deserve.

This means that saying goodbye to your bananas is not only good for you. It also is good for the people around you, the school, flock or herd of people you relate to and interact with. Not only will you be a nicer person to them, you will also inspire them to get rid of their bananas too. After all, we are all social animals that look at each other and copy each other's behavior. So, by applying the contents of this book, I hope you can set an example for them and thereby help reduce not only your own bananas, but also theirs. Enjoy.

About the Author

Jeroen Kraaijenbrink is a writer, advisor and lecturer on leadership and strategy. He lectures at the University of Amsterdam Business School and the TSM Business School in Enschede. He advises leaders in corporate and non-profit organizations and is also an active contributor on forbes.com.

Jeroen is also the founder of the strategy e-learning platform and community, **Better as Strategy** (www.betterasstrategy.com). On this platform, Jeroen shares what he does in his training and consulting work in the form of online courses, so that people can start practicing better strategy themselves. Better as Strategy shows that strategy can be engaging, practical and rewarding, at every level in an organization.

No More Bananas is Jeroen's third book. After writing two earlier books on strategy based on his professional expertise, No More Bananas reflects his personal journey to stand strong against the collective lunacy of today. Jeroen lives in the Netherlands, with his wife Caroline and their cat.

For more information about Jeroen, this book, or Better as Strategy, visit www.jeroenkraaijenbrink.com or www.betterasstrategy.com.